Our Daily Bread

Our Daily Bread

366 Recipes for Wonderful Breads

BY

Stella Standard

BONANZA BOOKS. NEW YORK

This edition is published by Bonanza Books ·
a division of Crown Publishers, Inc.
by arrangement with Funk & Wagnalls

c d e f g h
Manufactured in the United States of America

DESIGNED BY VINCENT TORRE

CONTENTS

I

White Flour and Mixed Flour Recipes

II

Whole Grain Recipes

Our Daily Bread

Bread, Wine and Oil, that blessed trinity of the kindly fruits of the earth, have been, ever since Biblical times, the symbol of peace —and plenty, the reward promised by angels in heaven to men of goodwill upon earth.

In all times and among all nations bread has been regarded as the staff of life, the foundation upon which all kinds of widely differing diets have been built, according to age, climate and custom. Among free and civilized peoples the head of the family is known as the breadwinner. And for close upon two thousand years Christians of all denominations have had and still have one prayer in common—the Lord's Prayer; they all ask, as they were divinely ordered to do, that they may be given their daily bread, even before asking to be forgiven their trespasses, to be delivered from evil and not to be led into temptation.

André L. Simon
President, Wine and Food Society

From *A Concise Encyclopaedia of Gastronomy*

Preface

Bread is a universal word like sun, moon, wind and stars, like earth, country, family, home. Bread has played such an important part in the lives of all peoples from time immemorial that now those in prosperous countries take it for granted and tend to forget that in some parts of the world drought and loss of crops cause fear in the marketplace, bread riots, famine and even death. It is no wonder then that bread enters into the religions, superstitions, folklore and history of all peoples. In war, armies depend on food as much as on guns. Retreating armies have always destroyed crops. The lack of bread has vanquished them both at home and in the field.

Bread figures in countless sayings in all languages. It connotes health, luck, one's own interest and great good fortune, as when one's "bread is buttered on both sides." When one breaks bread with a friend or neighbor it means to share food generally. We find bread and wine in its most beautiful and figurative sense in the Holy Communion. But bread is much older than Christianity —it dates back to prehistoric man.

Grains have been found dating back some twenty-five thousand years in the land that is now France. Some have been found in the United States dating back ten thousand years. In the prehistoric collections of the British Museum there are exhibits of peas, beans, and even cakes made of barley and millet. Excavations in the region of the lake dwellers of Switzerland have produced grains of wheat, corn, oats, millet and rye, ten thousand years old. The New Testament tells us that rye, millet, barley and wheat were cultivated in Palestine. Primitive man probably chewed the grains before he pounded and parched them. A hollowed-out basin of stone called a quern was used for grinding grain; a ball was used to crush it. Old querns have been found in the northern British Isles and in Norway, and in the more remote parts of these countries people were found as late as 1900 grinding with querns. Some crude, as well as some quite fine, examples of mortars that were used by the Egyptians and the Romans have been discovered by archaeologists.

It has not yet been settled which people made bread first—the Chinese or the Egyptians. The Chinese fermented but steamed their bread, as they do to this day. The Egyptians learned to bake theirs and probably invented and built the first ovens. They learned that wheat, when fermented, formed a gas that made bread light. Light bread was very soon preferred to the old flat bread. The Egyptians, too, were the first to develop a flour sieve or bolter. The Greeks brought bread to the Romans who then introduced it to Europe, where wheat agriculture had already begun. Bread became of great importance to Rome, where many Greek bakers were employed. There were 258 bakeshops in Rome by 100 B.C., at which time the Emperor Trajan organized the first Baker's Guild in Rome where the daily distribution of bread began. When the eruption of Mount Vesuvius destroyed Pompeii in A.D. 79, a public flour mill and oven were buried; they were found in the ruins when Pompeii was excavated.

In Scandinavia in the first half of the sixteenth century the farm crops included barley, oats and wheat, but rye was the principal crop. Early pictures show Swedish women doing public baking and today their breads, like the Danish, are famous, while their coffeecakes are among the best in Europe for variety and quality.

In the British Isles in the seventeenth and eighteenth centuries bread was made the way it is today except for the way yeast is made and the coarseness of the flour. Not until the eighteenth century was white flour improved, but even then it was still a luxury. White bread on the table was a sign of the degree of wealth the family had attained. F. Marian McNeill's *The Scots Kitchen* relates that

> in 16th century Scotland there were four kinds of wheaten bread, the finest called Manche; the second Cheat, or trencher bread; the third, Ravelled; and the fourth, Mashloch. The Ravelled was baked just as it came from the mill; flour, bran and all. For the Mashloch, the flour was almost entirely sifted, a portion of rye mixed with the bran; this composition was used by the poor people and the servants. Breid o' Mane was a very light and savory white bread. Breid o' Trayt was a superior kind of white bread. Ankerstock was a large loaf of rye, oblong in shape.

There are dozens of breads with such quaint names as sowens, farles and baps. Many were made with a mixture of oats and barley.

The English, too, had delightful names for small oval tea breads, made and baked very much like our rolls today. Some of them were called scones, East Kent huffkins, manchets, whigs or wigs, Cornish splits, Devonshire Chudleighs—named according to the county they were made in. They were sold or made at home. Our yeast-loaf breads of the last century followed the same lines.

The invention of the steam engine by James Watt in 1796, the introduction of the more efficient roller mill system, and the application of the middlings purifier combined to make modern milling possible. The steam engine could be geared directly to the turning of millstones or employed to raise water into reservoirs, freeing the miller from his dependence on sources of natural power. Watts designed an English mill, powered with steam in

1780. Less than thirty years later Oliver Evans used steam to power a Pittsburgh mill. By 1870 steam was used in 5,383 of some twenty-two thousand flour mills in America.

The first mention of a roller mill came in 1588 with the publication of an engineering handbook by an Italian, Agostino Ramelli. His drawings of devices, later generally adapted to milling, included a mechanically vibrated sieve and a hand-operated machine to grind grain, using a corrugated roller with spiral grooves. In 1662 another mechanical genius, G. A. Bockler, developed a mill using two corrugated rollers together with an agitating device for sifting the grind. But roller milling was not used again in flour production for more than a century. In 1833 rollers were again applied to flour milling by an unknown Swiss millwright, with later refinements by a countryman, Jacob Sulzberger. Their use spread to central and western Europe. A concentration of roller mills in and around Budapest gave the name "Hungarian" to the process.

In about 1800, the Hungarians became the first to separate the bran from the flour. This was done on stone mills which later reached a high degree of proficiency in the United States where, by 1870, a few more than twenty-two thousand mills (run by as little as three men per mill) served a total population of thirty million people. Today about two hundred and twenty-five major flour mills serve almost two hundred million people in our land.

In 1865 Edmund La Croix constructed the middlings purifier which filled an urgent need in making flour by the new method and which was later adapted to roller milling. Flour made from endosperm particles free of bran is usually the highest grade, and this middlings purifier improved the yield. The second half of the nineteenth century was a period of immense development and change in flour milling, as in all industry. Hundreds of machinery patents went into the improvement and refinement of the basic process—separating the outer bran and germ from the floury inner endosperm—all making possible the modern mill. An all-roller mill was constructed and operated briefly in Philadelphia in 1876. The first installation of commercial importance was made in Minneapolis in 1878.

The average bushel of wheat weighs about 60 pounds. The standard extraction rate provides 72 percent flour and 28 percent millfeed; some 2.3 bushels of wheat are required to produce 100 pounds of flour and 38 pounds of millfeed.

It has become evident from diet tests that doctors have made on obese patients that bread should not be eliminated from our diet. Now that white flour is enriched with the vitamins we need, it is usually part of the dieter's prescribed menu. One slice of bread contains 63 calories, an apple contains 70 and a cup of milk, 165. In an experiment at the University of Nebraska a group of students lost an average of 19.2 pounds in 8 weeks on a caloric-controlled diet containing large amounts of enriched bread. The other protein needs of the subjects were met and all daily requirements of other nutrients fulfilled. Other studies have shown that, with experimental diets high in cereals, potatoes and starchy vegetables, patients lost weight because of the bulkiness of the diet. If a completely balanced diet is adhered to—*i.e.,* a daily consumption of a choice of fish, meat, or poultry, with the addition of eggs, milk, cheese, butter, fresh vegetables and fruit—then bread can be added without fear of too much starch; the proper variety of necessary foods will take care of that.

Bread moved from the kitchen into the bakery where every day 40 million loaves are produced. It is high time it moved back into the kitchen. The satisfaction of producing a fine loaf is a thrill hardly possible to exaggerate.

High Altitude Baking

There is no difference from sea level to 2,000 feet in the amount of yeast used, period of fermentation, or baking temperatures. Adjustments begin at 5,000 feet, but there aren't many changes from the directions given in this book. The statistics given are from the Colorado State University Agricultural Experiment Station, Fort Collins, Colorado.

		RISING TIME	BAKING TIME
White Bread	5,000 feet	1st rising	45 to 55 min.
		60 minutes	375°
		2nd rising	
		30 minutes	
		pan rising	
		30 minutes	
	7,500 feet	1st rising	
		45 minutes	
		2nd rising	
		25 minutes	
		pan rising	
		25 minutes	
	10,000 feet	1st rising	
		40 minutes	
		2nd rising	

		RISING TIME	BAKING TIME
		20 minutes pan rising	
		20 minutes	
Whole Wheat Bread	5,000 feet	1st rising	55 to 60 min.
		55 minutes	375°
		2nd rising	
		30 minutes pan rising	
		30 minutes	
	7,500 feet	1st rising	
		45 minutes	
		2nd rising	
		25 minutes pan rising	
		25 minutes	
	10,000 feet	1st rising	
		40 minutes	
		2nd rising	
		25 minutes pan rising	
		25 minutes	
Rye Bread	5,000 feet	1st rising	15 min. 425°
		1 hour 15 minutes	and
		pan rising	30 min. 350°
		25 minutes	
	7,500 feet	1st rising	
		45 minutes pan rising	
		25 minutes	
	10,000 feet	1st rising	
		40 minutes pan rising	
		20 minutes	

		RISING TIME	BAKING TIME
Sweet Coffeecake Dough	5,000 feet	1st rising 1 hour 15 minutes pan rising 35 minutes	
	7,500 feet	1st rising 55 minutes pan rising 35 minutes	
	10,000 feet	1st rising 45 minutes pan rising 30 minutes	

At an altitude over 3,500 feet, it is suggested that the temperature be raised 25° F. for baking yeast bread.

I

White Flour and Mixed Flour Recipes

Yeast Breads

FLOUR, to make good bread, must be fresh. Nowadays millers are required by law to enrich white flour with nutrients. The chart shows the relative food value of various flours. The *white* flour referred to is a combination of all mill streams for white flour; *patent* flour is made from more highly refined streams; *bread* flour is made from hard wheat, the most suitable for making loaf bread. All-purpose flour is a mixture of hard and soft wheats, used for making white breads, hot breads and pastry. Some health stores and bakeries sell hard wheat but it is not always easy for everyone to get. Flour is bleached and matured, which the U.S. Department of Agriculture says improves its baking quality. Perhaps this is so after the bran, outer layers, and germ have been removed. I have been baking bread with whole grain flours for a great many years with marvelous results. Wheat flour, whether white or whole wheat, is the only grain with adequate proteins to produce elastic dough that contains gas for fermentation, hence the reason for adding wheat flour when other flours and meals are used, such as corn, rye, buckwheat and oat. There are, however, a few satisfactory loaves in the book that do not contain whole wheat.

Amounts of six specified nutrients in
1 pound of whole wheat flour and of different
types of white flour

Flour	Pro-tein	Cal-cium	Iron	Thia-mine	Ribo-flavin	Nia-cin
	Gm.	*Mg.*	*Mg.*	*Mg.*	*Mg.*	*Mg.*
Whole wheat (100 percent)..........	60.4	186	15.0	2.49	0.54	19.7
White, straight, hard wheat............	53.6	91	6.4	.53	.32	6.5
			Not enriched			
Patent: Bread.........	53.6	73	4.1	0.35	0.25	4.4
Patent: Family or all-purpose............	47.7	73	3.6	.28	.21	4.1
			Enriched			
Patent: Bread.........	53.6	73	13.0	2.00	1.20	16.0
Patent: Family or all-purpose...........	47.7	73	13.0	2.00	1.20	16.0

Source: Composition of Foods . . . Raw, Processed, Prepared (*11*). from the Agricultural Research Service of the United States Department of Agriculture.

YEAST in granular form comes in quarter-ounce envelopes. It is available everywhere. Cake yeast, which must be refrigerated, is not always easy to come by, so it is not specified here. When it is said that the latter achieves better results, one is reminded of those who say bleached asparagus is better than our plump green kind;

perhaps this is a bit of old-world nostalgia. One envelope of yeast is enough for 1 loaf of bread and up to 6 cups of flour, depending on the other ingredients. Individual recipes call for more. I often say to dissolve the yeast in warm water or milk with a little sugar, but it will act if sprinkled in the mixture. When I used the dissolving procedure it is because the liquid is part of the recipe.

PREPARATION OF PANS is generally done by oiling them with vegetable oil. I find this the best for bread pans. If other methods are used they are given in the recipes.

LIQUIDS, whether water, milk, buttermilk, sour cream, or beaten eggs, are in a 1 to 1½ cup ratio to 3 to 3½ cups of flour for bread doughs. Of course more liquid is used for batters but the recipes are specific. Before baking, eggs are part of the liquid. Sour milk, buttermilk and sour cream are excellent for baking because they are acids. Their use results in a fine, tender texture. In most cases they may replace milk, especially in hot breads. Formerly it was necessary to use baking soda with them but now all-purpose baking powder takes care of that. When sour cream replaces milk, the butter may have to be reduced somewhat.

CRUST can be made crisp by placing a pan of hot water on the oven floor while the bread is baking and brushing the top of the bread with water or salted water before baking. This is usually done for French bread.

GLAZES are made of egg white mixed with water; whole egg mixed with water or milk; egg yolk mixed with milk or cream. They are painted on the raised dough before baking with a feather brush. One tablespoon of cornstarch cooked with 1 cup of water until transparent is brushed on the bread as soon as it comes from the oven, otherwise it will be gummy.

SIZE OF THE RECIPES are generally for one loaf of bread. Any recipe may easily be doubled for large families or those who serve bread at every meal. I have never made a practice of freezing bread, so I make one loaf at a time for a family of two. If we serve it once or twice a day it will last a week or ten days. This is true if it is cut as needed (all homemade bread should be cut at table),

stored well, and is whole grain. Whole grain bread is so nourishing that it lasts twice as long as white. I find that guests are apt to
attack homemade bread like wolves, so these strictures are only for
ordinary circumstances.

TEMPERATURES are difficult to be certain about. The newer
electric stoves are quite dependable. Gas stoves depend on their
correct (or not) mechanism and the flow of gas, which can vary at
different times of the day. An oven thermometer is the only sure
gauge. Most breads bake at 375° F., some at 400° F. and some at
325° F. If they are to bake an hour, the oven is usually turned
down for the second half of the baking. If one's oven is tempera-
mental, the cook must learn to regulate it so that the bread doesn't
brown too much before it is cooked through. Some bakers preheat
their ovens before putting in yeast bread. I like to put bread, as a
rule, in a cold oven with the temperature set, so that it will
complete the rising. The pans are put on the lower third or fourth
of the oven, if possible on the same shelf. Bread baked at 400° F.
insures a crust. Temperatures are given in all recipes.

MEASURING cups and spoons are important because every recipe uses standard sizes. Flour sifters of 1½-cup size make for
neat measuring. They fit over the measuring cup. All measure-
ments are level. Whole grain flours are not sifted; white flour is
always sifted before measuring. Sifting makes a difference of as
much as ¼ cup of flour, which might affect a recipe. Guesswork
is done only by the experienced cook.

KNEADING. An old cookery book of the 1880s says "to make
good bread always be up in the morning early, just at the peep of
day," and a suggestion for kneading says "to raise the whole mass
and drop or dash it with considerable force upon the mixing board
or table for several minutes." In breadmaking, like everything
else, practices and times have changed. Kneading can be done
either on a board or in the mixing bowl. I have kneaded all kinds
of doughs for many years, from bread doughs to the finest pastry,
both in the bowl and on the board and I can truthfully say that I
have found no difference in the results. This should remove the

6

fear and fuss of breadmaking. One advantage of bowl-kneading is that there is no danger of kneading too much flour into the dough. Professional bakers today say that overkneading reduces the flavor of the bread. There are some who like the feel of kneading dough with their hands. I find a hard rubber spatula ideal for mixing and kneading the dough. For rolling dough on a board for shaping and cutting, most satisfactory cloth covers for both pin and board are available. After they have been used several times, the cloth becomes "treated" with flour, so little more is needed for each use. Dough doesn't stick so easily as on an uncovered wooden board.

PAN SIZES are important in all baking. The regulation loaf pan measures 9¼ x 5¼ x 3 inches. A loaf pan a little smaller is often needed. Small loaf pans measuring 5¾ x 3 x 2¼ inches are most useful for extra bread dough and for gifts of bread to friends. The ordinary 1-loaf recipe will fill 3 of these little pans. Bread made in them is attractive to serve on little breadboards for entertaining. Sandwich loaf pans measure 11 x 4½ x 2¾ inches. The 8 x 11-inch pan is necessary for many hot breads. A long dripping pan is indispensable for baking rolls. Cookie sheets, brioche, gugelhupf and charlotte molds are all useful for breads of different sizes and shapes. Often their name depends on their shape. Muffin tins, crêpe and pancake pans, etc., are all part of the equipment of a good kitchen.

EGGS nowadays come in Grade A only. It has been some years since eggs were graded other than for size. The recipes in this book call for large or extra large eggs. Bring eggs to room temperature before using.

BUTTER throughout this book is specified as sweet so that the salt may be regulated. Some pastries call for no salt. Some breads or pastry call for a quantity of butter and eggs; the flavor largely depends on these two ingredients, so they must be fresh and sweet. I can't think of another ingredient that adds so much in quality to a dish as country-fresh sweet butter no matter what dish is being prepared—meat, vegetables or bread. Some dark breads, however, are very good made with fresh chicken or bacon fat.

7

SUGAR is called for in nearly every recipe. It is usually brown or light brown sugar, for even the most delicate breads. My 5-pound cannister of white sugar is apt to last a very long time. It is sweet without any other flavor; white flour is also without much flavor. Both depend on the addition of other ingredients for character. Molasses and honey are two other favorites for sweetening.

REHEATING BREADS can be done by putting 2 Tbsps. of water in a paper bag and shaking the water out. Put in the rolls or muffins and heat them for 4 or 5 minutes in a 400° F. oven. They will be like new. Dip a French bread loaf quickly in and out of water and heat it in a 400° F. oven for 5 or 7 minutes. Croissants, or any buttery bread, are not covered but quickly heated in a hot oven.

STORING BREAD is different in dry and damp climates. In Nebraska where I grew up, the tin breadbox was all that was ever used. The earthen jar is ideal for doughnuts and even for bread if the climate is dry. In New York, where it is sometimes very damp, bread must be watched carefully to see that it does not mildew. I keep bread loosely in a plastic bag either in tin or earthenware. Infrequently do I have to resort to the refrigerator.

MALT SYRUP is made by Premier Malt Products. They produce plain malt syrup, hop-flavored light, and hop-flavored dark syrups. Hop-flavored syrup is especially suitable for rye breads. Their use gives bread the old-world professional flavor. If hop-flavored syrup is not available for use to make starter, use dark brown sugar instead. After the can of syrup is opened, it is kept refrigerated, tightly covered. When it is used it must be melted in warm water. Blue Ribbon Malt Syrups are used in making both bread and beer.

STARTER may be used in many kinds of breads. You may want to experiment with it. When you mix bread with the last cup of starter, mix in an extra cup of flour with the dough and reserve one cup of it. Refrigerate it, tightly covered, for the next batch of dough. Starter made with either whole wheat or rye may be used interchangeably in whole wheat or rye bread. One starter will be found in the recipe for Danish Sour Bread and another will be found in the recipe for Evangeline's Sourdough Rye Bread.

Orange Bread or Rolls

1 envelope yeast
6 Tbsps. light brown sugar
¼ cup lukewarm water
1¼ cups orange juice

3 Tbsps. butter
1½ tsps. salt
Grated rind of 1 orange
3½ cups sifted flour

Melt the yeast and the sugar in lukewarm water until frothy. Heat the orange juice with the butter just enough to melt it; add the salt. Grate the zest of the rind, without any white, into the flour. Mix the yeast with the lukewarm orange juice and add it to the flour. Beat the dough 3 or 4 minutes, then set to rise in a pan of warm water. When it is light, beat it down and put it in an oiled bread pan to rise again. Bake about 50 to 55 minutes at 350° F.

FOR ROLLS

After the first rising, ½ the dough at a time is rolled out ⅓ inch thick and cut in 2-inch rounds.

FOR THE GLAZE

2 Tbsps. butter
2 Tbsps. flour
½ cup sugar
1 cup orange juice
2 Tbsps. orange rind
½ cup hot water

Melt the butter in a saucepan and stir in the flour until smooth, then slowly add the liquids and the rest of the ingredients. Cook until mixture thickens a little. Pour this into a pan, large enough to hold 18 rolls. When it is cooled to lukewarm, place the rolls on the glaze and let them rise until double. Bake at 375° F. about 18 or 20 minutes.

Delicate White Bread

1 envelope yeast	2 eggs plus 1 white, beaten
1 cup flour	1 tsp. salt
¼ cup light brown sugar	⅓ cup melted butter
½ cup lukewarm water	½ cup warm milk
2¼ cups unsifted flour	2 Tbsps. rum

This is an elegant loaf with a fine texture and a lovely brown crust. Combine the first 4 ingredients in a large mixing bowl. Beat mixture well, set in a dishpan of warm water, cover with a tea towel and let the dough rise for about an hour. Beat the eggs and egg white until light, then beat them and all the remaining ingredients into the yeast mixture. Beat hard with a hard rubber spatula for 4 minutes. The dough should be light but with a good body. Set it back in the pan of warm water, cover, and let it rise 45 minutes to an hour. Beat it hard again, then put it in an oiled bread pan. Set the pan in warm water, cover lightly with a towel, and let the dough rise to the top of the pan. Put the bread in a cold oven. Set at 400° F. and bake 15 minutes. Turn the heat to 325° F. for another 25 minutes. Turn the bread out on a wire rack to cool, lightly covered with a cloth.

Nancy's White Bread

1 or 2 envelopes yeast	1 cup light brown sugar
½ cup lukewarm water	2 tsps. salt
1 Tbsp. sugar	7 to 9 cups sifted flour
2 cups milk, scalded	Glaze:
½ cup sweet butter (1 stick)	Egg
3 eggs, beaten	2 tsps. milk

Two envelopes of yeast make the bread rise more quickly but either 1 or 2 can be used. Combine the yeast with the water and 1 Tbsp. of sugar until it is frothy. Scald the milk, add the butter and cool. Beat the eggs until light and pour off 2 Tbsps. to be mixed with 2 tsps. of milk for the glaze. Add the sugar and salt to the beaten eggs and beat until thick. Light brown sugar makes the bread ivory color instead of pure white. Sift 7 cups of flour into a large mixing bowl. Combine the yeast, milk and butter and egg mixtures and add to the flour. Beat very hard for 10 minutes adding more sifted flour if necessary to make a light but stiff dough. Knead 3 or 4 minutes on a floured board. Put the dough into a greased bowl and set the bowl in a dishpan of warm water, cover with a tea towel, and let dough rise until double in bulk. Punch it down and let it rise again. Form into two or three loaves and put the dough in greased bread pans. Let rise in a warm place until the dough comes to the top of the pans. Brush with the glaze. Put the bread in a cold oven, turn the oven to 400° F. and bake for 20 minutes. Then reduce the heat to 375° F. and bake 20 to 25 minutes more. One large loaf can be made and rolls made from the rest of the dough. The rolls bake 20 minutes.

FRUIT BREADS

Recipe for Nancy's White Bread

Whole Wheat Bread or Rye Bread
1 to 1½ cups coarsely sliced fruit for each loaf

Choice of fruit
½ cup each citron & currants
Sliced dates
Sliced figs
Sliced pitted cooked prunes
Sliced cooked dried apricots
¾ cup currants soaked in ⅓ cup sherry or port
Sliced figs and ¼ cup preserved ginger
Raisins
Half fruit and half chopped nuts
1¼ cups coarsely chopped nuts
1 cup crunchy peanut butter

The addition is made before the last rising. It is beaten into the dough. When using peanut butter, decrease the butter in the recipe to half the quantity.

ALMA'S CINNAMON BREAD

Recipe for Nancy's White Bread

3 or 4 Tbsps. cinnamon

Alma's decade with our family was also the children's first decade. She frequently delighted us with this bread. She would divide the dough in half and roll it out to ½-inch thickness. This was after the first rising. The dough was liberally sprinkled with cinnamon, rolled up the length of the pan, molded into a loaf, put in the pan in a warm place to rise until light, and then baked. When it was cut each slice had a spiral of cinnamon. No sugar was added; Nancy's white bread is somewhat sweet so is perfect for this treatment.

Nut Bread

This is one of the most delicious tea breads and it may also be served with cheese. I have made it with 1 cup of ground browned almonds (measure the nuts before grinding and chopping) and ½ cup of chopped macadamia nuts. Hazelnuts, pecans or black walnuts, or a mixture can be used.

1 envelope yeast	1 tsp. almond extract
1 Tbsps. brown sugar	2 eggs, beaten
2 Tbsps. warm water	¾ cup warm milk
¼ cup sweet butter	3½ cups sifted flour
½ cup light brown sugar	1 cup nuts, ground
1 tsp. vanilla extract	½ cup nuts, chopped

Dissolve the yeast with the brown sugar and warm water until fluffy. Cream the butter and sugar until creamy then add the extracts and lightly beaten eggs. Combine the yeast mixture with the butter mixture and add the warm milk and the flour. Beat for 3 or 4 minutes. Put the bowl in a pan of quite warm water, cover with a towel and let the dough rise about 45 minutes until light.

Beat the dough down and add the nuts. Work the dough with a hard spatula for 3 minutes. The dough may be put in 1 oiled loaf pan and 1 small pan or 1 large loaf pan. Let it rise to the top of the pan, about an hour. Put the pan or pans in a cold oven set at 375° F. and bake the small loaf about 50 minutes and the large one 1 hour and 5 minutes. If it is baking too fast reduce the heat to 350° F. or even lower. The nuts make the loaf a rich brown.

Sally Lunn

1 envelope yeast	⅓ cup sweet butter
¼ cup lukewarm water	2 tsps. salt
3 Tbsps. honey or ⅓ cup light brown sugar	3½ cups sifted flour
2 eggs, beaten	Top:
¾ cup milk, scalded	4 Tbsps. light brown sugar
	2 tsps. cinnamon, cardamom or anise

Too much flour must not be used as this is a delicate, light bread. Dissolve the yeast in the lukewarm water with the honey or sugar until frothy. Have the eggs at room temperature and beat them very light. Scald the milk and add the butter and salt. When milk mixture is lukewarm combine it with the eggs and yeast. Add the liquid to 3 cups of sifted flour and beat until elastic, adding more flour if necessary so it will not be too thin. It must be spongy and light. Beat about 4 minutes. Set the bowl in a pan of hot water, cover with a towel and let the dough rise until light. Then beat it down and put it in a well-oiled pan. Set the pan in warm water. Cover loosely with a towel. When dough has risen, sprinkle with a mixture of the sugar and spice. This is optional. Put the loaf in a cold oven. Set oven at 400° F. and bake for 10 minutes, then turn the heat to 350° F. and bake 30 minutes more. This is a lovely tea bread. You may bake the dough in muffin tins, filling them ⅔ full and let them rise. Bake the same way but only about 20 minutes.

Dorothea's Dilly Casserole Bread

1 envelope yeast
¼ cup lukewarm water
1 cup of creamed cottage cheese
2 Tbsps. sugar
1 Tbsp. minced onion
1 Tbsp. butter
2 Tbsps. dill seed

1 tsp. salt
¼ tsp. soda
1 unbeaten egg
2¼ to 2½ cups flour
Soft butter
Salt

Melt the yeast in the lukewarm water in a large mixing bowl until it is foamy. Stir in the warmed-to-lukewarm cottage cheese, the sugar, and the onion which has been softened in the butter over a low flame. Add the dill seed, salt, soda and egg. Stir in the flour to make quite a stiff dough. Set the bowl in a pan of warm water, cover with a tea towel, and let the dough rise until light and double in size, about 50 or 60 minutes. Stir down a minute or 2, then put in a greased 1½- to 2-quart casserole. Let rise again 30 or 40 minutes. Bake at 350° F. about 45 minutes until a golden brown. Brush with soft butter and sprinkle with salt. This is a delicious and unusual bread.

Evangeline's Sourdough Rye Bread

This is absolutely delicious bread; served with sweet butter, one doesn't need much else for lunch or supper, except perhaps some good strong cheese and ale or beer. The starter takes about three days to make. It can be stored, well-covered, in the refrigerator, and a cup of it can be used in making other breads.

Sourdough Starter
1 envelope yeast
1 cup lukewarm water
1 cup rye flour
1 small peeled onion, wrapped loosely in cheese cloth
1 more cup lukewarm water
1 more cup rye flour

Bread
1 envelope yeast
⅓ cup lukewarm water
1 cup warm water
1 Tbsp. brown sugar
3 Tbsps. molasses
1 Tbsp. shortening
½ cup grated stale pumpernickel *or* ½ cup mashed potatoes
1 Tbsp. caraway seeds
1 Tbsp. salt
1 cup sourdough starter
2 cups white flour
¼ cup powdered milk (optional)
1 cup rye flour (about)
½ cup rye meal or more rye flour
Corn meal to sprinkle lightly on baking sheet

Melt an envelope of yeast in the cup of warm water until it froths, then add enough rye flour to make a soft paste. Sink the onion in it, and let it stand at room temperature, uncovered, or very loosely covered, until it is fermented and bubbly with a pungent and sour odor, about three days. The night before baking, when starter is at room temperature beat in the additional water and flour; leave at room temperature overnight. Measure out the amount needed for baking and refrigerate the rest. *Never* add any *leftover* dough to this starter. If it is not used again within 2 weeks, take out and mix well, discard ½ of it and add another ½ cup of water and ½ cup flour. Refrigerate again after several hours. This can be done any number of times. It should be tightly covered in the refrigerator.

To make the bread, mix the yeast and lukewarm water until frothy. Put the warm water, sugar, molasses, melted shortening, crumbs or potato in a large mixing bowl and stir until smooth, then add the frothy yeast. When mixture is smooth, add the caraway seeds, salt, and sourdough starter. Beat hard. Add white flour and powdered milk (if used) and beat hard for 3 minutes. Let dough rest 5 minutes, then gradually add the rye flour and meal or more rye flour and mix until it is stiff enough to turn onto a floured board. Knead hard, adding flour enough to make a stiff, elastic dough. Put the dough into a greased bowl, set it in a pan of quite hot water, cover with a towel, and let the dough rise until double, about 1½ hours. Then punch it down and let it rise again about 40 minutes. Punch down and divide into 4 small loaves. Sprinkle a baking sheet with corn meal and put the loaves on it. Slash across slantwise about 4 times with a very sharp knife. Put the dough in a cold oven, without turning on the heat, to rise again until double in bulk. Then turn the oven to 400° F. for 20 minutes; reduce the heat to 375° F. and bake 20 to 30 minutes more. A pan of hot water may be placed on the oven floor the first 15 minutes of baking to make the crust crisp. My aunt gave me the recipes for the wonderful sourdough and bread that follow.

Sourdough

If you are lucky enough to get hold of a bit of real sourdough starter, you can build it up in quantity by adding 2 Tbsps. of water and 2 Tbsps. of flour, letting it stand, preferably uncovered, overnight, and adding ¼ cup of water and ¼ cup of flour a day or 2 later. Let it stand long enough to become really pungent in odor, then store covered tightly in the refrigerator until you are ready to use it. If you can't get the real thing, you can start with 1 cup of water and 1 cup of flour beaten together well, and left several days until it is fermented. This doesn't make as tender a loaf as the genuine aged "wild yeast" gives. An even more delicate loaf is made from a starter using commercial yeast as a booster in the beginning. Every starter gives a different taste, so if you sample a loaf you especially like, you may be able to beg even a small scrap from which to build your own.

Potato Starter

Boil and mash 1 medium-size potato. Measure the potato water and add enough lukewarm water to make 2 cups. Mix it with the mashed potato in a Pyrex or crockery bowl. Sprinkle on it 1 envelope of yeast and 1 Tbsp. of granulated sugar. Cover very loosely with a plastic bag so air may reach the mixture, and leave it for at least 3 days at room temperature, stirring occasionally. It should ferment until it has a very pungent, sour odor. Refrigerate it, tightly covered, until you are ready to use it.

To Use Starter for Bread

The night before you use the starter, let it reach room temperature and then beat in 1 cup of water (potato water if you have it) and 1 cup of flour. In the morning take out what you need for bread and refrigerate the rest of it again. This can keep forever, if you renew it every two or three weeks. You beat it well, discard all but 1 cup, let it reach room temperature, add ½ cup of water and ½ cup of flour, let it stand several hours, then refrigerate it again.

Dissolve 1 envelope of yeast with ½ tsp. of sugar in 1 cup of lukewarm water. Put 1 cup of starter in a large mixing bowl, add the yeast, 1 tsp. of salt and 1 Tbsp. of melted shortening. Add 2 cups of flour, beat well, and let stand 10 minutes. Then add 1 or 2 cups of flour, enough to make a fairly stiff dough that can be kneaded on the floured board. Put dough in a greased bowl and let it rise until double in bulk, about 1½ hours, in a pan of quite warm water. Beat down and knead in ¼ tsp. of soda dissolved in 1 Tbsp. of warm water. Divide in 2 oblongs, each ½ inch thick. Roll up tightly into two loaves and place them on a baking sheet sprinkled with corn meal. Let them rise in a cold oven until double in bulk. When raised, turn the oven on at 425° F. and bake for 20 minutes (with a pan of hot water on the oven floor for crisp crust). Remove the water. Turn the heat to 375° F. and bake 15 to 20 minutes more. This makes grand breakfast toast.

Potato Bread

This is very light, lovely bread.

1 large potato	⅓ cup light brown sugar
⅓ cup hot water	½ cup skim milk powder
1 envelope yeast	2 eggs, beaten
¼ cup warm milk	3 cups sifted flour
2 Tbsps. light brown sugar	1½ tsps. cardamom *or* ½ tsp.
⅓ cup sweet butter	mace
1 Tbsp. salt	

Peel the potato and cut it in very fine dice so that it will cook quickly and not burn. Add the water, cover tight and cook over a low flame. Dissolve the yeast in the milk with brown sugar. Slice the butter into a large mixing bowl, add the salt, sugar and skim milk powder. When the potato is tender sieve it, undrained, into the mixing bowl. The hot potato will melt the ingredients. Stir until smooth. Stir in the yeast and the lightly beaten eggs. Beat in the 3 cups of sifted flour and cardamom, mace or your favorite spice. Beat for 3 or 4 minutes. If dough seems too stiff add 1, or at the most 2, Tbsps. of warm milk. Set the bowl in a pan of hot water, cover with a towel and let dough rise until light. It may be baked as 1 large loaf or 3 little loaves. Set them in lukewarm water until dough rises to the top of the pans. Bake the little ones 40 minutes and the large one 55 minutes. Begin the baking at 400° F. for 10 minutes then turn to 350° F.

If for any reason you must leave out the eggs, decrease the amount of water or the bread will fall in the center. Two or 3 Tbsps. of water will suffice to make the dough pliable. Remember there is moisture in the potato, and the eggs act as a thickener.

Whole Wheat Bread with Starter

1 cup starter   2 Tbsps. honey
  (see Danish Sour Rye)   1 envelope yeast
2 cups whole wheat flour   1 or more cups warm water
1 cup white flour   ¾ cup quartered prunes
1 Tbsp. salt

Remove 1 cup of starter (p. 172) from the refrigerator and bring it to room temperature by putting the cup in warm water. Put the flours in a mixing bowl and stir in the salt. Combine the honey, yeast and 1 cup of warm water. Make a well in the middle of the flour and stir in the starter and the yeast liquid. Stir hard until it is well mixed. A little warm water may be necessary to incorporate all the flour. Set the dough to rise in a pan of quite warm water covered with a tea towel. It will take 40 minutes to an hour. Sunsweet prunes used are convenient to cook with as they are delicious in breads, are pitted, and do not need soaking or cooking. Cut the prunes in quarters and stir them into the dough after it has risen. Punch it down well and put it in a large oiled pan. Let it rise until it is above the pan. Put it in a cold oven. Set oven at 400° F. and bake it 15 minutes, then turn the heat to 300° F. and bake 45 minutes more. This is a crusty, excellent bread.

Bran Bread

1 envelope yeast   1 cup bran flour
¼ cup lukewarm water   1¼ cups whole wheat flour
⅓ cup molasses   1 cup white flour
1 cup boiling water   Raisins ⎫
3 Tbsps. butter   Mace ⎬ Optional
1 Tbsp. salt   Cinnamon ⎭

Dissolve the yeast in the lukewarm water and molasses. Brown sugar or honey may be used instead of molasses, if preferred. Pour the boiling water over the butter and salt. Mix the flours together and, when the water is lukewarm, add it with the yeast and beat for 3 or 4 minutes. Then put the bowl of dough in a pan of quite warm water to rise, covered with a towel. When light, beat the dough down and put it in an oiled bread pan to rise again. When risen put the pan in a cold oven. Set the temperature at 375° F. and bake 20 minutes, then turn the heat to 350° F. and bake 35 or 40 minutes more. Raisins or a dash of mace or cinnamon can be added to the flour before liquids.

Indian Bread

1 envelope yeast	2 or 3 tsps. salt
¼ cup lukewarm water	2 large eggs, beaten
3 Tbsps. honey	¾ cup corn meal
⅔ cup scalded milk	2¼ cups flour
⅓ cup butter	½ cup powdered milk

Dissolve the yeast in the lukewarm water and honey until frothy. Scald the milk and pour it over the butter and salt. Beat the eggs until light. Mix the frothy yeast, lukewarm milk with melted butter and the eggs together and stir into the corn meal and flour mixed with the powdered milk. Beat very hard. To make a light spongy dough add 1 or 2 spoons of lukewarm milk or water if necessary. Put the bowl in a dishpan of hot water, cover with a tea towel and let the dough rise an hour. Punch it down and beat it 4 or 5 minutes. Put the dough in an oiled bread pan to rise again, set in warm water. When it is raised put it in a cold oven. Set the heat at 400° F. and bake for 15 minutes. Turn the heat to 325° F. and bake about 30 or 35 minutes more. When the heat is turned down, lightly paint the top of the loaf with beaten egg mixed with 1 Tbsp. of milk.

Salt Rising Bread

2 Tbsp. white corn meal	1½ Tbsp. sugar
1 cup milk, scalded	2 Tbsp. soft butter
Glass jar	1 to 1¼ cups sifted flour
2 cups sifted flour	½ cup hot water
2½ tsps. salt	

The directions must be carefully followed in every detail. It wasn't so difficult many years ago to make this bread. But I was told it is impossible in an air-polluted city like New York. After 3 tries I achieved a very fine loaf. I am sure it will be much easier and it will rise higher in areas where the air is relatively clean, because a "yeast" is formed during fermentation from the wild yeast that is in the air.

Put the *white* corn meal in a jar with a broad top, put a tablespoon in it to prevent its cracking, and pour the boiling milk in it. Set the jar in a pan of very hot water (120° F.) cover both with a tea towel and try to keep the water hot until gas issues from it with rather a sour smell and a hissing sound when you put your ear next to the opening. In clean areas it should take 6 or 7 hours. In New York it took from 10:30 in the morning until the next morning. It may have been ready at midnight, I don't know. Put 2 cups of flour sifted with the salt and sugar in a mixing bowl, make a hole in the center and add the soft butter and the corn meal-milk mixture and whisk it until it is light and smooth. It will be elastic. Set the bowl in a dishpan of very hot water and keep it hot for 2 or 3 hours. Then beat in the hot water and 1 to 1¼ cups of sifted flour. It may need 1 tablespoon of hot water to make it smooth and elastic. Put it in an oiled bread pan a little smaller than regulation size. Set it in a pan of warm (not hot) water and let it rise 2 or 3 hours. Preheat the oven to 375° and bake it 40 to 45 minutes. It will be a delicate light brown, have a fine crumb and a fascinating flavor. A good time to make it would be when you are home over a week end. You should be around to keep the water hot.

Raised White Corn Bread

1 cup scalded milk	1 envelope yeast
1 cup white corn meal	2 eggs, beaten
2 Tbsps. sweet butter	2 cups sifted white flour
¼ cup light brown sugar	2 tsps. salt

Scald the milk and pour it slowly over the meal, stirring it so there are no lumps. Add the butter and sugar and when the mixture is smooth and lukewarm, stir in the yeast. Beat the eggs until light and mix them with the sponge. Stir in the flour that has been sifted with the salt. Beat very hard for 4 minutes. The dough will be quite stiff. Set the bowl in a pan of very warm water, cover with a towel and let the dough rise until light. This will take perhaps 1½ hours. Beat dough down well and put it in a greased or oiled bread pan and let it rise to the top of the pan. This will take 1 hour. Put it in a cold oven. Set the heat at 375°F. and bake 25 minutes, then turn the heat to 350° F. and bake about 20 to 25 minutes. Brush with melted butter when it comes from the oven. This is a marvelous bread with a crisp crust.

Nebraska Oatmeal Bread

1 envelope yeast	2 cups rolled oats
¼ cup lukewarm water	2 Tbsps. lard (or butter)
⅓ cup brown sugar	4 cups sifted flour
2 cups scalding milk or water	1 Tbsp. salt

Put the yeast, lukewarm water, and sugar in a small bowl, and let stand until frothy. Pour the scalding liquid over the oats and lard or butter and let it stand until it is lukewarm. Sift the flour with the salt. Combine the yeast, oats and 1 cup of the flour and beat well. Set the bowl in a dishpan of quite warm water, cover with a tea towel and let the dough rise until light. Beat down and add the rest of the flour. If the dough is too heavy to be resilient add a very small amount of warm water. Beat dough with a hard spatula or knead it on a floured board until light. Let it rise again in a pan of warm water, covered, until it doubles. Beat down again and put the dough in two oiled bread pans to rise. When the dough is at the top of the pans put it in a 400° F. oven for 20 minutes, turn down the heat to 350° F. and bake 25 minutes more. A pan of hot water set on the oven floor while the bread is baking makes a fine brown crust. When adding water or milk to dough containing cereals, be careful not to add too much or the bread will sink in the middle when baked.

Wheat Germ and Olive Oil Bread

1 envelope of yeast	1 scant Tbsp. salt
¼ cup lukewarm water	3 cups flour
¼ cup liquid honey	¾ cup wheat germ
1¼ or more cups hot water	¼ cup olive oil

Put the yeast, lukewarm water and honey in a bowl, and let mixture become frothy. Liquid honey is honey that has been diluted with a very little water for convenient use. It should be thick but easy to pour. Mix the hot water with the salt and let it cool to lukewarm. Combine with the yeast mixture and add to the unsifted flour and wheat germ. Mix very well and, while mixing, pour the oil over it. More warm water can be added to make a malleable dough. Beat it hard in a kneading motion in the bowl for 5 minutes. Then put the bowl in a dishpan of hot water, cover with a tea towel, and let the dough rise. Beat down and put the dough in an oiled bread pan to rise again in the same warm place. Turn the oven temperature to 425° F. 10 minutes before you put the bread in the oven. Bake for 15 minutes. Turn the heat to 350° F. and bake 25 minutes more. If it is baking too fast turn the heat off the last 10 minutes. Put a pan of water on the oven floor to make a nice brown crust. This is a good bread with a fine texture.

Mixed Grains Bread

This is a delicious, filling bread. Spread with nut butter, this will give you energy and a feeling of well-being for half a day or longer.

1 cup rye flour
1 cup oat flour
1 cup buckwheat flour
⅔ cup brown rice flour
1 cup white flour
2 envelopes yeast
¼ cup warm water

½ cup molasses
2 eggs beaten
1 Tbsp. salt
1 tsp. anise powder, caraway seed *or* ½ tsp. mace
1 cup warm water, more or less
⅔ cup raisins

Mix all the flours in a large mixing bowl. Dissolve the yeast with lukewarm water and molasses. Combine it with the lightly beaten eggs, salt, spice and ½ cup of warm water. Make a well in the flour and stir in the liquid, adding more liquid to make a stiff dough. Add the raisins and beat and knead with a hard rubber spatula for 3 or 4 minutes. Set the bowl in a pan of hot water, cover with a towel and let the dough rise until light, about 50 minutes. Beat down and put some of the dough in a large oiled bread pan and the rest in a very small one. Set it to rise to the top of the pans—about 35 minutes. Put the pans in a cold oven. Set at 400° F., and bake for 20 minutes. Turn the heat to 375° F. and bake the small loaf 22 minutes more and the large loaf 35 minutes more 55 to 60 minutes altogether. Little bread pans are useful for that overflow dough, or else the oven floor will get it. Dough made with 3½ cups of flour just fills a regulation loaf pan.

Baguettes

This is the long slender French bread, gripped in the hand and carried home to lunch—in France. It is made with or without butter and with all water or ½ cup of milk as part of the liquid.

When made with butter (2 Tbsps. melted in warm water) and milk it keeps longer, but as the French buy it daily, it doesn't matter. The Italians make a crisp loaf using half white and half whole wheat flour. Use white hard wheat if available.

2 envelopes yeast
⅓ cup lukewarm water
1 Tbsps. sugar
4 cups white flour

1½ Tbsps. salt
1 cup lukewarm water
Corn meal for the pan
1 egg white
2 Tbsps. water

Melt the yeast in the warm water mixed with the sugar. Put the flour in a large mixing bowl and mix in the salt. Make a well in the center of the flour and stir in the yeast mixture, adding enough lukewarm water to incorporate all the flour. The dough must be well mixed but quite stiff. Knead it for 4 or 5 minutes, then put the bowl in a pan of warm water, cover with a tea towel and let the dough rise 2 hours. Punch it down for 2 minutes, then divide the dough in 2 parts. Stretch and roll each part into a long baguette, 1½ inches in diameter. Lay them on a baking sheet first sprinkled with corn meal.

There are two ways of baking baguettes. Let them rise 15 minutes, slash them 5 or 6 times diagonally with a razor blade and put them in a cold oven. Set oven at 350° F. and bake them 1 hour. Ten minutes before they are taken from the oven, paint them with a half-beaten egg white mixed with 2 Tbsps. of water. A pan of hot water is placed on the oven floor for a crisp crust. It is removed halfway through the baking. The bread finishes rising in the oven.

The other way of baking them is to let them rise 40 minutes, slashed as above, and put in a preheated 425° F. oven, with the pan of water on the oven floor, and bake 20 minutes. The water is then removed and the heat turned down to 325° F. if they are browning too fast; otherwise turn it to 375° F. and bake them 20 more minutes. Ten minutes before they come from the oven, paint with the egg-white glaze. Do not cover them before they are cut and served. If you like, sprinkle with sesame seeds before baking.

VARIATIONS

PAIN ÉPI is a fascinating craggy staff of a bread, with deep alternate slashes down the sides. When baked it looks like ears of corn on a stalk, hence the name. Pieces may be broken off the size of a roll.

PAIN DE FROMAGE   Take ½ the dough, work in ¼ cup of butter, ⅓ cup grated cheese and 1 egg, after the first rising. Put dough in an oiled round pan to rise and sprinkle the top with grated Gruyère cheese. Bake at 375° F. for 40 minutes.

PAIN DE SUCRE   This is made the same way as Baguettes, but can be made richer with ½ cup of butter, 1 egg and ¼ cup of sugar worked into the dough after the first rising. The top is sprinkled liberally with sugar before baking.

La Fouace aux Noix

Le Nègre, *Tours*

Tours calls to mind Chenonceaux, Loches, Amboise, Blois, Azay-le-Rideau—but Tours itself is a delightful city, full of ancient things, such as the Cathedral of St. Gatien, a step from the Musée des Beaux Arts which is housed in an old château. Within the gate spreads a tremendous Cedar of Lebanon, planted in 1804, next to a brilliant formal garden. A *passerelle* across the Loire brings the visitor to *Le Nègre,* one of the greatest 3-star restaurants in France, another important reason for visiting Tours. M. Charles Barrier, its director-chef, named his establishment for the simple *auberge* where he was apprenticed as a boy of fourteen. That simple restaurant catered to horse traders and carters and was called *Tête de Mort,* a corruption of *Tête de Maure* or moor's head. The present restaurant has an elegant dining room with crystal chandeliers and blown-up pictures of some of the châteaux of the region. One side of the room is all glass showing a plant-filled terrace and a fountain of a huge spouting fish. M. Barrier serves this nut bread, made in his kitchen, with the cheese. With the recipe he wrote this pertinent preamble:

La Fouace or hearthcake is, rather than a pastry, an embellished bread. *Les fouaciers de Lerné,* which Rabelais mentions in *Pantagruel,* were in reality bakers. The *fouace* was generally made at home, since bread was baked in the country oven or hearth. It was more or less rich, depending on the state of the house.

The ingredients composing it were flour, milk, salt, raisins, nuts —ingredients the countryman had at hand without buying them, so that they were available to use up in the most modest homes. When regular bread was made, a morsel of dough was set aside for the *fouace.* This was enriched with butter, some nuts and a few raisins. A ball was formed and baked in the oven with the bread. It provided their dessert.

It was eaten, preferably a little warm. Rabelais says somewhere on this subject, "there is nothing better than warm *fouace* with grapes and fresh Rosé Bourgueil or mellow Vouvray."

Here, then, is the recipe for *fouace.*

4 cups white flour	⅓ cup lukewarm water
½ cup whole wheat flour	1 cup lukewarm milk
1½ Tbsps. salt	¾ cup walnuts, coarsely
1 envelope yeast	chopped
	½ cup softened sweet butter

The flour used in France for *pain de campagne* is rougher than our white flour so I added the whole wheat. The result is a good approximation. Mix the flours with the salt in a large mixing bowl, make a well in the center and add the yeast which has been softened with the water. Add the milk and stir very well to make a spongy dough. Mix in the nuts and butter with a hard rubber spatula. The dough must be stiff so that it holds its shape. Set the bowl in a pan of quite warm water, cover with a tea towel and let the dough rise 2 hours. Punch down the dough and knead it with the spatula 3 or 4 minutes and form into a ball. Sprinkle a pan with coarse corn meal and put the ball on the meal. Let it rise 15 minutes, then turn the oven to 425° F. When the oven is hot, slash the top of the ball with a very sharp knife, put it in the oven on the middle shelf with a pan of hot water on the oven floor. Bake the bread for 30 minutes, remove the water and turn the oven to 300° F. and bake the bread 30 minutes more. This is perfect to serve with the *plateau des fromages*. If you wish to use starter (see Danish Sour Bread) for this bread, omit the whole wheat flour and add an extra ½ cup of white flour.

Pain de Mie

Restaurant Henri IV, *Chartres*
Maurice Cazalis, Director-Chef

Pain de Mie is all crumb with no crust. It is a delicate bread that is made in this fine restaurant, and is used to accompany some creamed dishes, for making sandwiches, or just for eating plain. This recipe just fits into a sandwich pan measuring 11 x 4½ x 2¾-inches.

4½ cups white flour
¼ cup sugar
1 Tbsp. salt
½ cup softened sweet butter

2 eggs, beaten
1 envelope yeast
1½ or more cups lukewarm water

Put the flour into a large mixing bowl, make a well in the middle and put in all the ingredients, mixing in the water gradually, adding enough to make a pliable dough. Mix with a firm rubber spatula until the dough is light and spongy. It must not be too soft. Set the bowl in a pan of warm water, cover with a tea towel and let the dough rise until double, about 1 hour. Punch it down for a minute or two, then put it in an oiled pan. Set the pan in warm water to rise again. This will take about 45 minutes. Bake about 40 minutes at 375° F. If it is baking too fast, turn the heat down to 325° F. after it has baked 25 minutes.

Pane Casalingo

This is Italian homemade bread—a large, crusty, round loaf made both in Italy and France. Resturants in both countries serve it toasted and it is very popular. It is made of hard wheat. To approximate its rough texture the corn meal is used in the starter and whole wheat may replace the white flour.

STARTER
1 cup scalded milk
2 Tbsps. malt syrup
¼ cup corn meal
1 cup hard wheat flour
1 envelope yeast

3 cups flour
4 tsps. salt
the starter
1 envelope yeast
2 Tbsps. butter
1 cup warm water

The starter can stand in a glass jar, covered with cheese cloth from 12 to 18 hours. Pour the scalded milk over the syrup and corn meal and when it is lukewarm, stir in the flour and yeast. For the dough put the unsifted flour in a large bowl and mix in the salt. Make a well in the center of the flour and add all the starter, the yeast and the butter melted in ½ cup of the water. Mix this well, adding just enough water to incorporate all the flour. If the dough isn't stiff enough the ball will flatten when baking. Mix it about 4 minutes, then put the bowl in a pan of warm water, cover with a tea towel and let the dough rise 2 hours. Punch it down 2 or 3 minutes, then put the dough in an oiled, round 7-inch fireproof bowl to rise about an hour until light. Preheat the oven to 500°. When the oven is hot, gently empty the dough onto a corn meal-sprinkled pan and slash the top across once each way with a razor blade, making shallow incisions so the dough won't sink. Put the bread in the oven with a pan of hot water on the oven floor, and bake it 20 minutes. Turn the oven down to 300° and remove the pan of water and continue baking 35 or 40 minutes more. Let it cool several hours before cutting it. This is as near as a home gas or electric oven can come to baking this bread as the old European ovens do with the even heat coming from all sides. You may sprinkle the dough with sesame seeds before baking.

VARIATIONS
PANE CRESCENTA from *Forno Flavio Gabrielli*

A visit to this rustic bakery 7 kilometers from Bologna proved both interesting and rewarding. Casalingo dough is the base for various breads seen in the bakeries. This one is made with cooked ham, such as prosciutto. The bread is particularly good when fresh and served with antipasto.

Casalingo dough	Salt
⅓ cup chopped ham	More chopped ham
¼ cup lard or butter	

Take half the casalingo dough for this bread (the other half may be made into a long narrow loaf). Work the ham and the soft shortening into the dough. Roll it out quite thin and put it in a round large pan, sprinkle with salt and ham. Let it rise then make 8 punches with a sharp knife over the surface. Bake it in a 375° F. oven about 25 minutes.

CIAMBELLA

Casalingo dough	½ cup sugar
½ cup butter	Sugar or sugar crystals
2 eggs, plus 2 yolks	

Soften the butter and add it to the beaten eggs and yolks. Beat in the sugar. After the dough has been mixed, work this into it before the first rising. Set the bowl in a pan of warm water, cover with a tea towel and let the dough rise until light. Divide the dough in half and roll each to fit an oiled 9-inch cake pan. Let the cakes rise and then sprinkle with sugar crystals. Bake at 375° F. about 25 minutes.

Pizza Romana

Piccolo Mondo, *Rome*

Marino Camponeschi, owner-chef of this gay restaurant, makes this pane himself for his restaurant and says it also makes marvelous sandwiches. It is crunchy, and great with a pasta.

DOUGH
1 envelope yeast
1 Tbsp. sugar
¼ cup lukewarm water
2 Tbsps. olive oil
4 cups white flour
1 Tbsp. salt
Lukewarm water

TOP
Olive oil
Salt

Dissolve the yeast with the sugar in the lukewarm water until frothy. Add the oil. Put the flour in a large mixing bowl, make a well in the middle of the flour and mix in the yeast mixture, salt and enough lukewarm water to make a light, spongy dough. Mix hard 2 minutes with a hard rubber spatula. Set the bowl in a pan of warm water, cover with a tea towel and let the dough rise until light and double in size. Punch down 2 minutes, then divide the dough in 3 parts, rolling each very thin. Put them on a greased sheet and let them rise. Punch holes over the surface with a sharp-pointed knife, brush with olive oil and sprinkle with some coarse or ordinary salt. Bake about 25 minutes at 375° F. This is cut in pie shapes (when cool) and served in a bread basket.

Danish Buttermilk Bread

1 envelope yeast
2 Tbsps. light brown sugar
⅓ cup lukewarm water
¼ cup sweet butter

4 cups white flour
2½ tsps. salt
2 or 3 tsps. caraway powder
1 cup buttermilk

Mix the yeast, sugar and warm water together until the yeast dissolves. Soften the butter so it can be whisked into the yeast mixture. Mix flour, salt and caraway powder in a mixing bowl. Warm the buttermilk to lukewarm and mix it with the yeast mixture. Make a well in the center of the flour and mix in the liquids. Beat very hard for 2 minutes, adding very little warm buttermilk to make a spongy, elastic dough. Set the bowl to rise in warm water, covered with a tea towel until the dough is light, about 1 hour. Beat down and put in an oiled bread pan, brush with oil or butter and let it rise again in warm water. Preheat the oven to 400° F. and bake 20 minutes; then turn the heat to 325° F. and bake 30 minutes more. Cardamom powder can be used instead of caraway if preferred.

Swedish Christmas Limpor Bread

Vörtlimpor

1 envelope yeast
¼ cup lukewarm water
2 Tbsps. light brown sugar
1½ cups white flour, unsifted
1 tsp. salt
1 Tbsp. aniseed

1 tsp. powdered fennel
Grated rind of 1 orange
⅓ cup molasses
1½ cups beer, ale or stout
1 tablespoon butter
2 cups rye flour

Combine the yeast, water and sugar and let stand in a small bowl until frothy. Put the white flour in a large mixing bowl and add the salt, aniseed, fennel, orange rind, and molasses. Heat the beer (ale or stout) in a saucepan to lukewarm and melt the butter in it, then make a well in the flour mixture and pour it in. Before mixing add the yeast and then beat it well. Set the bowl in a dishpan of quite hot water, cover and let the dough rise for 45 minutes to an hour. Add the rye flour and beat very hard; it should be a light, elastic dough. If necessary add a spoon or so of luke-warm water. Beat for 4 or 5 minutes then set in a pan of water again, cover and let rise until double in bulk. Beat the dough down well, then put it in a greased bread pan, set in warm water, cover loosely and let rise 1 hour or more. Put the pan in a cold oven. Set it at 375° F. and bake the bread 15 minutes; reduce the heat to 325° F. and bake 30 minutes more. This bread has a fascinating flavor.

Wheat and Wheat Germ Bread

1 envelope yeast
¼ cup lukewarm water
1¼ cups hot water
¼ cup butter
3 Tbsps. honey

1 cup wheat germ
1 cup whole wheat flour
2 cups white flour
1 Tbsp. salt

Dissolve the yeast in the warm water. Melt the butter in the hot water and when it is lukewarm add the yeast and honey. Mix the wheat germ with the flours and salt. Make a well in the center of the flour and stir in the liquids. Stir hard for 2 minutes, adding a very little warm water if necessary to make a pliable yet firm dough. Set the bowl in a pan of warm water covered with a tea towel for the dough to rise. After dough is light, punch it down with a wooden spoon for 2 or 3 minutes, then put it in an oiled bread pan and let it rise again. Bake it at 400° F. for 10 minutes, then turn the heat to 325° F. for 40 minutes. It can be brushed with oil before it rises the second time and sprinkled with sesame seeds. This is a very fine bread.

Holiday and
Fancy Yeast Breads

STOLLEN

Der Dresdner Christstollen

The custom of baking stollens is ancient, originating in Dresden about 1400. In those days the people tried to represent religious thought in their baking. For example, the doughnut represents the sponge by which the Lord received drink while on the cross, while the pretzel represents the chains He had to wear. The stollen is a representation of the Christchild in his swaddling clothes.

In olden times, the town of Siebenlehn was famous for its stollens. The bakers distributed them widely. In 1615 they had a fierce quarrel with the bakers of Meissen, who would not tolerate Siebenlehn bakery products to be brought to Meissen. In 1663 the Dresden bakers complained that the Siebenlehn bakers brought enormous quantities of baked goods to Dresden.

The recipe for stollen in those days may have been quite different from what it is today. Up to the year 1647, during the Lenten season, butter was not to be used for baking. Since the Advent season preceding Christmas was a time of fasting, the prohibition of butter left only oil to be used. This was quite inconvenient

34

and the cakes probably did not taste very good. Therefore the Archduke Ernst and his brother Duke Albrecht of Saxony petitioned the Pope to have the prohibition canceled. The way in which the two rulers worded their petition can be seen from the Pope's reply:

> Since, as you represent it to us, there are no olive trees in your lands, that there is not only not enough, but much too little oil, and it smells, and that it is expensive, or the kind of oil one makes from roots which is repugnant to the nature of human beings and unhealthy, and that its use brings all kinds of illnesses to the inhabitants of your lands—therefore we are well disposed toward your request and, by papal authority and the act of this letter, we grant permission that you, your women, sons, daughters and all true servants may freely use butter instead of oil without incurring penance.

Later, around 1691, others too were allowed to use butter for their baking. However, the condition for this permission was that a twentieth of one gold florin had to be contributed annually toward building the Cathedral of Freiberg. When Saxony became Protestant, this condition was canceled.

German Holiday Cake

2 envelopes yeast
⅓ cup lukewarm water
1 Tbsp. light brown sugar
1¾ cups scalded milk
1 tsp. salt
4 cups sifted flour
3 egg yolks, beaten
1 cup soft sweet butter
Grated rind of 1 lemon
Grated rind of 1 orange

2½ cups finely sliced fruit: citron, raisins, currants, glacéed cherries, pineapple, lemon peel, sultanas
⅓ cup sherry
1 cup almonds, chopped & browned
1 tsp. almond extract
1 tsp. vanilla
1 cup light brown sugar
1½ cups sifted flour
Melted butter
Soft sweet butter
Instant icing sugar

Dissolve the yeast in the lukewarm water with the sugar until frothy. Scald the milk with the salt and, when it is lukewarm, stir in the yeast and 4 cups of flour. Beat very hard for 3 minutes. Set the bowl in a dishpan of hot water, cover with a tea towel and let the sponge rise until light. Beat the egg yolks with the soft butter and add the two rinds. Pour the sherry over the prepared fruit so it won't stick together. Combine fruits with nuts, extracts, and sugar and toss them with 1½ cups of sifted flour. Combine this mixture with the sponge and yolk-butter mixture. Beat until light and spongy, adding a little more flour if necessary. The dough may be divided into 2 or 3 parts. Put each part on a floured board and roll into an oval a scant ½ inch thick. Fold one end over almost to the other end and with the heel of your hand press the fold gently to seal it. Put the cakes on a large greased, floured baking sheet to rise about 30 minutes. Since they are heavy with fruit, they do not rise as lightly as other cakes. Preheat the oven to 375° F. and bake the cakes about 45 minutes. If they are baking and browning too fast, turn the oven down after the first 25 minutes to 350° F. or 325° F. If 3 cakes are made they will take 10 to 12 minutes less time to bake. When they come from the oven, brush with melted butter. When cool, brush heavily with soft butter and sprinkle thickly with instant icing sugar which is more traditional than powdered sugar.

OTHER HOLIDAY BREADS

Panettone

This big, round, beautiful Christmas bread comes from Italy. It may be baked in a charlotte mold, 4 inches deep and 7¼ inches across. The dough is a little too large for this size mold so butter 3 or 4 muffin tins and fill them ½ full. The rum gives the bread a fine flavor and the saffron marinated an hour in the rum makes it a fine rich yellow.

¾ cup sweet butter
⅔ cup light brown sugar
1 tsp. salt
1 tsp. powdered anise
1 tsp. almond extract
2 envelopes yeast
¼ cup lukewarm milk
1 Tbsp. light brown sugar

2 eggs, beaten
1 tsp. saffron marinated in
3 Tbsps. rum 1 hour
4½ cups sifted flour
1 cup glacé fruits: cherries,
citron, pineapple, angelica,
currants
Honey and powdered sugar or
Egg White Icing (p. 40)

Cream the butter and sugar in a large mixing bowl until smooth. Add the salt, anise and extract. Dissolve the yeast in the milk and sugar and when it is foamy combine with the creamed butter mixture. Add the lightly beaten eggs and the saffron and rum. Stir in 3½ cups of the flour and beat for 3 minutes. Slice the fruit and toss it through the other cup of flour and mix it with the dough. When it is elastic set the bowl in a pan of lukewarm water, cover with a towel and let it rise until it is light—about an hour. Oil the mold, fill it ⅔ full of the dough and let it rise again until light. Preheat the oven to 375°, bake the cake 30 minutes, reduce the heat to 300° and continue baking it 30 minutes more. Let the cake stand 20 minutes, then remove it from the mold. Brush with honey and dredge with powdered sugar. Or if you wish to use the icing, cover the top of the cake and let it drip down the sides. It may be decorated with a little sliced candied fruit. Some of us like it served with sweet butter.

Vánočka

Czech Christmas Twist

2 envelopes yeast
¼ cup lukewarm water
2 Tbsps. light brown sugar
8 cups sifted flour
½ tsp. mace
1 tsp. anise
Grated rind 1 lemon
1 cup sweet butter

4 egg yolks, beaten
1 cup light brown sugar
1 cup warm light cream
1 cup warm milk, approximately
1 cup seedless raisins
½ cup sliced browned almonds
egg yolk
2 Tbsps. light cream

Dissolve the yeast in the lukewarm water with 2 Tbsps. sugar. Sift the sifted and measured flour with the spices and then toss the rind through it. Cut in the butter with a pastry cutter as you would for piecrust. Beat the egg yolks and add them to the sugar and warm cream. Make a well in the flour and pour in the yeast and egg-cream mixture. Mix well, then add enough warm milk to make quite a stiff dough and beat for 5 minutes. Set the bowl in a dishpan of quite warm water, cover with a tea towel, and let the dough rise an hour or more until double in bulk. Beat down the dough and add the raisins and nuts. With hands well floured, divide the dough in half. Make 4 long rolls of ½ of the dough; make 5 rolls of the other half. Let rolls rise 20 minutes, then braid the 4 large rolls and form a loaf in a pan lined with buttered parchment paper. Lightly flour the braid. Take 3 of the remaining rolls and make a braid and place it on top of the braid in the pan. Lightly flour the braid. Twist the 2 remaining rolls and lay them on top. Flouring each braid insures its remaining where it is put. Let it rise. Preheat the oven to 375° F. When the loaf has risen bake it for 30 minutes, then brush it with egg yolk mixed with light cream. Return it to the oven for 20 minutes more. If it is baking too fast, turn the temperature to 325° F. This is a most spectacular production of which any cook may be proud.

Babovka

from Czecho-Slovakia

1 envelope yeast	1 egg
¼ cup lukewarm water	½ tsp. salt
1 Tbsp. light brown sugar	1 cup warm milk
¼ cup flour	3 to 4 cups sifted flour
1 cup sweet butter	½ cup seedless raisins
½ cup light brown sugar	Powdered sugar
3 egg yolks	Cinnamon or anise

Melt the yeast in the lukewarm water with 1 Tbsp. sugar. Mix in ¼ cup of flour, set in a pan of warm water to become light. Cream the butter with the light brown sugar. Beat the yolks and egg until light, add the salt and warm milk. Combine with the creamed butter and sugar. Toss the raisins through 2½ cups of the flour. Combine the flour with the egg-butter mixture. When the yeast is light combine the two mixtures and beat very hard. Add more flour if necessary to make a light, spongy dough. Beat for 3 or 4 minutes. Butter a tube pan, add the dough and let it rise to double. The pan may be set in warm water, covered with a tea towel. Preheat the oven to 375° F. and bake about 45 minutes. If bread is baking too fast, turn oven down after 30 minutes to 325° F. After cake has been out of the oven 2 minutes, loosen the sides with a sharp pointed knife and turn the cake upside down onto a cake plate. Cover while hot with a thick sprinkle of mixed powdered sugar and spice.

Koulitch

This spectacular Russian coffeecake made to celebrate Easter is baked in a mold so that it is 12 inches high and it is frosted with yellow icing to make the Holy Day more festive. Hallelujah! If you haven't a cylinder, you can tie a buttered parchment paper collar around the top of a charlotte mold to hold the dough; or you may bake it in a 9-inch tube pan and decorate the cake while it is still a little warm, with frosting so that it drips casually down the sides. The top may have a few sugared violets placed here and there.

1 tsp. saffron
¼ cup dark rum
1 cup sliced glacé fruits: cherries, angelica, currants, pineapple, citron
½ cup sliced, browned almonds
2 or 3 bitter almonds, ground
1 cup sifted flour
3 envelopes yeast
¼ cup lukewarm milk
2 Tbsps. light brown sugar
¾ cup sweet butter

1 cup light brown sugar
1 tsp. anise extract
1 tsp. almond extract
3 egg yolks
1 cup light warm cream
4 cups sifted flour
3 egg whites, beaten

EGG WHITE ICING
1 beaten egg white
2 cups powdered sugar (10X)
4 or 5 drops yellow coloring
1 teaspoon rose or almond extract

First soak the saffron in the rum an hour or more. Prepare the fruits by slicing them. Grind both kinds of almonds together and mix them and the fruits in the cup of flour and set aside. Dissolve the yeast with the milk and 2 tablespoons of sugar until frothy. Cream the butter and sugar until smooth, then add the extracts, egg yolks and warm cream. Combine this mixture with the yeast. Add this mixture to the 4 cups of sifted flour and beat until smooth and elastic. Set the dough in a pan of warm water, cover with a towel and let it rise until light. Beat it down a minute, then work in the floured fruits and nuts and the saffron and rum. Beat the egg whites until stiff and fold them into the dough last. Set the bowl again in warm (not hot) water to rise until light. Butter your mold well and put in dough ⅔ full. Any dough that is left may be put in greased muffin tins. Let the dough rise to the top of the mold which may take 2 hours because of the butter and fruit. Preheat the oven 10 minutes set at 375° F. and bake the cake 20 minutes; then turn the heat to 325° F. and bake it 40 minutes longer. If the cake is baking too fast, turn the oven to 300° F. Bake the small cakes 25 or 30 minutes at 325° F. When the cakes are nearly cool frost them.

For the frosting, beat the egg white until stiff then beat in the sugar with a rotary beater and add the flavoring and coloring. If necessary add a teaspoon of rum or lemon juice.

This dough has various uses. It may be rolled thin, cut in strips, sprinkled with sugar, twisted, allowed to rise and then baked. It may be cut in squares, sprinkled with sugar and folded so that 2 opposite points meet. Or tiny rounds may be cut, covered with a teaspoon of jam, another round placed on top, allowed to rise and then baked.

Babka

from Russia

1 envelope yeast	2 or 3 Tbsps. dark rum
1 Tbsp. light brown sugar	1 tsp. vanilla
3 Tbsps. lukewarm water	2 cups flour, sifted
½ cup sweet butter	6 egg whites, beaten
½ cup light brown sugar	Powdered sugar
6 egg yolks	1 tsp. anise, cardamom, or cin-
½ cup heavy cream	namon
½ cup golden sultana raisins	

Dissolve the yeast with the Tbsp. of sugar in the lukewarm water until frothy. Cream the butter with the sugar until smooth; beat in the egg yolks, 1 at a time. Add the cream. Sprinkle the raisins with the rum and vanilla. Toss them through the flour. Combine the yeast with the butter-cream mixture and stir it into the flour. Beat hard for 2 minutes, then fold in the stiffly beaten egg whites. Butter a 9-inch tube pan well and sprinkle the bottom and sides with sugar. Pour in the dough and set the pan in a dishpan of warm water, cover with a tea towel, and let the dough rise to the top of the pan. This will take about 1 hour. Preheat the oven to 375° F. and bake the cake 15 minutes. Turn the heat to 350° F. and bake 20 minutes more. When cake comes from the oven let it stand a minute, then loosen from tube and sides with a slender sharp knife and turn it upside down onto a cake plate. Sprinkle thickly with powdered sugar mixed with anise. Serve warm or at room temperature.

Danish Coffee Braid or Ring

1 envelope yeast
¼ cup lukewarm water
1 cup warm milk
⅓ cup light brown sugar
¾ tsp. salt
½ cup soft sweet butter
4 cups sifted flour

2 tsp. cardamom seeds, crushed
1 egg yolk
1 Tbsp. cream
Chopped almonds
Light brown sugar
Cinnamon
Melted butter

Dissolve the yeast in the lukewarm water. Put the milk in a saucepan with the sugar, salt and butter. Heat milk just enough to melt the butter. Combine the yeast, milk mixture and 1 cup of the flour and beat until smooth. Mix the cardamom seeds through the rest of the flour, then add it to the sponge. Beat 4 or 5 minutes. Let the dough rise in a pan of warm water, covered, until light and doubled in bulk. Beat down and toss onto a floured board. For a braid, divide the dough in 3 parts, roll each into a long rope and braid them. Form into a greased shallow pan, paint with egg yolk mixed with 1 Tbsp. of cream. Sprinkle with chopped almonds, sugar and cinnamon. Let rise again in a warm place until light. Preheat the oven to 375° F. and bake the braid about 20 minutes; reset the oven to 350° F. and bake 25 to 30 minutes more.

For a ring, roll the dough ½ inch thick into an oblong. Brush with melted butter, sprinkle with chopped nuts, sugar and cinnamon. Roll up the long way, form into a ring and place in a greased shallow pan. Tuck the ends under. Brush with egg yolk mixed with cream. Sprinkle with cinnamon and sugar. With sharp scissors make diagonal cuts half through the dough ¾ inch apart. Let the ring rise until light, then bake about 35 to 40 minutes in a preheated 350° F. oven.

Czech Holiday Poppy Seed Cake

Buchta Makova

It takes less than two hours to begin and finish this wonderful, light cake. A beautiful coffeecake for teatime, dinner dessert or late supper.

2 envelopes yeast	½ cup heavy cream
¼ cup lukewarm water	½ cup browned sliced almonds,
1 Tbsp. light brown sugar	coarsely chopped
1 cup sweet butter	2 cups ground poppy seeds
8 egg yolks	½ cup light brown sugar
Grated rind 1 lemon	3 cups sifted flour
1 tsp. lemon juice	5 egg whites, beaten
¼ tsp. salt	2 tsps. almond extract
	Powdered sugar

Have all the ingredients at room temperature. Dissolve the yeast in the lukewarm water with 1 Tbsp. of sugar. Cream the butter with a single whisk and beat in 1 egg yolk at a time. Add the grated lemon rind, juice and salt. Warm the cream and whisk it in. Mix the almonds, poppy seeds and brown sugar together. Sift the flour and measure it. Beat the egg whites until stiff and add the almond extract. Mix the yeast with the butter mixture; then beat in all the prepared ingredients alternately, beating until light and resilient. Butter a 9-inch tube pan very well. When the batter is well mixed pour it into the tube pan and set it in a dishpan of warm (not hot) water. Cover with a tea towel to rise 50 minutes until the dough is within an inch of the top of the pan. Preheat the oven to 400° F. and bake the cake 5 minutes; reset the oven to 375° F. and bake 30 minutes more. After it comes from the oven let it stand a minute, then loosen the sides with a sharp pointed knife. Turn it onto a cake plate. If the pan has been well buttered, the cake will drop to the plate. Cover thickly with powdered sugar. It is best served with moderately soft sweet butter, the best you can obtain.

Czech Coffeecake

2 envelopes yeast	1 cup warm milk
¼ cup lukewarm water	4 cups sifted flour
1 Tbsp. light brown sugar	1½ tsps. salt
½ cup sweet butter	½ tsp. mace
½ cup light brown sugar	Grated rind 1 large lemon
4 egg yolks	2 egg whites, beaten stiff
	Cinnamon and Powdered sugar

Dissolve the yeast in the lukewarm water and Tbsp. sugar until frothy. Cream the butter and sugar until smooth and beat in the egg yolks, 1 at a time. Combine the yeast, butter mixture and the lukewarm milk. Put the flour in a large mixing bowl and stir in the salt, mace and lemon rind. Make a well in the center and pour in the liquid. Beat for 6 or 8 minutes with a hard rubber spatula. Then fold in the stiffly beaten whites of egg. Mix only until the whites are well incorporated. Put the batter in a 9-inch well-greased tube pan and set it in a pan of warm water to rise for 45 minutes. Cover it loosely with a tea towel. Put it in a cold oven set at 375° F. and bake for 15 minutes. If cake is browning too fast, turn the heat to 350 or even 325 and bake 30 minutes more. When it comes from the oven, let it stand 3 or 4 minutes, then loosen the edges with a narrow, sharp-pointed knife, turn it upside down onto a cake plate and sprinkle with a mixture of cinnamon and powdered sugar. This cake is delicious served with sweet butter and may be cut before it has completely cooled. It is fine for breakfast, tea or supper.

Rita's Julekake

Norwegian Christmas Bread

This is a great favorite among the Norwegians, who bake it throughout the winter.

2⅔ cups milk, scalded
1 cup butter
⅓ cup Crisco
2 envelopes yeast (rapidmix)
8 cups sifted flour

1 cup sugar
1 tsp. salt
2 tsps. cardamom
1⅓ cups raisins
8 ounces citron

Scald the milk and add the butter and Crisco. Let it stand until it is lukewarm. Thoroughly mix the undissolved yeast with all the dry ingredients including the cardamom, using 2 cups of the flour. Reserve ⅓ cup of flour for the kneading board. Stir in the milk-butter mixture. Toss the raisins and citron through the rest of the flour and add it to the batter. Mix thoroughly and set the bowl in a dishpan of quite warm water, cover with a tea towel and let the dough rise 3 hours. When it is double in bulk and light, knead the dough on a floured board until it is elastic. Divide the dough and put it in 2 greased bread pans. Put the pans in a warm place to rise 1 hour. Brush tops of loaves with warm milk and bake at 350° F. 1 hour. Let cool in the pans ½ hour.

German Coffeecake

2 envelopes yeast
¼ cup lukewarm water
1 Tbsp. sugar
1½ tsps. salt
4 cups sifted flour
⅔ cup gold sultana raisins
Grated rind of 1 lemon
1 cup milk, scalded
1 large egg, beaten

⅓ cup light brown sugar
⅓ cup butter
STREUSSEL
½ cup sweet butter, melted
½ cup light brown sugar
½ cup fine bread crumbs
½ cup sifted flour
2 Tbsps. cinnamon
½ cup browned almonds or
walnuts, ground

Combine the yeast, lukewarm water and sugar in a small bowl and set it in a saucepan of quite warm water; cover and let it become frothy. Sift the salt with 1½ cups of the flour and beat into the yeast mixture in a large mixing bowl. Set the bowl in a dishpan of quite warm water, cover with a tea towel and let sponge become light, about 30 minutes. Mix the raisins and rind with the rest of the sifted flour. Scald the milk and let it cool to lukewarm. Beat the egg until light and add it to the brown sugar and butter which have been lightly creamed together. Beat the flour, milk and butter mixture alternately into the yeast. Beat for 10 minutes until smooth and satiny. Set the bowl in a pan of warm water, cover with a tea towel and let the dough rise until double in volume. Beat it down well and roll it out on a well-floured board in an oblong ½ inch thick. Put the dough in a long, greased pan, cover with a towel, put it in a warm place and after 20 minutes strew the mixed ingredients of the streussel over the top. Let the dough rise another 25 minutes. Bake in a 375° F. oven 20 to 25 minutes. This may be served warm with butter.

The streussel is mixed so that it is in crumbles. It is a good mixture for many rolls and coffeecakes. The cinnamon may be replaced by 1 Tbsp. cardamom powder for Danish and Swedish coffeecakes.

Gugelhupf

Viennese Coffeecake

1 envelope yeast	¾ cup lukewarm milk
¼ cup lukewarm milk	⅓ cup raisins
2 Tbsps. light brown sugar	¼ cup sliced citron
⅔ cup sweet butter	2½ cups sifted flour
½ cup light brown sugar	½ tsp. salt
4 egg yolks	2 egg whites, beaten
1 tsp. almond extract	Powdered Sugar
1 tsp. rose extract	Anise (optional)

Dissolve the yeast in the lukewarm milk with 2 Tbsps. sugar until frothy. Cream the butter and sugar until fluffy and smooth and add the egg yolks and extracts. Combine the yeast and sugar-butter mixtures with the milk. Toss the raisins and citron in the flour sifted with the salt, combine with the liquids, and beat hard for 2 minutes. Fold in the stiffly beaten egg whites. Oil a gugelhupf, a fluted tube pan, and fill ⅔ full. Put the mold in a warm place, or in a pan of warm (not hot) water, cover with a towel and let the dough rise until it comes to the top of the pan. Preheat the oven to 400° F. and bake the cake for 10 minutes; turn the heat to 325° F. and bake 25 to 30 minutes more. Let it stand 2 minutes when it comes from the oven; loosen the sides with a sharp-pointed knife, turn it upside down over a cake plate and it will drop to the plate. Sprinkle generously with powdered sugar mixed with a little powdered anise, if you like. This has been a favorite coffeecake in Germany and Austria for generations.

Hungarian Mohn Cake

2 cups flour
¼ tsp. salt
½ cup sweet butter
1 envelope yeast
⅓ cup lukewarm water
3 Tbsps. light brown sugar
¼ cup sour cream

POPPY SEED FILLING
1 cup ground poppy seeds
Juice and grated rind of 1 small
lemon
½ cup light brown sugar
½ cup seedless raisins
Milk or light cream
GLAZE
1 egg yolk mixed with
2 Tbsps. heavy cream

Sift the flour with the salt. Cut in the butter with a wire pastry cutter. Dissolve the yeast in the lukewarm water with the sugar in a small bowl. Let sit in a pan of warm water, covered, until fluffy. Combine the yeast, flour and sour cream. Knead on a lightly floured board for 15 minutes, until it is light and springy. Roll the dough ½ inch thick and 12 inches long to fit a pan of that length. Grease and flour the pan. Combine the filling ingredients in a saucepan and moisten with a little milk or cream. Cook 2 or 3 minutes to a light smooth paste. Spread this on the dough and roll it up the long way. Put it in the pan and let it stand 10 minutes. It doesn't need to rise. Put the cake in a 350° F. oven and bake it 45 minutes. After it has been in the oven 20 minutes brush the surface with the glaze ingredients. This lovely dough has a variety of uses. After it is rolled it may be cut in 4-inch squares, filled with jam, rolled and baked about 25 minutes. Or it may be used for those little Russian filled pastries, pirozhki, for an entrée. They are filled with chopped hard-boiled eggs and mushrooms, or meat or chopped liver fillings.

Nut and Honey Ring

1 envelope yeast
1 Tbsp. light brown sugar
¼ cup lukewarm water
¾ cup warm milk
¼ cup sweet butter
¾ tsp. salt
1 large egg, beaten
3 cups sifted flour

FILLING
2 Tbsps. soft butter
2 Tbsps. heavy cream
2 Tbsps. thick honey
⅔ cup chopped nuts
1½ tsps. cinnamon
¾ cup raisins
1 egg yolk
1 Tbsp. cream
Ground nuts and sugar

Dissolve the yeast with the sugar in lukewarm water until frothy. Warm the milk enough to melt the butter. Add the salt and beaten egg and combine with the yeast; then stir into the flour. Beat 3 or 4 minutes until elastic. Put the bowl in a pan of warm water, cover with a towel and let dough rise until light. Mix the ingredients for the filling. When the dough has risen beat it down. Toss it onto a floured board and roll into an oblong ½ inch thick. Spread with the filling and roll the long way into a tight roll. Form into a ring on a greased pan and tuck the ends under. Brush with an egg yolk mixed with 1 Tbsp. of cream. Sprinkle with a few ground nuts and sugar. Using sharp scissors, make diagonal slashes on the top ¾ inch apart around the ring, an inch or more deep into the dough. Let the ring rise until light, then bake about 45 minutes in a preheated 350° F. oven.

Almond Coffeecake

2 envelopes yeast
¼ cup lukewarm water
2 Tbsps. light brown sugar
1 cup sweet butter
½ cup light brown sugar
8 egg yolks
½ cup warm heavy cream

2 tsps. almond extract
¼ tsp. salt
⅓ cup browned sliced almonds
⅓ cup finely chopped citron
4 cups sifted flour
5 egg whites, beaten
Powdered sugar

Dissolve the yeast and brown sugar in lukewarm water until frothy. Cream the butter and sugar until light and smooth; beat in 1 egg yolk at a time with a whisk. Mix the cream, almond extract and salt together. Combine with the yeast and butter-egg yolk mixtures. Toss the almonds and citron through the flour and stir in the first mixture. Beat very hard for 5 minutes, then fold in the stiffly beaten egg whites. Grease a 9-inch tube pan very well with butter and put in the dough. Let it rise about 50 minutes until it is almost to the top of the pan. Preheat the oven to 375° F. and bake for 10 minutes; reduce the heat to 350° F. and bake about 35 minutes more. Remove from the oven and after 2 minutes loosen the sides with a sharp-pointed knife, and turn upside down onto a cake plate. Cover with powdered sugar. Serve with sweet butter.

Sour Cream Coffeecake

2 envelopes yeast
1 Tbsp. light brown sugar
3 Tbsps. warm milk
½ cup sweet butter
⅔ cup light brown sugar
4 egg yolks
1 tsp. almond extract
1 tsp. vanilla extract
1 cup warmed sour cream
1½ tsps. salt
4 cups sifted flour

⅞ cup mixed candied fruits: pineapple, cherries, citron, currants, dates or prunes
2 egg whites, beaten
Streussel #2:
⅓ cup sweet butter
½ cup light brown sugar
1 Tbsp. cinnamon
1 cup sifted flour
½ cup browned chopped almonds

Dissolve the yeast with the brown sugar in the warm milk until foamy. Cream the butter and sugar until smooth then add the yolks, extracts and warmed cream. Combine the yeast and butter mixtures and add the salt and 3½ cups of the flour. Beat very hard with a hard rubber spatula for 2 or 3 minutes. Toss the fruits with the other ½ cup of flour and add it to the sponge. Use any combination of fruits you like. The dates and prunes must be sliced. After the dough is well mixed fold in the stiffly beaten egg whites. Set the bowl in a pan of warm water, cover with a towel and let the dough rise until light. This will take a little over an hour. Beat it down and put the dough in 2 oiled 8- or 10-inch pans. Or it may be baked in 1 long pan. Put the pans in a warm place to rise and make the streussel. Cream the butter and sugar until smooth, add the cinnamon and cut in the flour to make a crumbly mixture. Add the almonds. When the dough has risen, sprinkle the top with streussel. Bake at 375° F. for about 45 minutes. If the cake is baking too fast, turn the heat to 325° F.

This dough can be baked in a charlotte mold, gugelhupf or tube pan. When it is turned out the top is dredged with powdered sugar and the streussel is omitted. Or the dough can be divided in 2 parts, rolled out thin, spread with mohn filling (or some other), rolled, set to rise and then baked in a long loaf pan. The roll may also be sliced 1 inch thick, put cut-side down in a long pan, allowed to rise and then baked. A good dough has many uses.

Chocolate Bread

1 envelope yeast
¼ cup lukewarm water
1 Tbsp. light brown sugar
4 egg yolks, beaten
½ cup light brown sugar
½ cup soft sweet butter
½ cup Dutch cocoa

Few grains salt
2 tsps. vanilla
½ cup warm milk
2 cups sifted flour
4 egg whites, beaten
½ cup currants soaked in 2
Tbsps. rum

Dissolve the yeast in the lukewarm water with the sugar until frothy. Beat the egg yolks with the brown sugar until thick, then beat in the butter and add the cocoa, salt and vanilla. Beat until smooth; add the warm milk and flour. Beat 2 minutes. Fold in the stiffly beaten egg whites and currants. Grease a tube pan, set in a pan of warm water, cover it with a towel, and let the batter rise until it comes to the top of pan. Preheat the oven to 375° F. and bake the cake 15 minutes; reduce the heat to 350° F. and bake 25 to 30 minutes longer. Two minutes after it has come from the oven, loosen the sides with a sharp-pointed knife and turn upside down onto a cake plate. Sprinkle with powdered sugar or cover when cool with a thin chocolate icing.

CHOCOLATE ICING

4 Tbsps. black coffee
½ cup dark Dutch cocoa

1 tsp. butter
3 drops mocha extract

Mix the coffee, cocoa, butter and extract in a heavy saucepan and cook it over a low flame until blended, stirring with a rubber spatula continuously. This is a bitter glaze. If you wish a sweet glaze, add ½ cup of light brown sugar. Stir until it is thick and spread on cake. Chocolate Bread is suitable for tea or supper.

Saffron Bread

2 envelopes yeast
2 Tbsps. sugar
¼ cup lukewarm milk
½ tsp. saffron
2 Tbsps. rum or cognac
¾ cup seedless raisins
½ tsp. salt
6 cups sifted flour
1 egg beaten

1 cup sweet butter
1 cup light brown sugar
3 Tbsps. ground almonds
4 bitter almonds, ground *or* 1½
   tsps. almond extract
1¾ cups lukewarm milk
1 egg yolk
Sugar
Sliced almonds

Put the yeast, 2 Tbsps. sugar and the lukewarm milk in a mixing bowl until the yeast is frothy. Soak the saffron in the rum or cognac. Mix the raisins and salt with the flour. Beat the egg and mix it with the butter and sugar which have been creamed until light. Add the ground almonds. If bitter almonds aren't available, use the extract. Combine the rest of the milk with the yeast, the saffron and the flour. Beat hard. Let the bowl stand in a dishpan of warm water, covered with a tea towel, until dough is light. Beat in the sugar mixture and beat 5 minutes until the dough is elastic. Put a little over ½ the dough on a floured board, knead until light, then divide in 2 parts. Form each into long rolls 1½ inches thick. Twist the two rolls together and put in a greased pan. Two loaves may be made or the rest of the dough may be made into small twisted rolls. Brush the top with beaten yolk and sprinkle with sugar and sliced almonds. Set the pans in a warm place lightly covered with a cloth and, when raised, bake at 375° F. for 30 to 35 minutes. Small rolls take about 20 minutes.

Filled Tart

1 envelope yeast
3 Tbsps. lukewarm water
1 Tbsp. light brown sugar
½ cup sweet butter
2 Tbsps. light brown sugar
3 egg yolks
1 tsp. vanilla

¾ cup warm light cream
¼ tsp. salt
2 cups sifted flour
Filling: thinned jam, marmalade,
    poppy seed or streussel
1 egg yolk
1 Tbsp. light cream

Dissolve the yeast with the lukewarm water and 1 Tbsp. sugar until frothy. Cream the butter and sugar until smooth; beat in the egg yolks, 1 at a time. Combine the yeast and butter-egg yolk mixtures and add the vanilla, cream and salt. Beat in the flour, adding more if necessary to make a dough that can be rolled. Beat 4 minutes. Take half the dough and roll it in a round to fit a 10-inch round greased pan and spread with your choice of fillings. Roll the rest of the dough to fit the top, lay it on, and put the pan in a warm place to rise. Brush with beaten egg yolk mixed with 1 tablespoon light cream. Bake in a preheated 375° F. oven for 10 minutes; reduce the heat to 350° F. and bake about 20 to 25 minutes more.

See Mohn Cake or Valacky for poppy seed filling. See German Coffeecake for streussel.

Small Breads

ROLLS

Light Rolls

1 envelope yeast
1 Tbsp. light brown sugar
2 Tbsps. lukewarm water
½ cup sweet butter
1 Tbsp. light brown sugar

1 cup scalded milk
2 eggs, beaten
4 cups sifted flour
1 tsp. salt

Dissolve the yeast with the sugar in the lukewarm water. Cream sweet butter and sugar until fluffy and smooth. Cool the scalded milk to lukewarm and combine with the yeast and creamed butter and sugar, then add the eggs beaten until very light. Sift the flour, measure it and sift with the salt. Stir the yeast mixture into the flour and beat very hard for 3 or 4 minutes. This dough is too soft to knead. Set the bowl in a pan of quite warm water, cover with a towel and let the dough rise until double in bulk. Beat down again until spongy and elastic, then toss onto a floured board and roll to ⅓-inch thickness.

There are several ways of forming and cutting rolls. They may be cut in small rounds with a cookie cutter, the rounds brushed with butter and topped with another round. They may be cut in ovals, brushed with melted butter and folded over to make pocketbook rolls; or 3 tiny balls may be placed in greased muffin tins to make cloverleaf rolls. They may be rolled into thin strips, cut in triangles, sprinkled with a little cinnamon and sugar, rolled from the wide side to the point and curved into crescents.

Brush the tops with half-beaten egg white or melted butter. Let them rise until light in a warm place and bake about 18 to 20 minutes at 400° F.

Rich Egg Rolls

1 envelope yeast
3 Tbsps. lukewarm water
2 Tbsps. light brown sugar
2½ cups sifted flour
1 tsp. salt
½ cup sweet butter
¼ cup light brown sugar
2 large eggs

2 egg yolks
¼ cup warm heavy cream
Grated rind of 1 lemon
½ tsp. mace
GLAZE
1 egg yolk
2 Tbsps. cream

Dissolve the yeast and light brown sugar in lukewarm water in a small bowl until frothy. Stir in ¼ cup of the flour which has been sifted, measured and sifted with the salt in a large mixing bowl. Stir the flour and yeast until light and let it stand in a warm place while you prepare the rest of the ingredients, all of which must be at room temperature. Cream the butter and light brown sugar until smooth; beat in the eggs and yolks, one at a time. Add the cream, lemon rind and mace. When the yeast mixture is light beat it into the butter mixture. Add it to the 2¼ cups of flour in the mixing bowl and beat for 5 minutes. Set the bowl in a pan of warm (not hot) water, cover with a towel and let dough rise an hour. (Never let light doughs overrise as they collapse and then must be beaten down and set to rise again.) This dough is very hard to handle because it is so light.

Form the dough into rolls. Small spoonfuls (half of a kitchen spoon) may be put in oiled muffin tins. Or small pieces may be tossed in flour, rolled a little for finger rolls and placed in an oiled pan ½ inch apart. Or little ovals may be rolled on a well-floured board, a teaspoon of jam or glacé fruit put on one half and the dough folded over. Paint the tops with combined glaze ingredients and let rolls rise an hour in a warm place. Preheat the oven to 400° F. and bake rolls 7 minutes; turn the temperature to 325° F. and bake 8 minutes more. They are tender and delicious. Makes 30 finger rolls or 2 dozen muffin-tin size. These may be made in less than 3 hours.

Sour Cream Sweet Rolls

1 envelope yeast	1 cup sour cream
½ cup lukewarm milk	6 cups sifted flour
½ cup light brown sugar	1½ tsps. salt
1 cup sweet butter	Chopped nuts
2 large eggs, beaten	Brown sugar

Dissolve the yeast in the lukewarm milk. Cream the sugar and butter until smooth. Beat the eggs until light. Have the sour cream at room temperature. Sift the flour and use 4½ cups of it at first, sifting it with the salt. Combine the yeast, sugar-butter mixture, eggs and sour cream and stir it into the 4½ cups of flour. Beat for 3 or 4 minutes with a kneading motion with a hard rubber spatula. Wrap the bowl with a tea towel and refrigerate it several hours. When ready to use, remove from the refrigerator and let it stand until it doubles in bulk. Punch down and add the rest of the sifted flour or as much as necessary to make a light spongy dough. Beat 2 minutes. Divide into 2 or 3 parts and roll thin, into an oblong. Spread with sour cream, sprinkle with finely chopped nuts and brown sugar, and roll the long way like a jelly roll. Cut in 1-inch slices and put them cut side down in a greased, sugared pan to rise double. Bake at 375° F. about 25 to 28 minutes or until golden. This is a fine dough for fruit-filled coffeecake.

Potato Sour Cream Rolls

1 good-size potato
⅓ cup water
1 cup sour cream
⅓ cup sweet butter
¼ cup light brown sugar
2 large eggs, beaten
1 envelope yeast

2 Tbsps. warm water
2 Tbsps. light brown sugar
5 cups sifted flour
1 Tbsp. salt
GLAZE
1 beaten egg yolk
2 Tbsps. cream

Peel and dice the potato very fine so that when cooked tender most of the water will be absorbed. This is done over a very low flame. Mash potato through a sieve and stir until smooth with the sour cream, butter, sugar and lightly beaten eggs. Dissolve the yeast in the warm water and sugar until frothy, then mix with the potato mixture. Sift 4 cups of flour with the salt into a large mixing bowl and stir in the yeast mixture. Beat 2 minutes until smooth, then add the rest of the flour if needed. Beat 3 or 4 minutes, then set the bowl in a pan of quite warm water, cover with a towel and let the dough rise until light. Beat it down. It can be made into rolls or it can half-fill 2 very small greased loaf pans and 9 greased muffin tins. Let it rise to the top of the pans. Bake at 400° F. for 10 minutes, then turn the heat to 350° F. and bake the muffins 20 minutes more and the loaves 40 minutes more. It takes longer to bake this dough because of the potato. The texture is delicate and fine-grained. Ten minutes before the rolls or bread are done, brush with the glaze.

Buttermilk Rolls

1 envelope yeast
¼ cup lukewarm water
1 Tbsp. light brown sugar
1 cup buttermilk
¼ cup butter
3 cups flour

½ tsp. soda
3 Tbsps. light brown sugar
1½ tsps. salt
Melted butter
Corn meal

Dissolve the yeast in the lukewarm water with 1 Tbsp. sugar until frothy. Put the buttermilk and butter in a saucepan and heat just until the butter is melted. Sift the flour with the soda, sugar and salt. When the buttermilk is lukewarm, add it to the yeast and mix with the flour. Beat 3 or 4 minutes and if necessary add a very little more flour. The dough should be soft but spongy. Set the bowl in a dishpan of quite warm water, cover with a tea towel and let the dough rise an hour or until light. Beat it down and take pieces of dough the size of a pullet egg, roll in melted butter and fine corn meal and put them in a buttered pan to rise. When they have risen, bake at 400° F. about 18 minutes. This makes over 20 rolls.

Cinnamon Rolls

1 envelope yeast
1 Tbsp. sugar
½ cup lukewarm milk
2 cups flour
½ tsp. salt
1 egg, beaten
3 Tbsps. sweet butter
½ cup light brown sugar

2 Tbsps. butter
¾ cup light brown sugar
1 Tbsp. cinnamon
SYRUP
¾ cup light brown sugar
¼ cup water
1 Tbsp. cinnamon

Dissolve the yeast with 1 Tbsp. sugar in the lukewarm milk until it is frothy. Add ½ cup of flour. Beat hard; let sponge rise for 45 minutes. When the sponge is light add the rest of the flour sifted with the salt, the beaten egg and the sugar which has been creamed with 3 Tbsps. butter. Beat for 3 minutes; set the bowl in a pan of warm water, covered with a tea towel, to rise. Beat the dough down. Put it on a floured board and roll into an oblong ½ inch thick. Cream 2 Tbsps. butter with the sugar and cinnamon and spread it on the dough. Roll it up like a jelly roll and cut it in 1-inch slices. Put them in a well-greased pan cut side down, cover lightly with a cloth and let them rise 30 minutes. Bake the rolls at

375° F. about 20 minutes. Meanwhile make a syrup of the brown sugar, water and cinnamon and pour it over the rolls when they come out of the oven.

Bran Rolls

1 envelope yeast
¼ cup lukewarm water
⅓ cup molasses
1½ cups boiling water
⅓ cup butter
1 egg, beaten

1 Tbsp. salt
1 cup bran flour
1½ cups whole wheat flour
1½ cups white flour
¾ cup raisins

Dissolve the yeast in the lukewarm water and molasses. Boil the water and melt the butter in it; when lukewarm add the lightly beaten egg and salt. Combine with the yeast. Mix the flours and toss the raisins through them. If you can't get flaky bran in a health store, use wheat germ. Stir in the yeast mixture and beat very hard for 3 minutes. Let the dough rise in a warm place, covered with a tea towel, until double in bulk. The dough may be used immediately or stored in the refrigerator for 2 or 3 days and used when needed. Form into rolls or put 3 little balls in greased muffin tins for cloverleaf. Let rise again until light, then bake about 25 minutes at 375° F. If baking too fast reduce the heat to 325° F.

Orange Rolls

1 envelope yeast
½ cup lukewarm milk
½ cup light brown sugar
½ cup butter
2 eggs, beaten

1 tsp. salt
½ cup orange juice
4 to 4½ cups sifted flour
Grated rind 1 California orange

Dissolve the yeast in the lukewarm milk until it is frothy. Cream the sugar and butter until smooth. Beat the eggs until very light and combine with the salt, creamed butter and sugar, yeast and orange juice. Sift 4 cups of flour into a mixing bowl and stir in the rind and liquid mixture. Beat very hard until the dough is light and elastic. If necessary add more flour. Set the bowl in a pan of warm water, cover with a towel and let the dough rise until light and double in bulk. Beat down and form into rolls. Filled rolls can be made, if desired, by omitting the rind and mixing it with some sugar. Divide the dough in two parts, roll each in an oblong ½ inch thick, spread with soft butter and sprinkle with the rind and sugar. Roll up like a jelly roll and cut in 1-inch-thick slices. Put the slices, cut side down, in a greased pan and let them rise again. When they are light, bake about 20 to 25 minutes, ½ the time at 375° F. and ½ at 350° F.

Gladys' Special Orange Rolls

ROLLS
1 envelope yeast
1 Tbsp. light brown sugar
¼ cup lukewarm milk
½ cup sweet butter
¼ cup light brown sugar
2 eggs, beaten
¾ cup warm milk
¾ tsp. salt
4 (or more) cups sifted flour

DRESSING
½ cup light brown sugar
Grated rind 1 orange
½ cup orange juice
2 Tbsps. butter
If rolled:
½ cup light brown sugar
½ cup soft sweet butter
1 Tbsp. cinnamon

Dissolve the yeast with the brown sugar in lukewarm milk until frothy. Cream ½ cup of butter and ¼ cup of light brown sugar until smooth. Combine with the yeast and add the lightly beaten eggs and milk. Sift the salt with 3½ cups of flour into a large mixing bowl and make a well in the center. Pour in the mixture and beat hard for 2 minutes, then add more flour to make a soft and elastic dough. Beat another 3 minutes. Set the bowl in a pan of quite warm water, cover with a towel and let dough rise until light. Beat down and form into small rolls. For the dressing, boil up the sugar, rind, juice and butter and pour it into the baking pan. Put the rolls on top and let them rise until light in a warm place. Bake about 15 to 18 minutes at 375° F. This amount of dressing covers a 9-inch pan. Or the dough may be divided in half, each half rolled to a ½-inch-thick oblong, spread with sugar, soft butter and cinnamon. Roll the long way, cut in ½-inch slices, and put the slices cut side down on the dressing in the pan. Let rise until light and bake.

BUNS

Bath Buns

1 cup sweet butter	1 cup sifted flour
2 cups sifted flour	1 Tbsp. sherry
⅓ cup light brown sugar	1 tsp. rose extract
1 envelope yeast	2 tsps. caraway powder
2 Tbsps. honey	GLAZE
4 large eggs, beaten	1 egg yolk
	2 Tbsps. cream

Cut the butter into the flour with a wire pastry cutter as you would for pie crust. Stir in the sugar. Dissolve the yeast in the honey until it is frothy. Beat the eggs until very light, then sift in the flour, beating with a rotary beater so that there are no lumps. Add the seasonings. A few currants may be added if desired. Combine the flour-butter, yeast, and egg mixtures and beat until the dough is light. The dough should be stiff enough to form into rolls or balls. Add more sifted flour only if necessary. Put the rolls in a long greased pan or in greased muffin tins. Let them rise, covered with a towel, in a draftless place. Brush with the combined glaze ingredients. Bake about 30 minutes at 375° F.

Shrove Tuesday Buns

1 envelope yeast
¼ cup light brown sugar
¼ cup light warm cream
½ cup soft sweet butter
¼ cup light brown sugar
1 egg yolk
⅔ cup light warm cream
3 cups sifted flour
½ tsp. salt

GLAZE
1 egg yolk
2 Tbsps. cream
FILLING
½ cup browned ground almonds
4 bitter almonds, ground
1 beaten egg white
¼ cup light brown sugar
1 tsp. almond extract
1 cup heavy cream, whipped

Dissolve the yeast with the sugar and warm cream until frothy. Blend the soft butter, sugar, egg yolk and warm cream together. Combine with the yeast. Add the mixture to the flour sifted with the salt and beat for 2 minutes. Add more flour if necessary to make quite a stiff dough. Set the bowl of dough in a pan of hot water, cover with a towel and let the dough rise until light. Beat it down and form into 12 balls. Put them in an oiled pan to rise again. When light, brush lightly with the mixed glaze ingredients and bake about 20 minutes at 400° F.

For the filling, grind the almonds together. Beat the egg white until stiff, add the sugar and beat again. Add the almond extract and the nuts. Fold in the cream whipped until stiff. When the buns are cool remove a triangle from each top and a little of the crumb underneath. Fill and return the triangle to the top. Let the filling rise over the top.

Good Friday Hot Cross Buns

2 envelopes yeast
¼ cup lukewarm water
1 Tbsp. light brown sugar
1½ cups scalded milk
½ cup sweet butter
½ cup brown sugar
1½ tsps. salt
2 eggs, beaten
4 (or more) cups sifted flour
2 tsps. cinnamon

1 tsp. clove
½ tsp. nutmeg
½ cup currants
⅓ cup finely diced citron
FROSTING
2 Tbsps. hot milk
Powdered sugar
Grated rind 1 lemon

Dissolve the yeast in the lukewarm water with 1 Tbsp. brown sugar until frothy. Scald the milk and add the butter, sugar and salt. Beat the eggs until light and combine with the milk mixture and the yeast. Sift 3 cups of the flour with the spices into a mixing bowl; add the yeast mixture. Beat for 4 minutes. Toss the currants and citron with ½ cup of the flour and mix it with the sponge. If necessary add more flour to make a firm dough. Beat well and set the dough in a pan of quite warm water to rise, covered with a towel. When dough is light, beat it down well and form into 2 dozen balls. Put them in a long well-greased pan, loosely covered with a towel, to rise again. This will take about 45 minutes. Bake them about 20 minutes at 400° F. If baking too fast turn the heat down to 325° F. When they come from the oven, brush with melted butter. For the icing, mix the hot milk with as much powdered sugar as it will take and not run; add the lemon rind. When the rolls are cool, make a cross over the tops with icing.

MUFFINS, ETC.

English Muffins

1 envelope yeast	1 tsp. salt
1 cup boiling water	2 cups sifted flour
¼ cup sieved boiled potato	

Put the yeast in a bowl and when the water is lukewarm stir it into the yeast. Add the lightly sieved potato and the salt. Stir until yeast is dissolved, then add the flour and beat 2 or 3 minutes. Cover lightly and let the dough rise in a warm place. Remove pieces of dough the size of an egg and pat them into rounds ⅓ inch thick on a well-floured board. Cover so that the towel does not touch the very light dough. Let rise to double in bulk. Lift the muffins onto a hot lightly greased griddle with a spatula, gently so they don't fall. Fry slowly 15 minutes, turn and fry 15 minutes on the other side. See that they do not burn. They may be eaten with butter while hot or allowed to cool then torn apart with a fork, toasted and spread with butter. This makes about 8 or 9 muffins.

Crumpets

2 cups boiling water	1 tsp. salt
2 envelopes yeast	2 cups sifted flour
¼ cup sieved boiled potato	

Boil the water and let it cool to lukewarm then combine all the ingredients. The ingredients are the same as the English muffin except twice as much liquid is used. Beat the batter 4 minutes then let it rise in a warm place. Let the dough rise three times, beating it 3 or 4 minutes after each rising in order to create a porous texture. Grease 3½-inch muffin rings and set them on a greased griddle. Pour the batter into the rings ⅓ inch deep and bake 20 minutes. Do not turn them. After the crumpets cool, they are toasted and spread with butter to serve. Makes 18 or 20.

Brioche

2 envelopes yeast
4 Tbsps. light brown sugar
¼ cup lukewarm milk
4 cups sifted white flour
2½ tsps. salt

1 to 1¼ cups fresh sweet butter
4 large eggs plus 4 yolks
GLAZE
1 egg yolk
2 Tbsps. cream

Mix the yeast with the sugar, add the warm milk and let it become frothy. Sift the flour with the salt into a large mixing bowl. Use the very freshest farm butter you can get and let it stand in a bowl until it is soft. Break the eggs and yolks into a bowl and let them stand until they are at room temperature. I like this mixture of yolks and whites, as the latter give the dough lightness. Dump the yeast, butter and eggs into the flour and mix for 10 minutes. Either quantity of butter is excellent; the greater quantity makes a richer brioche, which keeps longer. A hard rubber spatula is perfect for mixing. The dough should be elastic and softer than bread dough. Set the bowl in a dishpan of warm (not hot) water, cover with a tea towel and let the dough rise until light, about 1 hour. Beat the dough down, wrap the bowl with two tea towels and refrigerate 6 hours or overnight. Dough rises under refrigeration and if it falls before you use it, it may be coaxed back into a soft dough by adding 2 Tbsps. of warm water and setting in a dishpan of lukewarm water for 1½ hours, covered with a towel. Beat the dough until it is elastic, then fill well-buttered molds half full. This recipe fills 20 to 22 small fluted brioche molds (or muffin tins) or two fluted molds, one 6 inches across and one 8 inches across. For the small ones, roll balls the size of a large marble in flour, make a hole in the center of the dough; insert a ball in each, paint the tops with the mixture of egg yolk and cream, then let them rise until light. Preheat the oven to 450° and bake them 10 minutes, reduce the heat to 325° and bake them 7 minutes more. The brioches should be crusty on the outside and soft in the inside, achieved only in a very hot oven to begin the baking. For the larger molds, fill them ⅔ full and insert balls the size of a pullet egg, first rolled in flour. Brush with the glaze. Set the molds in warm water, covered, to rise to the top of the tins. Bake them in a preheated oven at 450° for 10 minutes, turn the heat to 325° and bake the smaller one about 18 minutes more and the larger one about 20 minutes more. They are very pretty brought to the table on a breadboard and served with sweet butter.

I have wanted brioches in a hurry to serve with a sweetbread dish and have made them in two hours; they were delicious but I think that refrigerating the dough for some hours makes a finer and mellower brioche. I cut the recipe down to ¼, *i.e.,* 1 envelope yeast, 1 Tbsp. milk, 1 Tbsp. sugar, 1 cup flour, ¾ tsp. salt, 1 egg and 1 yolk. It made 6 brioches. The proof of a good recipe lies in its ability to be divided or multiplied without changing its quality.

Saucisson en Brioche

Le Bossu, Lyon

Mme. Blanc made this for a dinner of welcome when we visited Lyon. It was a very handsome entrée indeed. Hers was a home-made sausage but very fine ones may be obtained in shops specializing in pork products. It should be plump—a good 1½ to 2 inches in diameter and at least 8 inches long.

½ recipe for Brioche   a fine Czech or German sausage

Roll out the dough before the last rising, just long enough to enclose the ends of the sausage and wide enough so that it just overlaps. Lay the filled roll seam side down in an oiled mold just to fit and let it rise until light. Bake it 10 minutes at 450° then turn the heat down to 325° and bake it 15 to 18 minutes more. Serves 8 or 10. This is a classic use for liver pâté or pâté de foie gras. It is molded and enclosed in the brioche dough and baked the same way but in a round fluted mold.

Brioche Niçoise

Au Chapon Fin, *Thoissey*

When in France last summer, we drove through Burgundy to visit our friend Paul Blanc, one of the very greatest chefs of France. His delightful country inn, about thirty miles north of Lyon, is just the place to spend days for quiet walks and drives through the countryside, then return to enjoy some of the very best food imaginable. This is the way little brioches are gilded here, but they really come from southern France, where they must have a sweet tooth, at least when it comes to brioche.

Recipe for Brioche ½ cup sugar
  ½ cup heavy cream

Put the sugar and cream in a saucepan and cook until mixture thickens and colors a little. Brush the tops of the freshly baked brioches and run them under the flame to glaze.

Croissants

1 envelope yeast
3 Tbsps. lukewarm water
1 Tbsp. sugar
½ cup sifted flour
2 cups sifted flour

1 tsp. salt
¾ cup milk, room temperature
1 cup sweet butter
GLAZE
1 egg yolk
2 Tbsps. cream

Make a sponge of the yeast dissolved in the lukewarm water with sugar. When it is frothy stir in ½ cup flour and set it in a warm place to rise. Sift the 2 cups of sifted flour with the salt and mix with the milk until smooth. When the sponge is light, mix in the flour-milk mixture. Let this stand 10 or 15 minutes. Dust two sheets of wax paper with flour; put the cup of butter between them. Flatten to a scant ½ inch; chill. Take the dough and on a floured board roll it ½ inch thick into an oblong strip. Put ½ the butter in the middle of the strip and fold one end over the butter. Put the other piece of butter on the folded dough and fold the second end over the butter. Roll out again and fold in 4 layers. Wrap in wax paper and chill 4 or 5 hours or overnight. An hour and a half before baking, remove the dough from the refrigerator and make two more turns, that is, roll it in a strip, fold four times and repeat this. Chill ½ hour, then roll in two strips ⅛ inch thick and 4½ inches wide, and cut in triangles. Beginning at the wide side roll so the point is outside. Put the rolls, point side up, on a baking sheet and curve into crescents. Brush with egg yolk mixed with 2 Tbsps. of cream. Let rest 30 minutes or until light. Preheat the oven to 400° F. and bake 5 minutes; turn the heat to 375° F. and bake 10 minutes more or until golden. Makes about 2 dozen small croissants.

Danish Crescents

2 envelopes yeast
2 Tbsps. sugar
¼ cup lukewarm water
3 eggs, beaten
1¾ cups cold milk
6 cups sifted flour
1½ cups sweet butter, softened
　(¾ pound)
Melted butter
Sugar

ALMOND FILLING
2 Tbsps. sweet butter
⅓ cup sugar
1 tsp. almond extract
4 ounces browned almonds,
　ground
1 egg, beaten

VANILLA CREAM FILLING
1 egg yolk, beaten
1 Tbsp. flour
2 Tbsps. sugar
¾ cup scalded milk
1 tsp. vanilla

Dissolve the yeast and the sugar in lukewarm water until frothy. Beat the eggs until light and add them to the yeast with the cold milk. Add the flour to make a soft dough. This dough is not kneaded but handled as little as possible. Roll out the dough and spread with the softened butter. Fold over to incorporate the butter. Make 3 more turns, as the rolling and folding process is called. Cover the dough well and refrigerate 4 or 5 hours or overnight. When ready to make the crescents let the dough stand at room temperature for 20 minutes. Roll out in thin strips 5 inches wide, using only part of the dough at a time. Cut in triangles, add 1 tsp. of the chosen filling at the wide end, and roll up so the point is on the outside. Bend slightly into crescents and put them on a baking sheet. Bake them in a preheated 450° F. oven about 10 minutes. While hot brush with melted butter and dip in sugar. These are divine morsels and I was able, fortunately, to persuade a certain Danish pastry cook to give me the recipe. For the *Almond Filling:* Cream the butter and sugar and add the other ingredients. For the *Vanilla Cream Filling:* Beat the egg yolk, flour and sugar together and stir it into the scalded milk. Cook until it thickens; when it cools, add the vanilla.

Danish Pastry

Reinhard Van Hauen, Copenhagen

2 envelopes yeast	1 tsp. cardamom powder
2 Tbsps. sugar	1¼ cups sweet butter, softened
2 eggs	FILLINGS
1⅓ cups cold milk	Almond Filling (p. 69)
4 cups flour	Vanilla Custard Filling (p. 74)
1 tsp. salt	

Mix the yeast, sugar, beaten eggs and milk together. Put the flour in a large mixing bowl and mix in the salt and cardamom. Add the liquid to the flour and make a soft dough. This dough is not kneaded but handled as little as possible after it is well mixed. Roll the dough out into a square ½ inch thick and spread with the butter which is not too soft. Fold the dough like a handkerchief, once each way and roll out gently. Repeat this two more times so the butter is well incorporated. Put the dough in a bowl, wrap in a tea towel and refrigerate for 5 hours or overnight. When you are ready to form it into pastries, remove it from the refrigerator and let it stand 20 minutes. Roll part of the dough at a time. Roll the dough thin in 4-inch-wide strips. For crescents, cut in triangles 4 inches at the base. Put a teaspoon of filling in the center and roll up so the point is on the outside. Put them on a baking sheet, curving them into crescents. For square pastries, cut the pastry in 4- or 5-inch squares, put a teaspoon or two of filling in the center and bring the points together over the top, pinching them together a little. For long pastry, roll out a strip 5 inches wide, fill along the center, then bring the sides together over the top. For cockscombs, cut the long filled roll in 4-inch lengths, making 4 slashes along one side. Bake in a preheated 450° F. oven about 10 to 22 minutes, according to the size and thickness of the pastry. When they come from the oven they may be painted with melted butter and sprinkled with icing sugar, or a sugar icing and chopped browned almonds. See miscellaneous recipes and the index for various fillings. See Koláčky for Vanilla Custard Filling.

Swedish Rusks

1 envelope yeast	1 cup rye flour
1 Tbsp. sugar	1½ cups white flour
⅓ cup lukewarm water	1 or 2 tsps. powdered fennel
1 Tbsp. butter	2 tsps. salt
⅔ cup lukewarm orange juice or milk	¼ cup butter
	¼ cup light brown sugar

There are several ways of making rusks. Instead of using rye flour and fennel, they can be made of all white flour and flavored with 2 Tbsps. of grated orange rind, using milk for the liquid. Or they can be made with half white flour and half whole wheat and flavored as you choose. Dissolve the yeast with 1 Tbsp. of sugar in ⅓ cup of warm water. Melt the butter in the warm juice or milk and combine the mixtures. Put the flour in a large bowl and mix with the fennel, if used, and the salt. Make a well in the center of the flour and mix in the liquid-yeast mixture. Stir for 3 minutes until the dough is well mixed. It must be quite stiff. Set it to rise an hour in a bowl of warm water, covered with a tea towel. Meanwhile cream the butter and sugar together until smooth. When the dough has risen, work in the creamed mixture and knead with a hard rubber spatula until light. Nip off small pieces and roll them into balls the size of a walnut. Put them on a lightly oiled baking sheet with space between. There should be 50. Let them rise 20 minutes in a warm place out of a draft. Put them in a cold oven. Turn heat to 400° F. and bake rusks 10 minutes, then turn the heat to 350° F. and bake 15 minutes more. When they are thoroughly cool, cut them in half and let them dry out in a 275° F. oven for 15 or 20 minutes. They stiffen more as they cool and should not be hard but just delicate and crisp. This makes 100 rusks.

Maritozzi

This is a little Italian sugar bun filled with fruit. The *pasticceria* in the cities of Italy are filled with culinary works of art.

1 envelope yeast	1 tsp. salt
3 Tbsps. lukewarm water	3½ (about) cups sifted flour
1 Tbsp. light brown sugar	⅓ cup chopped orange peel
½ cup sweet butter	⅓ cup currants
⅓ cup light brown sugar	1 tsp. almond extract
¾ cup scalded milk	⅓ cup pignoli nuts
2 eggs plus 1 yolk, beaten	Beaten egg and sugar

Dissolve the yeast with the lukewarm water and sugar until fluffy. Cream the butter and sugar until smooth. Scald the milk and cool to lukewarm. Add the well-beaten eggs. Sift the salt with 3 cups of flour and toss the peel, currants that have been sprinkled with the almond extract, and the nuts through it. Combine the yeast with the creamed butter and the milk-egg mixture. Make a well in the flour and stir in the liquid. Beat very hard for 3 minutes, adding more flour if necessary to make a light, spongy dough. Set the bowl in a pan of warm water, cover with a towel and let the dough rise until light. Beat it down and take pieces the size of a pullet egg. Roll them in ovals and dip in beaten egg and roll in sugar. Put them in a greased pan to rise and when light bake at 375° F. about 15 minutes.

Koláčky

Bohemian Tarts

The bakeries in Czech neighborhoods always display *Koláčky* but if you are fortunate enough to be served them in a Czech home you will savor something quite different. This recipe will show you one reason why *homemade* is a magic word.

1 envelope yeast
¼ cup lukewarm milk
2 Tbsps. light brown sugar
¼ cup sifted flour
½ cup sweet butter
¼ cup light brown sugar
2 egg yolks
⅓ cup warm heavy cream

Grated rind of 1 lemon
¼ tsp. cinnamon or mace
¾ tsp. salt
2¼ cups sifted flour
2 egg whites, beaten
GLAZE
1 egg yolk
2 Tbsps. cream
FILLINGS
Apricot or plum jam, or
    Poppy seed filling, or
    Vanilla custard

Dissolve the yeast with the lukewarm milk and sugar until frothy in a small bowl set in warm water. Stir in ¼ cup of flour and let it become light. Have all the ingredients at room temperature. Cream the butter and sugar until smooth; beat in the egg yolks, then the cream, rind, spice and salt. Combine the yeast sponge with the butter mixture and beat very well; add it to the sifted and measured flour. Beat for 5 minutes. The dough should be light and elastic. Fold in the stiffly beaten egg whites and when well mixed, put the bowl of dough to rise in a pan of warm (not hot) water. This will take about an hour. Beat it down. Nip off small balls of dough and put them on a floured board. Roll to ½-inch thickness with the hand or rolling pin. Brush with combined glaze ingredients. Make 3 dents with your finger to hold a little jam or 1 tsp. of either filling. These are left open, or if you wish, make squares of the dough, fill and bring opposite points together, pinching them together. There will be openings on the sides. Brush the top with glaze and put them on a long oiled pan. Cover and put in a warm place to rise again. When they are light bake them about 20 minutes in a preheated 375° F. oven. This makes about 24 to 30 tarts.

POPPY SEED FILLING
1 cup ground poppy seeds
Grated rind and juice of 1 lemon
½ cup light brown sugar or ¼
    cup honey
⅓ cup seedless raisins or
    currants
Milk or cream

Put all the ingredients in a saucepan with 2 or 3 tablespoons of milk or cream and cook 2 or 3 minutes to a smooth, light paste. Add more liquid if necessary. Stir constantly. Let cool before using.

VANILLA CUSTARD FILLING
1 cup light cream, scalded
¼ cup light brown sugar
1½ Tbsps. flour
2 egg yolks
2 tsps. vanilla

Scald the cream. Sift the sugar and flour together, then beat it into the egg yolks. Whisk the hot cream into the egg yolk mixture and return it to a low flame, stirring constantly until it thickens. (This must be thick.) Let cool thoroughly and add the vanilla.

Quick Breads

Orange Bread

Gild the lily by serving this bread for tea with orange marmalade.

Grated rind of 2 California
  oranges
1 cup orange juice
1½ cups sugar
1 egg, beaten

1 cup milk
2 cups sifted flour
1 cup oat flour
½ tsp. salt
3 tsps. baking powder

Grate the rind into a saucepan, add the orange juice and simmer uncovered 5 minutes. Add the sugar and boil to a syrup until it threads slightly. Let it cool. Beat the egg and add it and the milk to the syrup. Mix the flours, salt and baking powder; combine with the syrup mixture. Bake in an oiled bread pan about 50 minutes at 350° F.

VARIATION A cup of thinned orange marmalade and ½ cup of sugar may replace the syrup (rind, juice and sugar).

Raisin Nut Bread

1 egg, beaten
¾ cup molasses
¾ cup light brown sugar
1½ cups buttermilk
¾ cup chopped browned
   almonds, pecans or black
   walnuts

¾ cup raisins
1½ cups whole wheat flour
1½ cups white flour
2 tsps. baking powder
1 tsp. salt

This is a fine tea bread and worthy of very good nuts. Beat the egg and add the molasses, brown sugar, buttermilk, nuts and raisins. Mix the flours with the baking powder and salt. Combine the mixtures. Two or 3 Tbsps. more of buttermilk may be needed to make a soft but firm batter. Bake about 1 hour at 350° F., in an oiled bread pan.

Almond Tea Bread

2 Tbsps. butter
1 cup light brown sugar
1 cup milk
1 egg, beaten
2 cups flour

1 cup whole wheat flour
½ tsp. salt
2 tsps. baking powder
1 cup sliced browned almonds
¾ cup seedless raisins

Cream the butter with the sugar. Stir in the milk and add the beaten egg. Mix the unsifted flours with the salt and baking powder. Toss the almonds which have been chopped a little, and the raisins, with the flours; combine with the first mixture. Grease a bread pan, fill with the batter and let it stand 20 minutes. Bake it an hour, 20 minutes at 350° F. and 40 minutes at 325° F.

Apricot Almond Bread

1½ cups dried apricots
½ cup orange juice
½ cup light brown sugar
2 Tbsps. butter
1 egg, beaten
1½ cups sifted flour

1 cup whole wheat, oat, bran
    flour, or corn meal
½ cup chopped browned
    almonds
3 tsps. baking powder
¾ tsp. salt
½ cup sour cream or buttermilk

Wash and slice the apricots quite fine, cover with the orange juice and cook 6 or 7 minutes. While hot stir in the sugar and butter. Beat the egg until light. You can use all white flour but 1 cup of any of those mentioned gives more flavor to the bread. Mix the flours with the nuts, baking powder and salt. Combine the apricots and beaten egg and flour adding enough sour cream or buttermilk to make a firm but soft dough. Bake in an oiled bread pan an hour at 350° F. This is better a day old.

Prune Bread

1 cup stewed prunes
1 cup light brown sugar
2 Tbsps. melted butter
1 egg, beaten
¾ cup prune juice
1 cup buttermilk

2 tsps. baking powder
½ tsp. salt
1 cup whole wheat flour
1½ cups sifted white flour
⅔ cup chopped browned
    almonds
1 tsp. almond extract

Pit and cut the prunes up fine. Add the sugar, melted butter, beaten egg, juice, and buttermilk. Mix the baking powder, salt and flours with the almonds. Combine the two mixtures and stir in the almond extract. Bake 1 hour at 350° F. If baking too fast, turn the heat to 325° F. the second ½ hour.

Date or Fig Bread

2 cups chopped dates or figs
½ cup boiling water
1 cup hot light cream
1 cup light brown sugar
2 Tbsps. melted butter
3 eggs, beaten

1 cup sifted flour
1¾ cups whole wheat flour
2 tsps. baking powder
½ tsp. salt
¾ cup chopped browned
  almonds
1 tsp. vanilla

Pit and slice the dates very thin. If figs are used, choose very soft Smyrna or other soft figs and slice them very thin. Cover fruit with the boiling water and hot cream and let it cool. Stir in the sugar, melted butter and lightly beaten eggs. Mix the flours with the baking powder, salt and nuts. Combine the two mixtures and stir in the vanilla. Bake in oiled bread pans, 1 of ordinary size and 1 very small one. Bake the larger 50 to 60 minutes and the smaller about 40 minutes at 350° F. Turn down the heat to 325° F. if baking too fast after they have been in the oven 25 minutes.

Banana Bread

½ cup sweet butter
1 cup light brown sugar
4 medium-size ripe bananas,
  mashed
2 eggs, beaten
1 Tbsp. lemon juice

¼ tsp. nutmeg
½ cup raisins or chopped
  pecans
¼ tsp. salt
1 tsp. baking powder
2 cups sifted flour, or 1½ cups
  flour and 1 cup 100%
  crumbled bran

Cream the butter and sugar until creamy and smooth. Mash the bananas through a coarse sieve and mix with the sugar-butter mixture. Add the lightly beaten eggs, lemon juice, nutmeg and raisins or nuts. Sift the salt and baking powder with the flour. Combine the two mixtures and bake in an oiled bread pan 1 hour at 350° F.

Norwegian Citron Bread

½ cup sweet butter
1½ cups light brown sugar
2 large eggs, beaten
4 cups sifted flour
3 tsps. baking powder

¾ tsp. salt
2 tsps. cardamom
½ cup raisins
1 cup moist sliced citron
1½ cups milk

Cream the butter and sugar until smooth, then add the beaten eggs. Sift the flour with the dry ingredients; toss the raisins and citron through them. Add the dry ingredients and the milk, alternately, to the creamed mixture. Bake in 3 little oiled loaf pans or in 1 large one, 1 hour at 350° F. for the large loaf and 35 to 40 minutes for the little ones.

Irish Soda Bread

½ cup currants
3 Tbsps. Irish whiskey (for St. Patrick's Day)
3 cups sifted flour
1 tsp. salt
1½ tsps. baking powder

1 tsp. soda
1 Tbsp. light brown sugar
¼ cup chopped candied orange peel
2 tsps. caraway powder
1½ cups or more buttermilk

Soak the currants in the whiskey an hour or more. Sift the flour with all the dry ingredients and toss the currants and marinade through the flour. Mix in the candied orange peel and the caraway powder. Caraway seeds may be used if desired. Stir in enough buttermilk to make a nice light dough, like muffin dough. Bake it in a greased, floured 10-inch circular pan or skillet about 35 minutes at 350° F. The cake should shrink from the sides of the pan when done. Cool a couple of hours before serving.

Crumbled Bran Bread

1 cup brown sugar
2 Tbsps. butter
1 tsp. soda
2 Tbsps. milk
½ tsp. salt
2 eggs, beaten

1 cup buttermilk
1½ cups crumbled bran
1½ cups sifted white flour
½ cup raisins
½ cup nuts

Cream the sugar and butter. Dissolve the soda in the milk and add it to the sugar mixture, with the salt, lightly beaten eggs and buttermilk. Mix the bran, flour, raisins and nuts together; add to the first mixture. Put in a greased bread pan and bake 30 minutes at 350° F. and then 30 minutes at 300° F.

Corn Meal Loaf

This fine loaf may be served hot from the oven, cold, or toasted. It can be made of white corn meal or fine yellow corn meal or half fine and half coarsely ground meal. The last combination gives the bread a crunchy, crustlike quality.

2½ cups corn meal
2 Tbsps. light brown sugar
1 tsp. salt
3 egg yolks
2½ cups milk
3 Tbsps. melted butter

1 cup sifted white flour
1 tsp. baking powder
1 tsp. cream of tartar
1 tsp. soda
3 egg whites, beaten stiff

Mix the meal with the sugar and salt in a large mixing bowl. Beat the egg yolks and add the milk and melted butter. Instead of the butter and milk, you may use ½ cup sour cream and 2 cups of buttermilk. Either combination is very good. Combine with the meal. Sift the white flour with the baking powder and cream of tartar and add it to the corn meal mixture. Add the soda dissolved in 2 tablespoons of hot water then fold in the stiffly beaten egg whites last. Put the batter into a well-greased bread pan and bake at 375° F. for 1 hour. If your oven bakes fast turn the heat down to 325° F. the last 20 minutes.

Boston Brown Bread

1¼ cups whole wheat, rye, oat,
or buckwheat flour
1 cup corn meal
1 cup sifted white flour
1½ tsps. salt

2 tsps. baking powder
1 cup raisins
2 cups buttermilk
1 cup molasses

Mix all the dry ingredients and toss the raisins through them. Mix the buttermilk and molasses together and stir it into the flours. Fill coffee cans ⅔ full, cover with plastic lids and steam 3 hours in a large kettle of simmering water halfway up the cans. Cover the kettle. This must be watched from time to time to see that the water is replenished with boiling water. The white flour can be replaced by one of the whole grain flours, choosing 2 different ones so that there will be 3 grains. Corn meal is always used.

Steamed Indian Bread

3 cups buttermilk
3 cups corn meal
1 cup flour
2 tsps. baking powder

2 tsps. salt
½ tsp. soda
1 cup light molasses

Mix 1 cup of cold buttermilk with the corn meal. Heat the rest of the buttermilk and mix it with the meal. Sift the flour with all the dry ingredients; add them and the molasses to the corn meal. When well mixed, fill 2 well-greased cylinder containers ⅔ full. Cover and steam 3 hours. Coffee cans are good for this as they have plastic lids to cover the bread while it is steamed in a large kettle. Keep simmering water halfway up the cans and cover the kettle. A melon mold can be used to steam breads in; the shape looks festive when the bread is brought steaming to the table.

Muffins and Popovers

MUFFINS

Plain Muffins

¼ cup butter
¼ cup light brown sugar
1 large egg, beaten
1 cup milk

2 cups sifted flour
4 level tsps. baking powder
½ tsp. salt

Cream the butter and sugar until fluffy and smooth. Stir in the lightly beaten egg, the milk and the sifted dry ingredients. Mix as little as possible to attain a light tender muffin. The mixture can be a little rough. Bake in 9 large greased muffin tins at 375° F. about 18 or 20 minutes. This can also make 18 little muffins, which are baked 12 minutes.

VARIATION For a richer muffin, cut ½ cup of butter into the mixed dry ingredients as you would for piecrust. Add the beaten egg, sugar and milk together, mixing as little as possible.

NUT MUFFINS Mix ½ cup coarsely chopped nuts (almonds, pecans, walnuts, macadamia, peanuts, or black walnuts) with the flour before it is mixed with the other ingredients. A whole or half nut may be put on top of the batter before baking.

Sour Cream Muffins

½ cup light brown sugar
½ cup butter
2 eggs, beaten
1¼ cups sour cream

2 cups flour
3 tsps. baking powder
½ tsp. soda
½ tsp. salt

Cream the butter and sugar until light and fluffy, then add the well-beaten eggs, sour cream and sifted dry ingredients. Mix as little as possible and bake in greased muffin tins 20 to 25 minutes at 375° F. Buttermilk (1½ cups) can be used instead of sour cream.

Cherry, Blueberry, or Fresh Currant Muffins

1 cup fresh fruit
Sugar to taste
⅓ cup butter
¼ cup light brown sugar
2 eggs, beaten
1 cup milk

2 cups sifted flour
4 tsps. baking powder
½ tsp. salt
Fruit and light brown sugar
Sugar
Cinnamon

Prepare a full cup of fruit sprinkled with sugar to taste just before using. Cream the butter and sugar until fluffy and smooth. Add the well-beaten eggs, milk and sifted dry ingredients, mixing as little as possible, to attain a light tender muffin. Half-fill the greased muffin tins with batter, then add a small spoon of fruit, cover with batter and sprinkle with cinnamon and sugar. Bake at 375° F. for 25 minutes. Makes 9 large muffins or 18 small ones. NOTE: Many other fruits can be used: sliced cooked prunes, sliced dates, apricots, raisins. Half a cup of dried currants soaked in 2 Tbsps. of sherry or port can be added to the batter. Half a cup of glacé fruits can be stirred into the flour before mixing with the other ingredients. *Sunsweet* ready-to-eat prunes are excellent for baking as they need no cooking, washing or pitting.

Sweet Potato or Yam Muffins

¼ cup butter
3 Tbsps. light brown sugar
1½ cups flour
¾ tsp. salt
3 tsps. baking powder
½ cup coarsely chopped pecans

2 egg yolks
1 cup mashed sweet potatoes, or
 yams
¼ cup milk or more
2 egg whites, beaten
Mixed cinnamon and sugar

Cream the butter and sugar until fluffy and smooth. Sift the dry ingredients together and toss the nuts through them. Mix the egg yolks with the mashed potato and add the milk. Combine the two mixtures and fold in the stiffly beaten egg whites. Put the batter in 9 greased muffin tins and sprinkle the tops with a mixture of cinnamon and sugar. Bake about 35 minutes at 375° F.

Oatmeal Gems

1 cup steel-cut oats
1 cup buttermilk
1½ cups sifted flour
1 tsp. soda

2 Tbsps. molasses
½ tsp. salt
1 egg, beaten

Soak the oats in the buttermilk at least 5 hours. They can be soaked overnight to make muffins for breakfast. Add the flour to the oats. Dissolve the soda in the molasses and add it to the flour mixture with the salt and beaten egg. Bake in greased muffin tins 10 minutes at 375° F., then reduce the heat to 325° F. for 10 minutes more. Serve hot with butter and honey or jam.

Bran Gems or Quick Bread

2 cups flour
1 tsp. baking powder
1 tsp. soda
1 tsp. salt

2 cups sour cream
2 cups flaky bran or wheat germ
⅓ cup molasses

Sift the flour with the baking powder, soda and salt. Stir in the sour cream, bran (or wheat germ) and molasses. These can have chopped prunes, raisins or dates added. Bake in greased gem tins or in a bread pan. Bake the gems 30 minutes at 350° F. and the bread close to an hour. Whole wheat flour can take the place of white flour.

Cornstarch or Potato Starch Muffins

½ cup sifted cornstarch or
  potato starch
½ tsp. salt
1 tsp. baking powder

1 tsp. anise
2 Tbsps. light brown sugar
3 Tbsps. currants
3 or 4 eggs, separated

Mix all the dry ingredients and toss the currants through them. Three extra large eggs are used or 4 large eggs. Add the yolks to the dry ingredients and stir until smooth then fold in the stiffly beaten egg whites. Bake in 8 or 9 oiled and floured muffin tins, 10 minutes at 400° F. and 5 minutes at 325° F. Serve hot with butter. They are very light.

Munkpan* Balls with Fruit

1 cup sweet cream
4 eggs, separated
2 Tbsps. light brown sugar
½ tsp. salt
1¼ cups sifted flour
Butter for frying

Choice of fruit:
Pitted cherries
Raspberries
Raisins or currants
Sliced dates or prunes
Chopped apple

Sour cream may be used instead of sweet and ½ tsp. soda added. Beat the yolks with the sugar until very light; add the rest of the ingredients, folding in the stiffly beaten whites last. The prepared

* The munkpan is a heavy iron pan with 7 half-globe hollows each 2¼ inches in diameter. They are both Swedish and Hungarian.

fresh fruit may be sweetened a little with light brown sugar. Heat the munk form with plenty of oil or a mixture of oil and butter in each depression. Add a tablespoon of batter then a spoon of fruit and top with more batter. They are fried on top of the stove. When they are a light golden on the bottom, loosen them with a sharp knife and turn them over with 2 sharp-pointed knives. Continue frying until they are done. Serve hot with a sprinkle of powdered sugar. Pass sour cream to serve with them.

POPOVERS

Popovers

1 cup plus 2 Tbsps. sifted flour   1 cup plus 2 Tbsps. milk
¾ tsp. salt   3 eggs
1 Tbsp. melted butter or oil

Sift the flour with the salt and blend until smooth with the butter or oil and the milk, using either a rotary beater or the electric blender. Beat the eggs in a bowl with the rotary beater until light, then add the milk-flour mixture. Beat very well. This batter can stand in the refrigerator or can be baked immediately. Grease 11 iron popover forms very well and fill ⅔ full with the batter. Bake 45 to 50 minutes at 425° F., beginning in a cold oven; or bake at 375° F. 50 minutes. Don't open the oven door until the last 10 minutes.

VARIATIONS

YORKSHIRE PUDDING

Put ¼ cup of beef drippings in a large loaf pan, greasing the sides well, add the popover batter and bake 35 or 40 minutes before the roast is done. This is a beautiful puffed up loaf. If the batter is poured into the roasting pan, you may have a greasy product and no gravy with the meat, therefore use a greased loaf pan.

CHEESE POPOVERS

Add ½ cup of grated cheese to the popover recipe.

Buttermilk Popovers

1¼ cups buttermilk	1 Tbsp. oil
1 cup sifted flour	2 egg yolks
¾ tsp. salt	2 egg whites, beaten
1 tsp. light brown sugar	1 tsp. baking powder

Blend the buttermilk and the flour with a rotary beater or in an electric blender. Beat in the salt, sugar, oil and egg yolks. Beat the egg whites until stiff and add the baking powder. Combine with the batter. Fill 11 well-greased iron popover forms and bake 40 minutes at 375° F. They are very light and a little custardy inside.

Cocktail Cheese Popovers

1 cup boiling water	Few grains salt
½ cup butter	Few grains nutmeg
½ cup sifted flour	2 eggs
½ cup Parmesan cheese	

Put the water in a saucepan and when it boils melt the butter in it. Stir in the flour, cheese and seasonings all at once. Beat very hard, slipping pan on and off a very low flame as you would for pâte à chou. Let the mixture cool. Half an hour before you serve the popovers, beat in the eggs, 1 at a time. Beat well. Grease and flour a cookie sheet. Drop 30 little tsps. of mixture on the sheet and bake 15 minutes at 375° F. and 15 minutes at 350° F. Serve immediately.

Hot Breads: Coffeecakes, Corn Breads, Gingerbreads

Gougère

Hostellerie du Vieux Moulin
Bouilland, Côte d'Or

This delightful Burgundian pastry was given to me by Raymond Heriot, owner-chef of this lovely inn a short way from Beaune, the seat of *the* red wine of the world. The pastry makes a good accompaniment for a lunch or supper dish of creamed chicken or seafood or a salad.

PÂTE À CHOU
1 cup milk
⅓ cup butter
¼ tsp. salt
1 cup sifted flour
4 large eggs

1 Tbsp. heavy cream
½ cup shredded Swiss or
    Gruyère cheese
3 Tbsps. diced cheese

Preheat the oven to 375° F. Put the milk in a saucepan with butter and, when it is hot and the butter is melted, add the salt and dump in the flour all at once. Stir vigorously over a low flame until the mixture leaves the sides of the pan. Add 1 egg at a time beating very hard. This must not burn so move it off and on the heat. The mixture is very thick. Add the cream and ½ cup of cheese, and after it is well mixed, put it in a mound on a well-greased 10-inch glass pie plate, one that can be brought to the table. Sprinkle the top with the diced cheese. Bake 25 minutes in preheated oven; turn the heat to 350° F. and bake 10 minutes more. Makes 6 or more slices and serves 4 to 6. It is served with butter and as soon as it comes from the oven.

COFFEECAKES

Sour Cream Coffeecake

½ cup sweet butter
1 cup light brown sugar
2 cups sifted flour
2 tsps. baking powder
3 Tbsps. Madeira
3 Tbsps. currants
2 eggs, beaten

1 cup sour cream
FILLING
⅓ cup light brown sugar
⅓ cup raisins
½ cup ground almonds
2 Tbsps. cinnamon

Cream the butter with the sugar until creamy and smooth. Sift the flour with the baking powder. Marinate the currants in the Madeira an hour; toss them through the dry ingredients. Beat the eggs until light and stir in the sour cream. Combine the butter-sugar mixture, flour and liquid. Put ½ the batter in a greased, floured 8 x 11-inch pan and sprinkle with ½ of the mixed ingredients for the filling. Add the rest of e batter and sprinkle the top with the rest of the filling mixture. Bake at 350° F. about 35 to 40 minutes. Serve hot with butter.

Hot Raisin Bread

2 cups sifted flour
1 cup light brown sugar
1 Tbsp. cinnamon
¼ tsp. nutmeg
½ cup sweet butter
½ cup raisins or currants

2 tsps. baking powder
3 Tbsps. molasses
1 egg, beaten
1 cup buttermilk
½ tsp. salt

Sift the flour, sugar, cinnamon and nutmeg together and cut in the butter with a pastry cutter as for piecrust. Reserve ½ cup of these crumbs for the top of the batter. Toss the raisins or currants into the rest of the crumbles. Mix the baking powder with the molasses, add the egg, well beaten, the buttermilk and the salt. Combine with the flour crumbles and pour the batter into an 8 x 11-inch greased, floured pan, sprinkle the top with the reserved crumbles and bake at 350° F. about 25 minutes. Serve hot with butter.

Apple Hot Bread

1½ cups diced tart apples
1 Tbsp. cinnamon
2 Tbsps. brown sugar
3 Tbsps. butter
⅓ cup butter
½ cup light brown sugar
1 egg, beaten
¾ cup evaporated milk

2¼ cups sifted flour
1 tsp. cinnamon
½ tsp. salt
3½ tsps. baking powder
¼ cup light brown sugar
2 tsps. cinnamon
½ tsp. clove

Peel, core and dice tart apples. Mix them with the cinnamon and sugar. Melt 3 Tbsps. butter in a heavy saucepan and add the apples. Cover and steam 2 or 3 minutes over low heat. This is to soften them without their losing their shape. Cream the butter and sugar until smooth, then add the beaten egg and evaporated milk. Sift the flour with the cinnamon, salt and baking powder. Combine the two mixtures and, when blended, fold in the apples. Put the batter in a greased, floured 8 x 11-inch baking pan and sprinkle the top with the mixed sugar, cinnamon and clove. Bake 25 or 30 minutes at 350° F. Serve hot with heavy cream or butter.

Hot Cinnamon Bread

½ cup sweet butter
2 cups light brown sugar
1 Tbsp. cinnamon
¼ tsp. clove

2½ cups sifted flour
1 large egg, beaten
¾ cup buttermilk
2 tsps. baking powder

Cream the butter and sugar until smooth and creamy, add the spices and work in the flour so the mixture is crumbly. Reserve ¾ cup of the crumbles for the top. To the rest of the crumbles add the beaten egg and the buttermilk mixed with the baking powder. Grease and flour an 8 x 11-inch baking pan and add the batter. Sprinkle the top with the reserved crumbles. Bake at 350° F. about 20 to 25 minutes. Serve immediately with butter.

CORN BREADS

Light Corn Bread

¼ cup sweet butter
⅓ cup light brown sugar
2 egg yolks, beaten
1¼ cups buttermilk
⅞ cup corn meal

2 cups cake flour, sifted
1 tsp. salt
3 tsps. baking powder
½ tsp. soda
2 egg whites, beaten

Cream the butter and sugar until smooth. Add the egg yolks. Stir in the buttermilk and the mixed dry ingredients alternately. Fold in the stiffly beaten whites last. Bake in a greased, floured 8 x 11 x 1½-inch pan about 20 minutes at 375° F.

Cream Corn Bread

1 cup corn meal	1 tsp. salt
¾ cup sifted flour	2 Tbsps. melted butter
4 tsps. baking powder	2 eggs, beaten
3 Tbsps. light brown sugar	1 cup cream

Sift the dry ingredients together. Mix the melted butter with the well-beaten eggs and cream. For ordinary purposes, use light cream; for special occasions, heavy cream makes a rich and lovely bread. Combine the two mixtures and bake in a greased, floured 8 x 11-inch cake pan about 20 minutes at 350° F. Serve hot with sweet butter.

Southern Corn Bread

¼ cup sifted flour	2 eggs, beaten
½ tsp. soda	¾ cup buttermilk
1 tsp. baking powder	1½ cups boiling water
1 tsp. salt	2 cups corn meal
1 Tbsp. light brown sugar	

Sift the first 5 ingredients together and mix with the well-beaten eggs and buttermilk. Pour the boiling water gradually over the corn meal; mix until smooth. Add it to the first mixture. Bake in an 8 x 11-inch greased, floured pan 20 to 25 minutes at 350° F.

Old-Fashioned Sour Cream Corn Bread

¾ cup sifted white flour	3 Tbsps. light brown sugar
1 tsp. soda	¼ cup milk
1½ tsps. cream of tartar	2 Tbsps. melted butter
1 tsp. salt	1 large egg, beaten
1 cup corn meal	1 cup heavy sour cream

Sift the flour with the soda, cream of tartar and salt. Mix in the corn meal. Mix the sugar, milk, melted butter, well-beaten egg and cream together; combine with the dry ingredients. Bake in a greased, floured 9-inch square cake pan or round pan, 10 minutes at 375° F. and 10 minutes at 350° F. This is a fine textured bread as are all buttermilk or sour cream breads.

Buttermilk Corn Bread

2 cups buttermilk
4 Tbsps. melted butter
2 eggs, beaten
1 tsp. salt

2 tsps. baking powder
1 cup sifted flour
2 cups corn meal
⅓ cup brown sugar or molasses

Combine the buttermilk with the melted butter, well-beaten eggs and salt. Sift the baking powder with the flour and mix it with the corn meal. Combine the liquids with the flours and add the sugar or molasses. Bake in a greased, floured 8 x 11-inch baking pan 20 to 25 minutes at 375° F. If baking too fast turn to 350° F. after 10 minutes. Serve hot with butter.

Skillet Custard Corn Bread

1½ cups corn meal
½ cup flour
1 tsp. baking powder
1 tsp. soda
1 tsp. salt

1 Tbsp. brown sugar
2 eggs, beaten
1 cup buttermilk
2 cups sweet milk
3 Tbsps. butter

Mix all the dry ingredients together. Beat the eggs until light and then mix them with the buttermilk and 1 cup of the milk. Combine the liquid mixture with the dry ingredients. Melt the butter in a large 10 inch iron skillet. Tip the skillet so the butter coats the bottom and sides. Put in the batter and add the second cup of milk to the center. Do not stir again. Bake 30 minutes at 350° F. Serve in wedges with butter as soon as it is done.

Pumpkin Corn Bread

1½ cups corn meal
1 cup pumpkin, cooked and
  mashed
½ cup sifted flour
1 tsp. salt
3 tsps. baking powder

½ tsp. cinnamon
½ tsp. clove
3 Tbsps. honey or brown sugar
2 eggs, beaten
¾ cup sour cream
¾ cup (or more) buttermilk

Mix the corn meal and pumpkin in a mixing bowl and add the flour sifted with the dry ingredients. Beat the eggs until light and mix in the honey (if used) and the sour cream. Combine with the dry ingredients, adding enough buttermilk to make a medium soft batter. Bake in an 8 x 11-inch greased, floured pan at 350° F. about 20 to 25 minutes.

Coconut Corn Bread

1¾ cups corn meal
½ cup light brown sugar
1 cup sifted white flour
1 tsp. ginger
1 tsp. salt

2 tsps. baking powder
2 eggs, beaten
2 Tbsps. melted butter
2 cups buttermilk
1 can moist coconut

Put the corn meal and sugar in the mixing bowl and add the mixed and sifted dry ingredients. Beat the eggs until light and add the melted butter and buttermilk. Combine the two mixtures and stir in ⅔ of the coconut. Put the batter in a greased, floured 8 x 11-inch pan and sprinkle the top with the rest of the coconut. Bake about 20 to 25 minutes at 350° F. Serve hot with butter. It is also good cold.

Fresh Corn Corn Bread

2½ cups corn cut from ears or
    white shoe peg canned corn
½ cup flour
½ cup corn meal
2 tsps. salt
2 tsps. baking powder

2 egg yolks
⅓ cup heavy sweet or sour
    cream
1 Tbsp. light brown sugar
2 egg whites, beaten

Score the kernels then cut them from the ears, scraping all the milk out of them. Le Sueur brand fine white corn is also very good. Mix corn with the flours, salt and baking powder. Add the yolks, cream and sugar. When well mixed, fold in the stiffly beaten egg whites. Bake in a greased, floured 8 x 11-inch pan at 350° F. about 25 minutes. Serve hot with butter.

GINGERBREAD

Gingerbread is old-fashioned but should be revived because it is a delicious and versatile cake. When I was young we always had it for lunch, hot with butter. I don't think it goes with whipped cream, but of course that is a matter of taste. A thin chocolate frosting is better with it if you wish to dress it up. Raisins can be added, and grated orange rind gives a good flavor. A Tbsp. of cocoa can be added with the spices if desired, to give it just a little richer flavor.

Sour Cream Gingerbread

½ cup sweet butter
1 cup brown sugar
⅔ cup light molasses
2 egg yolks
½ cup sour cream
1½ cups sifted flour
1 tsp. ginger

1 tsp. cinnamon
¼ tsp. nutmeg
¼ tsp. clove
1 tsp. soda
2 Tbsps. hot water
2 egg whites, beaten

Cream the butter and sugar until light and smooth. Add the molasses, egg yolks and sour cream. Sift the flour with the spices and add to the butter mixture. Dissolve the soda in the hot water and add it. Fold in the stiffly beaten egg whites last. Bake in a greased, floured 8 x 11-inch pan at 350° F. about 25 to 30 minutes. When it shrinks from the sides of the pan or springs back to the touch of the finger to the top, it is done. This is delicious served hot with butter.

Eggless Gingerbread

1 cup molasses
1 cup sour cream
2 tsps. baking powder
2¼ cups sifted flour

2 tsps. ginger
⅛ tsp. salt
¼ cup melted butter

Mix the molasses with the sour cream and baking powder. Sift the flour with the dry ingredients and combine with the sour cream mixture. Add the melted butter last and bake in a shallow 8 x 11-inch greased, floured pan 35 minutes at 350° F.

Mame's Gingerbread

This is one of the finest gingerbreads, no matter which liquid you use. It is served hot with butter, or a thin chocolate frosting can be spread on it when it is cool.

¾ cup sweet butter	1 tsp. cinnamon
¾ cup brown sugar	1 tsp. ginger
¾ cup light molasses	1 tsp. clove
2 eggs, beaten	2 tsps. soda
2½ cups sifted flour	1 cup boiling water, orange juice or strong black coffee

Cream the butter and sugar; when smooth add the molasses. Beat the eggs until light and add them. Sift the flour with the spices and add to the egg mixture. Dissolve the soda in the hot liquid and add it to the batter. Bake in a long shallow greased, floured pan at 350° F. about 35 to 40 minutes.

Orange Gingerbread

(*white flour*)

½ cup sweet butter	½ cup cold strong tea
½ cup light brown sugar	1¾ cup pastry flour
½ cup light molasses	¾ tsp. soda
1 egg, beaten	1 tsp. ginger
Juice and grated rind of 1 orange	

Cream the butter and sugar until smooth, then add the molasses, beaten egg, juice and rind. Beat well; add the tea, and the flour sifted with the soda and ginger. Bake in an 8 x 11-inch pan, which has been greased and floured, 30 minutes at 350° F. This is very fine, especially hot with butter. Very good for tea with marmalade.

Pancakes, Crêpes, Waffles

PANCAKES

There are so many ways to make pancakes, it is hard to know when to stop. They can be made simply with all white flour, or enriched with wheat germ, an extra egg and extra milk powder. They can be made lighter by beating the egg whites until stiff and folding them in last.

2 cups sifted flour *or* 1½ cups flour and ⅔ cup wheat germ
2 tsps. baking powder
1½ tsps. salt
2 Tbsps. light brown sugar

2 or 3 large eggs (separated, optional)
3 Tbsps. melted butter
2 cups milk
½ cup milk powder (optional)

Sift the dry ingredients together. Beat the eggs or egg yolks until very light and combine with the melted butter, milk and milk powder (if used). Mix the liquids into the flour until smooth. If eggs are separated, fold in the stiffly beaten whites. Fry in butter or a mixture of butter and oil on a hot griddle. When the top of the cakes bubble, turn them once and fry to a golden brown on the other side. This makes about 18 pancakes.

VARIATIONS

CHILDREN'S PANCAKES

When you melt the butter mix in ⅓ cup of peanut butter and add it to the beaten eggs, mixing thoroughly with a rotary egg beater. Follow the foregoing recipe in all other respects. Thinned honey is good on these.

CHERRY PANCAKE FROM THE AUVERGNE

Medium thick pancake batter	¼ cup corn syrup
Pitted pie or black cherries	¼ cup light brown sugar
¼ cup melted butter	1 pat butter

Put 2½ cups of batter in a greased deep pie dish and sprinkle liberally with cherries and melted butter. Bake in a 350° F. oven until the batter is set. Serve with hot cherry sauce, made by cooking 1 cup of pitted cherries 3 minutes with ¼ cup of corn syrup and ¼ cup of light brown sugar and a pat of butter.

Grandma's Buttermilk Pancakes

2½ cups buttermilk	1 tsp. baking powder
2½ cups sifted flour	¾ tsp. soda
3 eggs, beaten	1 Tbsp. hot water
1 tsp. salt	2 Tbsps. light brown sugar

Mix the buttermilk and flour and refrigerate 12 to 24 hours, the longer the better. (But of course you can fry them at once.) When ready to make the cakes, beat the eggs until light and add them to the salt, baking powder, soda (dissolved in the hot water) and sugar. Combine with the flour and buttermilk. Fry in butter on a hot griddle.

Mother's Graham Pancakes

⅔ cup graham or whole wheat
  flour
1⅓ cups sifted white flour
2 tsps. baking powder
¾ tsp. salt

1 Tbsp. brown sugar
2 eggs, beaten
2 cups buttermilk
¼ cup sour cream or more

Mix all the dry ingredients. Beat the eggs until light; add the buttermilk and sour cream. Combine the 2 mixtures and if you like a rich but thin pancake, just add more sour cream. Fry in plenty of butter on a fairly hot griddle. Serve with butter and syrup.

Corn Meal Pancakes

¾ cup corn meal
1 cup sifted flour
1 tsp. salt
2 tsps. baking powder
1 or 2 Tbsps. light brown sugar

2 egg yolks
3 Tbsps. melted butter
2 cups buttermilk
2 egg whites, beaten

Mix the dry ingredients. Beat the egg yolks, melted butter, and the buttermilk together and combine with the dry ingredients. If a thinner pancake is desired, add a little more buttermilk. The whites don't thin the batter to any extent. Fold in the stiffly beaten egg whites last. Fry on a hot griddle in a mixture of oil and butter. Orange syrup is very good on these.

Flannel Griddle Cakes

1 cup sifted white flour
1 cup whole wheat, rye, oat or
  buckwheat flour
½ cup wheat germ (optional)
2 tsps. baking powder
1 tsp. salt

2 Tbsps. light brown sugar
2 eggs, beaten
2¼ cups buttermilk or more
2 Tbsps. sour cream *or* melted
  butter

Mix the dry ingredients and add the well-beaten eggs and buttermilk. The thickness of the batter is a matter of taste. Add more buttermilk if necessary and the sour cream or melted butter. Fry in butter and oil on a hot griddle. When they bubble on top, turn them once and fry until golden brown. These are hearty and will serve 4 or 5, especially if the wheat germ is added. They make a fine children's supper with crisp bacon or little fried pork sausages.

Apple Pancake

3 apples, peeled, cored and
  finely shredded
¼ cup lemon juice, sherry or
  Madeira
1 cup sifted flour
½ tsp. salt
1½ tsp. baking powder
3 Tbsps. light brown sugar

1 cup sour cream
4 egg yolks
Milk
4 egg whites, beaten
Butter
Powdered sugar with cinnamon
  or anise

Shred the apples into a plastic container or bowl with an airtight lid so they won't darken, and marinate them an hour sprinkled with juice or one of the wines. Sift the flour with the dry ingredients, and combine with the sour cream mixed with the egg yolks. If necessary add a little milk to make a medium thick batter; add the apples and marinade. Fold in the stiffly beaten egg whites. Fry the cakes, small or large, in butter. Sprinkle the top with a mixture of powdered sugar and a spice. Serves 4. Berries, cherries or sliced peaches may be used instead of apples.

Green Corn Cakes

2 cups corn cut from ears	½ cup sifted flour
1 cup milk	1 tsp. baking powder
2 Tbsps. melted butter	2 tsps. salt
2 egg yolks, beaten	2 egg whites, beaten
1 tsp. light brown sugar	Butter for frying

You will need 3 ears of corn. Put the ears in hot water, bring to a boil and remove the corn from the water immediately. Score the kernels with a sharp-pointed knife and cut them from the ears. Add the milk, melted butter, egg yolks and sugar. Sift the dry ingredients together and mix them with the corn. Fold in the stiffly beaten egg whites last. Fry on a well-buttered griddle. Serve with chicken or for lunch or supper with maple syrup. Serves 4.

Rice Batter Cakes

1 cup cooked patna, brown or Indian rice	3 Tbsps. light brown sugar
2 cups milk	⅓ cup sour cream
1 cup sifted flour	2 egg yolks
1½ tsps. baking powder	Milk
1 tsp. salt	2 egg whites, beaten
	Butter and oil

Soak the cooked rice in the milk 2 hours. Mix the dry ingredients together and add the sour cream and egg yolks. Combine with the rice and milk. If the batter is too thick, thin it with a little milk. Fold in the stiffly beaten egg whites. Fry in a mixture of butter and oil on a hot griddle. These are good with apricot or damson plum jam.

Raised Rye Pancakes

1 envelope yeast	2 Tbsps. brown sugar
1 cup warm milk	¼ cup cream
1 cup rye flour	¼ cup melted butter
¾ cup sifted white flour	2 tsps. baking powder
1 tsp. salt	2 eggs, beaten

Mix the first 6 ingredients and beat well together. Wrap the bowl in a towel and set in a warm place for several hours or all night. Mix the cream, melted butter, baking powder and well-beaten eggs together when ready to make the pancakes. Add the mixture to the sponge, mix well and fry like other pancakes.

Raised Pancakes

3 eggs, beaten	¼ cup lukewarm milk
2 Tbsps. light brown sugar	1 Tbsp. sugar
3 Tbsps. melted butter	1¾ cups lukewarm milk
1 tsp. salt	2 cups sifted flour or more
1 envelope yeast	

Beat the eggs until light, add the sugar, butter and salt. Mix the yeast with the lukewarm milk and sugar. When it is frothy add it to the egg mixture, with 1¾ cups of milk and enough flour to make the consistency of pancake batter. Set the bowl in warm water, covered with a tea towel, for about 30 to 40 minutes until batter rises. Fry like any other pancake on a well-greased griddle, turn once. Serve with a mixture of sugar and cinnamon; maple syrup; ground poppy seeds mixed with sugar and melted butter; or anything you choose.

VARIATION Omit the melted butter and replace ¾ cup of the milk with 1 cup of sour cream.

Raised Corn Meal Pancakes

1 cup corn meal
1 cup boiling milk
1 envelope yeast
¼ cup lukewarm water
2 Tbsps. light brown sugar

2 eggs, beaten
½ cup sifted flour
2 tsps. salt
1 tsp. baking powder
½ cup sour cream

Put the corn meal in a large mixing bowl and stir in the boiling milk until it is smooth. Dissolve the yeast in the lukewarm water with sugar until it is frothy. Combine the two mixtures when the corn meal is lukewarm. Cover and let it stand several hours or overnight. Twenty minutes before you are ready to fry the cakes beat the eggs, which should be at room temperature, until light. Sift the flour with the salt and baking powder and mix it with the eggs; stir in the sour cream. Combine the mixture with the yeast and corn meal and beat very hard for 2 minutes. Set it in a pan of quite warm water, cover and let it become light. Fry on a fairly hot griddle with butter and oil, the best combination for frying pancakes. This serves 4. The pancakes are very light and tender. They can be served with syrup for breakfast or supper or with chicken or pork instead of potatoes.

Potato Pancakes

4 medium-size raw potatoes, shredded
Salt and freshly ground pepper
3 Tbsps. flour
1 egg, beaten

¼ cup grated onion
½ cup shredded Swiss or Gruyère cheese
Heavy cream
Butter for frying

As the potatoes become watery after they are shredded, it is suggested all the ingredients be ready before you begin with the potatoes. Then work fast. Peel the potatoes and use the finest shredder. Mix with all the other ingredients adding just enough cream to make a moist but not wet batter. Fry the pancakes on a very hot griddle with plenty of butter so they have a golden crust on both sides and slide them onto a baking sheet. They finish cooking in about 4 minutes in a 400° F. oven. If prepared and fried ahead of time, they can be reheated just before serving for guests. They are wonderful with anything, but traditionally they are served with pot roast.

Cottage Cheese Pancakes

½ cup sieved cottage cheese
½ cup sour cream
2 large egg yolks
1 Tbsp. honey or light brown
  sugar
½ cup sifted flour

1 tsp. baking powder
½ tsp. salt
¼ tsp. nutmeg
2 egg whites, beaten
Butter for frying

Mix the cheese, cream, egg yolks and honey or sugar. Sift the dry ingredients together and combine with the cheese mixture. Fold in the stiffly beaten egg whites. Fry in plenty of butter on a griddle, turning once when they are a light brown. This makes 11 or 12 very delicate pancakes. This makes for a festive breakfast or a dessert with syrup, orange for instance.

Swedish Pancakes

Plättar

These are made in a Swedish pancake iron with its depressions for each small cake. They are piled and kept hot on a platter over boiling water. The proportion of flour and liquid is 1 to 3, somewhat thinner than ours.

3 eggs, beaten
1 cup heavy cream
1 cup sifted flour
¼ tsp. salt

¼ cup melted butter
1 Tbsp. light brown sugar
2 cups milk
Butter for frying

Beat the eggs until light, add the cream and gradually beat in the flour and salt until smooth; then add the butter, sugar and milk. Let stand 2 hours before frying. Brush the forms with melted butter and heat until quite hot. Put 2 or 3 small spoons of batter in each form and tip the pan so the bottom is covered. Fry until golden on each side. Serve with fruit sauce, sugar and cinnamon, or syrup.

Norwegian Pan-Cake

1 cup sifted flour	1 Tbsp. oil
½ tsp. salt	Soft sweet butter
1 Tbsp. light brown sugar	Light brown sugar
3 eggs, beaten	Cinnamon or cardamom powder
1½ cups milk	Butter and oil for frying

Sift the flour with the salt and sugar. Beat the eggs until very light. Combine the flour, eggs, milk, and oil, and let the batter stand an hour or more before frying. Put plenty of oil and butter on a hot griddle and add 1 serving spoon of batter. Tip the griddle so that each cake is 7 inches across. When done, spread each cake with soft butter and sprinkle with sugar seasoned with 1 Tbsp. cinnamon or a less amount of cardamom. Put each cake on a fireproof plate and top it with the next and so on until all are baked. Let the cakes stand in a warm oven with the door open until finished and then serve immediately. Syrup or orange syrup can be served with it. The stack of cakes is cut in pie-shape wedges. Serves 4 or 5.

French Apple Pancake

3 Tbsps. butter
3 large tart apples
2 tsps. lemon juice (if needed)
3 or 4 Tbsps. brown sugar
1 tsp. cinnamon
1 cup sifted flour *or* ½ cup white flour and ½ cup whole wheat flour

1 tsp. baking powder
½ tsp. salt
1 Tbsp. brown sugar
2 eggs, beaten
1 cup milk
Powdered sugar
Cinnamon

Melt the butter in a skillet and add the peeled, cored, finely sliced apples. Sprinkle with lemon juice and mixed sugar and cinnamon. Sauté the apples gently until tender. For the batter, sift the dry ingredients together. Beat the eggs until very light, add the milk and combine with the flour. When the apples are tender pour the batter over them and bake in a 350° F. oven until the batter is set and the top is lightly browned. Slide off onto a hot platter, fold over and sprinkle the top with mixed cinnamon and powdered sugar and serve immediately.

VARIATION The apples can be mixed with the batter and fried in butter on a pancake griddle. Serves 4.

Syrnikis with Berries and Sour Cream
Russian Cheesecakes

1 cup sieved cottage cheese
½ tsp. salt
3 Tbsps. cornstarch
1 egg, beaten
Butter
Honey

GARNISH
Strawberries, raspberries, blueberries or blackberries
Sour cream
Powdered sugar with anise

Mix the sieved cheese with the salt, cornstarch and beaten egg. Melt butter on a pancake pan with a dash of honey and fry big spoonfuls of the mixture; brown on both sides. Serve with bowls of fruit and sour cream, and a shaker of mixed powdered sugar and anise. This serves 3 but can easily be doubled.

Filled Rolled Pancake

⅔ cup sweet butter
1⅔ cup sifted flour
¼ tsp. salt
3 Tbsps. light brown sugar
2 cups milk

2 large eggs plus 1 yolk
3 egg whites, beaten
FILLING
1 cup jam (apricot or raspberry)
¾ cup heavy cream, whipped; or sour cream

Melt the butter in a saucepan and add the sifted flour, salt, sugar and milk. Beat hard over a low flame until it is thick and smooth. Remove from the heat and beat in the eggs and yolk, 1 at a time. When the mixture cools a little, beat the egg whites until stiff. Stir ¼ of the whites into the batter, then fold in the rest. Butter a jelly roll pan, lay a buttered parchment paper on it, then spread the batter over it in an oblong a scant ½ inch thick. Bake about 25 minutes in a 350° F. oven. Turn onto a well-sugared paper, spread with the jam and cream and roll the long way. Sprinkle heavily with powdered sugar. Cut in thick slices. Serves 4 to 6.

Swiss Pancakes

1 cup shredded Gruyère or Emmenthaler cheese
2 Tbsps. flour
¼ tsp. salt
Few grains nutmeg

1 tsp. mustard or grated lemon rind
2 eggs, beaten
½ cup sour cream
Butter for frying

Toss the finely shredded cheese with the flour, salt, nutmeg, mustard or lemon rind. Beat the eggs until light and mix with the sour cream. Combine the two mixtures. Fry small cakes in butter on a medium-hot griddle. They may be served with a salad or with fish or chicken. Serves 4 to 6.

CRÊPES

Crêpes for Entrées

2 cups sifted flour
½ tsp. salt
1 tsp. light brown sugar
1½ cups milk

½ cup light or heavy cream
4 egg yolks plus
2 whole eggs

Sift the flour with the dry ingredients and add the milk and cream, beating with a rotary beater until mixture is smooth. An electric blender is good for this. Beat the yolks and eggs in a bowl until light, then add the flour batter and mix well. Let batter stand an hour before frying. Follow the directions for French crêpes for frying.

FILLINGS

1. Thick cream sauce and cheese sauce (Mornay) spread to cool and stiffen on a platter. Cut in strips and fill and roll crêpes. Add a big spoon of cream sauce or sour cream to the top of each crêpe and sprinkle with grated cheese. Reheat and glaze under flame.
2. Choice of diced chicken, chicken livers, mushrooms, shellfish, ham and Mornay Sauce, or sweetbreads in a thick cream sauce. Additions to sauce: chopped browned almonds and currants marinated in Madeira.

French Crêpes

(*Entrée*)

These crêpes are mixed and then allowed to stand 3 hours at least before frying. They are extremely light and perfect for filling and rolling for serving as an entrée (first course) for 8 persons or for 4 or 5 as a main lunch or supper dish. Recipe makes about 18 crêpes. (Ingredients and directions continued on next page.)

1 cup sifted flour
1/8 tsp. salt
4 eggs
2 Tbsps. oil

1/4 cup sweet butter
1/2 cup milk
1 cup beer

Sift the flour and salt into a mixing bowl; make a well in the center and break the eggs into it. Beat with a rotary beater until mixture is smooth, then add the oil and beat again. Heat the butter in the milk until it is just melted, add to the batter and then add the beer. Mix well and let stand. Rub the crêpe pan quickly with a stick of butter before each crêpe is fried. The pan should be quite hot. Put two or three spoons of batter in the pan and tip it so the bottom is covered. A thin layer of batter is used to make a delicate crêpe. Time it 1 minute before turning it or it will break; fry about 30 seconds on the second side. Turn them first side down onto a large plate, so the good side will be on the outside when they are rolled. It is all right if there are a few little holes here and there—that means it is lacy and tender. They can be filled and placed in an oven-proof shallow pan or they may stand with wax paper between the layers and be filled shortly before reheating and serving. A lasagne pan is fine for these. Use any of previous Crêpes Fillings.

Crêpes Suzette

1½ cups milk
1½ cups flour
1 tsp. grated orange rind

1/4 cup melted sweet butter
1/4 cup orange liqueur
4 eggs, beaten

Beat milk and flour together with a rotary beater until smooth and without lumps. An electric blender is good for this. Add the rind, butter, and liqueur. Beat the eggs in a bowl until light. Add them to batter. Refrigerate the batter for 2 hours before frying. Follow directions for frying for French crêpes. Makes 18 or 20 crêpes to serve 6.

SUZETTE SAUCE
1 Tbsp. grated orange rind
⅓ cup orange juice
¾ cup sweet butter
½ cup light brown sugar

¾ cup orange liqueur: Grand
   Marnier, Cointreau,
   Chartreuse, or curaçao
Powdered sugar
½ cup Cognac

Put the rind, juice, butter and sugar in a chafing dish and stir over a medium flame until the butter is melted. Add the liqueur and when mixed dip each crêpe on both sides, fold twice and remove each to the side of the pan until all are dipped in the sauce. Put them back in the middle of the pan, sprinkle with sugar, pour the cognac over them and blaze. Spoon the sauce over the crêpes until the flame dies. Serve 3 on each dessert plate and sprinkle again with powdered sugar.

Crêpes alla Capocabana

Hotel Kraft, Florence

Maître d'hôtel Marino Coppetti makes lovely chafing dish specialties for guests at this hotel's roof restaurant. It is one of the best places to lunch or dine in Florence and certainly one of the most attractive. Not its least attraction is being situated on *quiet* via Solferino.

12 crêpes (for 4)
12 sticks pineapple

SAUCE
½ cup sugar
¾ cup strong coffee or espresso
2 tsps. powdered coffee
1 jigger cognac, blazed
1 jigger curaçao
2 or 3 Tbsps. Grand Marnier
Whipped cream

Make the crêpes ahead of time and wrap each around a pineapple stick. If fresh pineapple is not available, drain canned pineapple sticks and marinate them an hour in one of the liqueurs. For the sauce put the sugar and 2 or 3 Tbsps. of the coffee in a chafing dish. Melt and lightly caramelize the sugar over a low flame, stirring it until it is a little thick and golden color. It must not be black. Remove from the flame and stir in the rest of the coffee and the powdered coffee. Cook until it thickens and is syrupy. Lay the crêpes in the syrup and blaze them with the cognac. Extinguish the flame by covering it, then add the curaçao and Grand Marnier. Spoon the sauce over the crêpes and when they are hot, serve three on each plate with sauce. Pass a bowl of whipped cream separately.

Filled Dessert Crêpes

CRÊPES
1 cup plus 1 Tbsp. sifted flour
¾ tsp. baking powder
1½ Tbsps. powdered sugar
⅜ tsp. salt
5 eggs, beaten
1⅞ cups milk
1½ tsps. vanilla
3 tsps. melted butter

FILLING
½ cup sweet butter
1 cup powdered sugar
2 Tbsps. lemon juice
Grated rind 1 small lemon
3 Tbsps. Chartreuse or Grand Marnier

Sift all the dry ingredients. Beat the eggs until light and add the milk, vanilla and butter. Combine with the dry ingredients and beat until smooth. Let stand two hours before frying. Fry the crêpes and let them cool thoroughly before filling them with 1 Tbsp. of chilled filling. Fold like a package so they are airtight. Dredge with powdered sugar and heat quickly in a 450° F. oven for 4 minutes, then glaze under the flame for about 40 seconds. The surprise filling inside forms their sauce. The filling is made long ahead of time so it may chill and stiffen. Cream the butter and sugar until smooth, add the rest of the ingredients and store in refrigerator several hours.

Crêpe Dauphine

I almost changed the name of this recipe to *crêpe murmure*, because they are so light, they are like a whisper. You mix them rather like a pâte à chou. They fold easily and may enclose a little jam. They can be made any size you like. They are delicious with a few honeyed fresh raspberries spread on one side, folded over and a dash of *crème fraîche* on top, if desired. Suzette sauce served in a tureen or pitcher with these would produce a delicious and simple Crêpe Suzette.

4 Tbsps. sweet butter
½ cup plus 2 Tbsps. sifted flour
⅞ cup milk
3 large egg yolks
¼ tsp. salt
2 Tbsps. light brown sugar

½ cup plus 1 Tbsp. heavy cream
3 egg whites, beaten
DRESSINGS
Apricot jam, syrup, or fresh
   honeyed raspberries and
   crème fraîche

Melt the butter in a saucepan, add the flour; stir a little, then add the milk and cook over a low flame until the mixture leaves the sides of the pan and is thick, creamy and smooth. Remove from the heat and beat in the yolks, 1 at a time, then the salt, sugar and heavy cream. This can stand for a half hour. When ready to fry the crêpes, beat the egg whites until stiff and fold ¼ of them into the batter; then lightly mix in the rest of the whites. Fry on a medium-hot well-buttered griddle until golden on one side, then turn them and cook a short time on the other. This batter is easy to use as it has body and doesn't drip when turned. This makes 16 3-inch oval cakes.

Crêpes Parmentier

Parmentier (1737 to 1817) popularized the potato in France. It is hard to believe it was ever scorned in that country, for now it is served practically every day at least once. No man could have a better monument than these utterly delicious pancakes. They are popular all over France but they have achieved their peak of perfection at the *Chapon Fin,* a charming country inn at Thoissey, Burgundy, under the tutelage of Paul Blanc.

3 good-size potatoes	4 to 6 large eggs
Warm heavy cream	Sweet clarified butter for frying
¼ cup sifted flour	Powdered sugar
1 tsp. salt	

Peel the potatoes, boil them until tender, then rice them through a sieve along with perhaps ¼ cup of warm heavy cream to make a soft but thick purée. When cool, add the flour sifted with the salt. Beat 3 eggs until light and mix with the potato then add eggs as needed, 1 by 1 to make a thick rich batter. The recipe calls for clarified butter, which is melted butter poured off from the white residue. It is discarded. I find sweet butter often has no residue. Fry small pancakes in plenty of butter until a golden color on both sides. If you aren't careful, you will find yourselves eating 8 or 10 of these. Pass the sugar shaker for those who want it.

Sour Cream Crêpes

1 cup flour, sifted	1 cup heavy sour cream
½ tsp. salt	4 egg whites, beaten
1 tsp. sugar	GARNISH
½ tsp. baking powder	Fresh raspberries and *crème*
4 egg yolks, beaten	*fraîche*

Sift the dry ingredients together. Mix the beaten egg yolks with the sour cream and combine with dry ingredients. Last fold in the stiffly beaten whites. Fry the cakes in butter a delicate brown on both sides, turning once. They are very delicate and are not to be stacked. Serve garnished with any berries in season with a jug of *crème fraîche.* (See syrups.) Or they may be served with jam and sour cream. Serves 4. Spread thinned jam over 1 or 2 cakes, put them together and serve with Crème Fraîche or heavy cream. This must be done quickly as they are very delicate.

Apple or Banana Pandowdy

1 cup sifted flour *or* ½ cup each
   whole wheat and white flour
½ tsp. salt
2 cups milk
1 Tbsp. melted butter
1 Tbsp. light brown sugar
3 egg yolks

3 egg whites, beaten
3 bananas, sliced *or* 1¼ cups
   shredded tart apple
Nutmeg or cinnamon
⅓ cup light brown sugar
Cinnamon
Powdered sugar

Mix the flour and salt. Mix the milk with the melted butter, sugar and egg yolks. Combine the mixtures and beat until smooth. This can be done in the electric blender, then pour batter into a bowl so the stiffly beaten egg whites can be folded in. Lavishly grease a shallow baking dish or iron skillet and add half the batter. Arrange the sliced bananas over the top and sprinkle with nutmeg and brown sugar. If apples are used, sprinkle with cinnamon instead of nutmeg. Add the rest of the batter over the fruit. Bake at 375° F. for 15 minutes and 10 or 12 minutes more at 325° F. Serve immediately as this is similar to a popover batter. The top may be lightly sprinkled with a mixture of either nutmeg or cinnamon and powdered sugar. Serve with maple syrup. Serves 4. Other fruits may be used, such as any berry or sliced peaches or apricots.

WAFFLES

Waffle batter is like pancake batter except that more melted butter is added to prevent their sticking to the irons—if they do, add 1 to 3 more tablespoons of butter. The irons must be preheated to make sure that the first waffle will be as good as the last. After each waffle is removed the irons must be reheated before another is added. The waffle is done some few seconds after the steaming stops, but it will be crisper if allowed a few seconds more. A medium-thin batter assures crispness. Pancake syrups are served with waffles. Favorite dressings are sliced fresh peaches, honey and thick cream, sour cream or ice cream.

Sour Cream Waffles

⅓ cup soft sweet butter
4 egg yolks
1 cup sour cream
1 cup sifted flour

1½ tsps. baking powder
¾ tsp. salt
4 egg whites, beaten

Beat the soft butter with the egg yolks, adding 1 at a time. Combine with the sour cream. Sift the flour with the baking powder and salt and stir in the cream mixture. Fold in the stiffly beaten egg whites last. Grease the irons well and preheat until quite hot.

Sweet Milk or Buttermilk Waffles

1½ cups sifted flour
3 tsps. baking powder
½ tsp. salt
2 or 3 egg yolks

1½ cups milk or buttermilk
6 Tbsps. melted butter
2 or 3 egg whites, beaten
2 Tbsps. light brown sugar

Sift the flour with the baking powder and salt. Beat the egg yolks and add them to the milk or buttermilk and melted butter. Combine with the flour. Beat the egg whites until stiff then beat again with the sugar; fold into the batter and fry.

VARIATIONS

WHOLE GRAIN WAFFLES One third or ½ the quantity of flour may be replaced by oat, bran, whole wheat, rye or buckwheat flour, or corn meal.

FRUIT WAFFLES 1 cup blueberries may be added to the batter. Serve with blueberries and sour cream. ¾ cup chopped apples may be added to the batter.

RICE WAFFLES Add ½ cup fluffy, cooked rice to the batter and use ½ cup melted butter in recipe.

Cream Waffles

1 cup sifted flour
1 tsp. baking powder
½ tsp. salt
1 Tbsp. light brown sugar

1 cup heavy cream
2 or 3 egg yolks
2 Tbsps. melted butter
2 or 3 egg whites, beaten

Sift the flour with the dry ingredients. Beat the cream with the egg yolks, add the butter and combine with the flour. Fold the stiffly beaten egg whites in last. Fry as directed. If the batter is too thick, thin with a little milk. Irons should never be filled too full.

Swedish Crisp Waffles

1⅔ cup heavy cream, whipped
1⅓ cups sifted flour
½ tsp. salt
¾ cup ice water

2 Tbsps. melted butter
GARNISH
Cinnamon and powdered sugar,
    or fruit sauce or jam

Whip the cream until stiff. Sift the flour with the salt and combine with the water, beating until smooth. Add the melted butter and fold in the cream. Preheat the waffle iron and butter it lightly. If a Swedish iron is used, just cover the design with batter. Bake to a golden color on each side. Do not stack them. Serve hot, divided into sections. In Sweden they are served for tea. The grated rind of ½ lemon can be added. Two beaten eggs can be added, in which case reduce the water to ½ cup and the cream to 1¼ cups.

Fried and Boiled Breads: Doughnuts, Fritters, Dumplings

DOUGHNUTS

Doughnuts are really easy to make. All one needs is a good recipe, a frying thermometer, a heavy 4-quart kettle and some happy appetites. A very pleasant culinary memory of mine is the time when we ate our fill from frying kettle to mouth, so to speak. Here are 3 good ones.

Sweet Milk or Buttermilk Doughnuts

3 eggs or 2 eggs plus 1 yolk
1 cup light brown sugar
⅓ to ¾ cup sweet butter, melted
1 cup sweet milk or buttermilk

4 cups sifted flour, more or less
3 tsps. baking powder
¼ tsp. salt
Oil for deep frying
Powdered sugar

Beat the eggs until very light, add the sugar and beat until thick and creamy. The amount of butter you use depends on how rich you like your doughnut. I should use at least ½ cup with buttermilk. Add the melted butter and liquid to the sugar mixture. Sift 3 cups of flour with the baking powder and salt. Mix it with the batter and add more flour to make a dough that can be rolled. Do not add any more flour than is necessary. Too much flour makes a bready and uninteresting doughnut. Roll the dough with a very light hand, ½ inch thick on a lightly floured board, ½ the dough at a time, and cut with a doughnut cutter. Heat 5 or 6 cups of oil 370 to 375° F. and lift the rings into it, taking care not to crowd them. Turn 2 or 3 times until they are golden on both sides. The balls take a little less time to fry. Drain them on brown paper. Put plenty of powdered sugar in a paper bag and shake the doughnuts in it. When serving put a ball on each doughnut. They are best stored in an earthenware jar with a well-fitting lid.

Sour Cream Doughnuts

2 cups light brown sugar	3 tsps. baking powder
3 eggs, beaten	¼ tsp. salt
1 cup sour cream	3½ to 4 cups sifted flour
½ cup buttermilk	Oil for deep frying
⅛ tsp. nutmeg	Powdered sugar

Measure 2 cups of light brown sugar, packed lightly. Beat the eggs until very light, add the sugar and beat until thick and creamy. Add the cream and buttermilk to the egg mixture. Sift the dry ingredients together with 3 cups of the flour. Combine the mixtures and if necessary add a little more flour, just enough so the dough may be rolled. Cut the doughnuts and let them stand 20 minutes before frying. Follow frying directions in preceding recipe.

VARIATION
POTATO DOUGHNUTS In either of the above recipes, replace ½ to ¾ cup of flour with that quantity of boiled, riced potatoes. Add

the sugar and butter to the hot potato. Beat the eggs until very light and combine with the potato. Then add the sifted dry ingredients, using 2 cups of flour and adding more if necessary. Fry as directed.

Potato Doughnuts

1 cup hot mashed potatoes	2 tsps. baking powder
1 cup light brown sugar	½ tsp. salt
1 cup evaporated milk	⅛ tsp. powdered clove
2 eggs, beaten	Fat for deep frying
3⅓ cups flour (about)	

Add the sugar to the hot potatoes and stir until smooth. Add the milk and beaten eggs. Sift 3 cups of flour with the dry ingredients and combine with the potato mixture. If not firm enough to roll, add more flour but no more than is necessary. Roll out about ⅓ inch thick, cut with a doughnut cutter, and fry in deep oil or fat at 370° F. until brown on both sides, turning once. Drain on brown paper until cool, then shake in a bag with plenty of powdered sugar. Makes about 24 doughnuts.

Gina Ford's Hjortebakkles

Norwegian Doughnuts

The recipe for these lovely little rich crisp doughnuts was given by a lady ninety years old who has been delighting her children and grandchildren with them for many years. She brought the recipe from Norway.

4 eggs, well beaten	4 cups sifted flour
1⅓ cups sugar	2 tsps. baking powder
1 cup sweet butter, melted and cooled	2 pounds lard for frying

Beat the eggs until light, then add the sugar and beat until thick. Put the butter in a saucepan set in a larger saucepan containing boiling water, to melt it. When butter is lukewarm, add it to the egg mixture. Sift the flour with the baking powder and stir it into the first mixture. The dough will be thick. Nip off small pieces, roll them between lightly floured hands into about a 5-inch cigarette-slender tube, then pinch the ends together to make a ring. Fix 8 or 9 of them on a floured paper, then fry them in a kettle of lard heated 370 to 375° F., until they are a light golden color. Drain on brown paper. These doughnuts are not to be rolled and cut. Vegetable oil may be used for frying but the lard is greatly preferred. If your family is small, half a recipe will produce more than 50 little doughnuts. I have tried them using light brown sugar and they are just as good. I used extra large eggs for ½ the recipe and had to add ⅓ cup of sifted flour. They can be shaken in a bag with powdered sugar.

FRITTERS

Plain Fritters

1 cup sifted flour	1 egg or 2 eggs, separated
1 tsp. baking powder	½ cup milk or beer
½ tsp. salt	Oil for deep frying
2 Tbsps. melted butter	

Sift dry ingredients together, then add butter and egg yolks, milk or beer and mix. Fold in stiffly beaten egg whites. The proportions for fritter batter are 1 cup of flour to ½ cup of liquid and 1 egg. This makes 12 to 18 fritters depending on their size. They are taken up by big spoonfuls, or as much as desired, scraped off the spoon into the 370° F. vegetable oil. If the eggs are beaten separately with the stiffly beaten whites added last, they make a light and delicious dessert fritter to serve with powdered sugar, wine or fruit sauce. This batter is also used for dipping prepared fruits, such as apple slices first marinated in lemon juice or kirsch. The fruit is drained, dipped in batter and fried. A frying basket is lowered into the hot fat and the batter added, not crowding the fritters. When they are golden on both sides they are drained on brown paper. If raw fish or meat is cooked, begin the frying at 365° F. and let the heat rise to 375° F. This gives the raw food a chance to cook thoroughly. Some French recipes add 2 Tbsps. of brandy to the batter and use milk or water as the liquid.

Chinese Fritter Batter

This is one of the best batters for dipping fruit, vegetables, chicken, spareribs, and shrimp, etc., for deep frying.

2 eggs, beaten	½ tsp. salt
4 Tbsps. flour	2 tsps. sugar

Beat the ingredients together, dip pieces of food and fry in deep fat or oil. If more batter is needed, simply increase by adding 2 Tbsps. of flour to every additional egg and a little salt and 1 tsp. of sugar. The sugar does not make the coating sweet but makes it brown nicely.

Breading for Cutlets, Croquettes, etc.

Flour
Beaten egg
Fine fresh crumbs, *or*
Corn meal, *or*
Whole grain flours
Parmesan cheese (optional)

Beaten egg clings better to food if it is first rolled lightly in flour. The food is then dipped in beaten egg, then in ingredient chosen for breading. Fine crumbs may be mixed with ⅓ to ½ the quantity of Parmesan cheese. This makes a rich crust. Corn meal, whole wheat, rye or oat flour are excellent for breading either with or without the cheese. The foods are deep fried in oil or fried in a mixture of butter and oil in a skillet.

Hominy Fritters

1½ cups cold boiled hominy	1½ tsps. baking powder
⅓ cup sifted flour	Milk
1 large egg yolk	1 egg white, beaten
1 tsp. salt	Oil for frying

Mix first five ingredients, adding enough milk to make a very stiff batter. Fold in the beaten egg white last. Drop from a spoon into 375° F. oil and fry to a golden color. Fine with chicken.

Corn Fritters

2 cups corn, scored, cut from ears	1 Tbsp. light brown sugar
1 cup sifted flour	¼ cup butter, melted
2 tsps. salt	2 eggs, separated
1 tsp. baking powder	Oil for deep frying

Cut the corn from the ears or use a very good brand of white shoe peg canned corn kernels. If canned is used, drain it. Sift the flour with all the dry ingredients and stir in the corn. Mix the melted butter and egg yolks and stir them into the corn mixture; fold in the stiffly beaten egg whites last. Heat 5 cups of vegetable oil to 365° F., then drop spoons of batter into the oil, letting the oil come up to 375° F. Do not crowd the fritters. When they are golden brown on both sides, drain them onto brown paper. Serve hot with powdered sugar, syrup, or with pork or chicken. Serves 4 to 6. When the oil is cool, drain it, and store in the refrigerator to use again.

Raised Fritters

Any roll or bread dough makes fritters. Pinch off small pieces of dough, roll in balls the size of a marble, let them rise 20 minutes on a greased pan, then fry at 370° F. in hot oil. They may be filled before rising with an apricot or other fruit, or jam. When they are golden, drain them on brown paper. Sprinkle with powdered sugar and serve hot. Serve 3 to a person.

Beignets

Soupirs de Nonne

These puffed fritters ("nun's sighs") are pâte à chou and can be slit and filled with flavored fruit: apricots, strawberries, raspberries, or chocolate cream filling or jam. This makes 12 fritters.

¼ cup sweet butter
½ cup boiling water
½ tsp. salt
½ cup sifted flour
2 eggs
Powdered sugar

Put the butter, water and salt in a saucepan and when the butter is melted, dump in the flour and stir vigorously over a low fire until the mixture forms a ball and leaves the sides of the pan. Remove from the fire and beat in the eggs, 1 at a time. Have the oil heated to 370° F. and drop small spoonfuls into the oil; cook until golden brown. Drain onto brown paper and fill. Sprinkle with powdered sugar and serve immediately.

Calas

These hot rice fritters were a delicacy purveyed by Negro women in earlier days for breakfast. The women carrying napkin-lined baskets of these freshly deep-fried cakes called *Cala' Cala' tout chaud,* a street cry of Old New Orleans. This is my own version with a full-flavored rice. It makes a wonderful luncheon, supper, or Sunday morning treat.

½ cup patna or Indian rice
1½ cups water
1 envelope yeast
3 Tbsps. lukewarm water
¼ cup light brown sugar
3 medium-size eggs, beaten
¼ tsp. salt

¼ cup light brown sugar
½ tsp. fresh grated nutmeg
1 cup (or more) sifted flour
Oil for deep frying
Powdered sugar or syrup
Fruit sauce (optional)

Wash the rice and cook it tightly covered in 1½ cups of water over a slow flame until the water is absorbed. When rice is cooked, turn off the heat and let it stand 10 minutes. The steam will loosen all the rice from the bottom of the pot. Dissolve the yeast and sugar in the water in a large mixing bowl and mix it with the rice when it is lukewarm. For this use regular-size eggs, as the larger the egg, the more flour is required and the less flour the better. They should be at room temperature. Beat them until they are light; add the salt and the sugar and beat again. Add the nutmeg. beat this into the rice and yeast for 2 or 3 minutes, then add the cup of flour. Set the bowl in a dishpan of hot water, cover with a towel and let batter become light for 2 hours. Heat 5 or 6 cups of vegetable oil in a 4-quart pan to 340° F. or 350° F. Drop 1 spoonful into the fat and if holds together, no more flour will be needed. If it dissolves, add a little more flour. When Calas are golden, turn and fry on the other side. Drain and serve immediately sprinkled with powdered sugar; or they may be served with syrup or, if for a supper dessert, with a fruit sauce. Serves 4, liberally.

DUMPLINGS

Dumplings for Stews

2 cups sifted flour
4 tsps. baking powder
1 tsp. salt

1 tsp. butter
1 tsp. lard, bacon fat or vegetable shortening
¾ cup milk

Mix the dry ingredients and cut in the fat with a wire pastry cutter. Stir in the milk, mixing very lightly, just enough to wet the batter. The dumplings can be rolled and cut with a biscuit cutter or dropped from a spoon onto actively simmering stew. Cover tight and cook 12 minutes without lifting the lid. There is enough shortening to make light, tender dumplings. Lift them with a slotted spoon to the edge of a large platter and heap the stew in the center. Makes 8 or 10 dumplings.

BOILED FRUIT DUMPLINGS

Dough:
1 cup sifted flour
2 tsps. baking powder

⅛ tsp. salt
1 Tbsp. butter
½ cup milk

SYRUPS FOR BOILING DUMPLINGS

Berry:
3 cups raspberries and red currants *or* cherries, blackberries, etc.
1 cup boiling water
1 cup light brown sugar
1 Tbsp. butter
(With strawberries use 1 cup of orange juice instead of water and grated rind of 1 orange.)

Orange:
1 cup light corn syrup
½ cup sugar
1¼ cups orange juice
Rind and juice of 1 lemon
1 Tbsp. butter
Peach:
1 pound skinned quartered peaches
Grated rind of 1 orange
1 cup orange juice
1 cup light brown sugar
1 Tbsp. butter

Lemon:
1 cup light brown sugar
1 cup light corn syrup
Grated rind 1 lemon
Juice of 2 large lemons plus
    water to make 1 cup
2 Tbsps. butter

Plums:
1 pound tart red plums, sliced
1 cup hot water
1 cup light brown sugar
1 Tbsp. butter

Choose the fruit and make a syrup with all the ingredients given for each fruit by putting them in a good-size saucepan equipped with a tight lid. Bring to the boil for a scant minute, drop the dough from a big spoon in 6 equal parts. Cover and simmer gently for 20 minutes. Serve the dumplings in six sauce dishes with the sauce divided over them. Serve with heavy cream if you like. For the dough, sift the flour with the dry ingredients and cut in the butter with a wire pastry cutter. Stir in the milk to make a soft dough.

Corn Meal Dumplings

¾ cup corn meal
1 cup sifted white flour
3 tsps. baking powder
1 tsp. salt

1 Tbsp. chopped onions or
    chives
2 Tbsps. sour cream
1 egg, beaten
Buttermilk

Sift the dry ingredients together. Add the onion or chives. Parsley or dill also makes a good flavor. Mix the sour cream, egg and ¼ cup of buttermilk and combine with the dry ingredients. If necessary add a little more buttermilk to make a soft but stiff dough. Drop from a spoon onto slowly simmering stew, cover and cook slowly 12 to 15 minutes without lifting the lid. The stew must not stop simmering. Makes 8 dumplings.

Hungarian Dumplings

Cheese Knoedel

½ pound creamed cottage
  cheese
Grated rind of 1 lemon
½ tsp. salt
⅓ to ½ cup farina (cream of
  wheat)
2 egg yolks
2 egg whites, beaten
Boiling salted water

GARNISH
3 Tbsps. butter
⅓ cup fine crumbs
½ tsp. cinnamon
1 Tbsp. light brown sugar
Fruit sauce and sour cream
  (optional)

Sieve the cheese and mix it with all the other ingredients, folding in the stiffly beaten egg whites last. Form into dumplings the size of a walnut and drop them into actively simmering salted water, cover and cook for 10 minutes. Drain from the water and swish around in the melted butter mixed with the crumbs, cinnamon and sugar. Serve with the meat course; or, for dessert, with fruit sauce and sour cream.

Liver Dumplings

¾ pound calf, pork or yearling
  liver
Butter
¼ cup chopped onion
1 egg, beaten
1 Tbsp. chopped parsley
Salt and pepper

½ tsp. thyme
¼ tsp. nutmeg
½ cup bread crumbs
¼ cup sifted flour
Boiling consommé or salted
  water

Have the liver sliced thin. Sear the slices in butter, then grind it fine with the onion which has been sautéed 3 minutes in 1 tablespoon of butter. Stir in the beaten egg and all the other ingredients except the consommé. Roll into 12 dumplings. Try one in boiling liquid and if it holds together no more flour will be necessary. Boil 6 minutes. These are excellent served with spaghetti, sauerkraut or boiled rice or a risotto. If tiny dumplings are made they may be served in consommé or soup.

Biscuits, Crusts, Scones

BISCUITS

Baking Powder Biscuits

This recipe embraces three choices or variations of the standard recipe. The dry ingredients are sifted together. The sugar may be omitted but it enhances the flavor somewhat, and the biscuits brown better with it. Part butter and part other fat makes for a more tender biscuit than all butter. The amount used depends on how rich you want the biscuit. If a well-beaten egg is used, the liquid is reduced a little. The standard recipe calls for sweet milk; buttermilk can be used, which makes a fine and tender biscuit.

2 cups sifted flour
3 tsps. baking powder
¾ tsp. salt
1 tsp. sugar (optional)

4 or 5 Tbsps. butter and lard or
    vegetable shortening, mixed
1 egg, beaten (optional)
⅔ (about) cup sweet milk or
    buttermilk

Sift the dry ingredients together and cut the shortening in with a wire pastry cutter; the ingredients should be cold. Add the egg and liquid to the flour, just enough so the dough is light, soft, but stiff enough to handle. Put the dough on a floured board and mold it lightly into a ball, handling as little as possible. Roll very gently to ½-inch thickness and cut with a 1½-inch or 2-inch cutter. Place the rounds on a greased and floured pan. If you aren't in a hurry they can be chilled ten minutes. Pre-heat the oven to 450° F. and bake from 12 to 15 minutes. Serve immediately with room-temperature sweet butter and jam (if for breakfast or lunch), or chicken gravy if for dinner. Serves 4 to 6.

BISCUIT ADDITIONS AND VARIATIONS

PEANUT BUTTER BISCUITS: 3 Tbsps. peanut butter (or other nut butters) beaten with an egg and added with the milk.

SOUR CREAM BISCUITS: 1 cup thick sour cream and 1 Tbsp. melted shortening used in place of other liquid.

HERB BISCUITS: Three Tbsps. chopped fresh dill, parsley, or chervil, etc., added to the mixed dry ingredients.

CURRANT BISCUITS: Three or 4 Tbsps. currants soaked in 2 Tbsps. Madeira or sherry added to the dry ingredients. Sprinkle the tops with a mixture of sugar and cinnamon, cardamom or anise.

ORANGE BISCUITS: Replace ½ liquid with orange juice. Add the grated rind of 1 orange to the dry ingredients. Use 1 Tbsp. sugar with the dry ingredients.

MASHED POTATO BISCUITS: Replace 1 cup of flour with fluffy mashed potatoes. Mashed sweet potatoes can be used instead of white.

CHEESE BISCUITS: Two-thirds cup of grated Cheddar cheese is added to the dry ingredients.

VERMONT BISCUITS: Roll out the dough as for jelly roll, spread with maple cream, roll up the long way and cut in inch-thick slices; put them cut side down on a greased pan. Bake in a preheated 400° F. oven for 15 minutes. Lovely for tea.

ORANGE-SYRUP BISCUITS: Boil up 1 Tbsp. grated orange rind, ½ cup of orange juice, ½ cup of sugar and 2 Tbsps. butter. Roll the dough into an oblong, roll up the long way and cut in

¾-inch slices. Put them in a greased 9-inch square pan and pour the cooled orange syrup over them. Bake 15 minutes at 400° F.

FRIED BISCUITS: Make the dough with the beaten egg. Cut in 3 x 1-inch strips and fry them on a well-buttered griddle until puffed and golden on all sides. Serve with syrup or marmalade or a mixture of sugar and cinnamon.

Almond Rolled Biscuits

2 cups sifted flour
3 tsps. baking powder
2 tsps. light brown sugar
¾ tsp. salt
¼ cup butter and vegetable
   shortening mixed
⅔ cup milk (about)

1½ tsps. almond extract
FILLING
¼ cup soft sweet butter
½ cup sliced browned almonds
¼ cup honey
¼ cup light brown sugar

Mix the sifted flour with the dry ingredients. Cut in the shortening with a wire pastry cutter. Mix ½ cup of milk with the almond extract and add to the dry ingredients. Add more milk to make a light, soft dough which is rolled out ½ inch thick. Make an oblong 6 x 14 inches. Spread with soft butter and sprinkle with the almonds. (Put the almonds on before the mixed liquid honey and brown sugar as it will keep the honey mixture from running off.) Dribble the sweetening over the surface keeping at least an inch from the edges. Roll up the long way and cut in inch-thick slices. Put them cut side down on a greased pan. Preheat the oven to 400° F. and bake about 15 minutes.

VARIATION

ROLLED CHEESE BISCUITS Cheese rolled biscuits are made exactly the same way as Almond Rolled Biscuits except omit the sugar and mix 2 tsps. of dry mustard with the dry ingredients. Sprinkle 1 cup of grated Cheddar cheese over the rolled surface which has been spread with butter. Omit the nuts and sweetening. Roll the long way; slice and bake 15 minutes at 400° F.

Fruit Biscuit Roll

BISCUIT DOUGH
2 cups sifted flour
2 tsps. baking powder
½ tsp. salt
2 Tbsps. light brown sugar
½ cup butter and vegetable shortening mixed
¾ cup milk (about)

CHOICE OF FRUIT
2 cups berries, cherries, sliced peaches, apricots, plums *or* 1 cup thinned damson jam or apricot or prune purée
SYRUP
1 cup orange juice
½ cup light brown sugar
3 Tbsps. butter
Almond extract, cinnamon or clove
GARNISH
Heavy cream or *crème fraîche*

This makes a great summer lunch with, perhaps, a bottle of chilled wine. Sift the flour with the dry ingredients and cut in the cold shortening with a wire pastry cutter. Then stir in just enough milk so that dough can be handled. Roll out ½ inch thick and 10 inches wide. The fruit has been prepared. Boil up all the ingredients for the syrup and pour it over the fruit (except the jam or purée, if used) and let it stand 3 minutes. Reserve the syrup for the pan. Sieve the fruit and spread it over the dough, roll the dough up like a jelly roll and lift it into a well-greased oblong pan. Put it into a 375° F. oven for 10 minutes, then pour the boiling syrup over it and bake it 20 minutes more at 325° F. Lift the roll onto a platter with pancake turners and scrape the pan syrup over it. Serve immediately with cream or *crème fraîche*. Blackberries are especially good for this and so are red currants and raspberries, half and half. Serves 4 or 5.
If jam is used in the roll, boil up the syrup and pour it over the partially baked roll, as directed.

CRUST

Crust for Chicken or Meat Pies

⅓ cup white flour
⅓ cup whole wheat flour
⅓ cup corn meal
1 tsp. salt

2 tsps. baking powder
2 tsps. light brown sugar
¼ cup corn oil
Buttermilk

Mix the dry ingredients together. Mix the vegetable oil with ½ cup of buttermilk and stir it into the flours. Add more buttermilk to make a soft mixture but one that will keep its shape when dropped by tablespoonfuls onto the top of the baking dish of stew, leaving vents between the blobs of dough for steam to escape. Bake in a preheated 375° F. oven for 12 minutes, then reduce the heat to 350° F. and bake 12 minutes more. This is a delicious, tender crust.

Potato Scones

1¼ cups seasoned mashed
  potatoes
1½ tsps. baking powder
½ tsp. salt

½ cup sifted flour
1 egg, beaten
¼ cup buttermilk

The potatoes should be fluffy and soft. Mix the dry ingredients together and blend with the potato; add the beaten egg and buttermilk. Mix and pat into a ¾-inch-thick cake and put it in a greased, floured pie plate. Bake 8 minutes at 400° F. Turn the temperature to 350° F. and bake 4 minutes more. Cut in 6 pie-shape wedges and serve hot with butter. These are light and delicious. If for tea, sprinkle the top with a mixture of sugar and cinnamon when you turn the heat to 350° F.

SCONES

Cream Tea Scones

2 cups sifted flour	¼ cup sweet butter
4 tsps. baking powder	2 eggs, beaten
¾ tsp. salt	¾ cup heavy cream
1 Tbsp. light brown sugar	Sugar and anise or cinnamon

Sift the dry ingredients together and cut in the butter with a wire pastry cutter. Beat the eggs until light, then mix with the cream. Add the liquids to the dry ingredients, stirring as little as possible. Divide the dough in two parts, pat or roll and place in two greased and floured round 6- or 7-inch cake pans. Cut in quarters so they may be easily broken apart when they are served. Sprinkle the tops with a mixture of sugar and a spice, very lightly. Bake at 425° F. about 18 minutes. Serve hot with butter and jam.

Oat Scones

¾ cup oat flour	¼ cup sweet butter
1¼ cups sifted white flour	½ (or more) cup buttermilk
3 tsps. baking powder	1 egg, beaten
1 tsp. salt	
3 Tbsps. light brown sugar	

Mix the dry ingredients and cut in the butter with a wire pastry cutter. Mix ⅓ cup of buttermilk with the well-beaten egg and mix it with the flours. Add more buttermilk to make a soft batter that can be rolled. Roll into a neat strip 5 inches wide and ¾ inch thick. Cut in triangles and bake on a greased, floured sheet at 400° F. about 15 to 18 minutes. Serve hot with butter and jam. Three or 4 minutes before removing from the oven, sprinkle with a mixture of sugar and spice, if you like. Three tablespoons of currants may be added to the dough.

Miscellaneous

SYRUPS FOR HOT BREADS

Orange Syrup

1 cup orange juice
¼ cup honey or brown sugar

⅓ cup sweet butter
2 Tbsps. lemon juice

Boil up the juice and other ingredients to melt the butter. Serve in a pitcher.

Brown Sugar Syrup

1 cup light brown sugar
⅓ cup water
1 tsp. cinnamon (optional)

⅓ cup butter
3 Tbsps. brandy or rum (for supper dishes only)

Boil the sugar and water for 2 minutes; add the other ingredients. Serve in a pitcher.

Maple or Honey Syrup

1 cup maple syrup
⅓ cup butter   *or*
1 tsp. cinnamon (optional)

½ cup honey
¼ cup water
⅓ cup butter

Heat the ingredients. Water is used to thin out very heavy honey.

Honey with Sweet or Sour Cream

Dilute the honey if very thick with 1 or 2 Tbsps. of boiling water. Combine equal quantities of honey and heavy sweet cream or sour cream. This is delicious over hot breads, cereal or shortcakes.

Molasses and Honey

Molasses may be heated alone with butter or it may be diluted with honey to soften the strong flavor. The tonic quality of molasses is liked by many over breakfast dishes.

FILLINGS FOR SWEET ROLLS, COFFEECAKES, TARTS, ROLLED PANCAKES AND DANISH PASTRY

Cottage Cheese Filling

1 cup sieved creamed cottage cheese or ricotta
⅓ cup light brown sugar
3 egg yolks

⅓ cup chopped brown almonds, *or* ⅓ cup raisins (soaked in 2 Tbsps. Madeira)
Grated rind of 1 lemon

Mix all the ingredients together. Suitable for filling pancakes or crêpes to be rolled and heated.

Prune or Apricot Filling

1½ cups cooked dried prunes or
   apricots, puréed
⅓ cup light brown sugar
2 Tbsps. sweet butter, melted

1 tsp. rose extract
1 tsp. almond extract
¼ cup ground browned
   almonds

Mix all ingredients together.

Apple Butter Filling

¼ cup currants or raisins
¼ cup brandy or rum
1½ cups dark spicy apple butter

Marinate the currants or raisins an hour in the liquor, then add to
the butter. This is good to fill Vánočka.

Peach Jam Filling

Peach butter or jam
Orange juice or rum (if
   necessary)

¼ cup ground browned
   almonds
1 tsp. almond extract

If the butter or jam is very thick, it may be thinned with 2 or 3
Tbsps. orange juice or rum. Add the almonds and extract. This is a
delicious filling for little rolls such as Rich Egg Rolls. Other jellies
or thinned jams can be used, such as blackberry, currant, raspberry,
or grape.

Poppy Seed Filling

1 cup ground poppy seeds
⅓ cup light brown sugar
¼ cup soft sweet butter
⅓ cup heavy cream

½ cup raisins *or* ⅓ cup
   chopped browned almonds
3 egg yolks
2 tsps. vanilla

Mix the poppy seeds, sugar, butter, cream, and raisins or almonds and bring to the boil for 30 seconds, stirring continuously. Remove from the fire when smooth; add the egg yolks and, when cool, the vanilla. Fine for coffeecakes, rolls, Vánočka, etc.

Raisin Filling

1 cup raisins
½ cup white corn syrup
1 tsp. cornstarch

Juice of ½ lemon
1 tsp. vanilla or almond extract

Put the raisins and corn syrup in a saucepan and bring to the boil. Cover, turn off the heat and let the raisins puff up and steam until cool. If the syrup is too thin, blend the cornstarch with the lemon juice and stir into the raisins and cook until it thickens. When cool add the extract.

Hazelnut Filling

¼ cup sweet butter
⅓ cup light brown sugar
2 egg yolks

1 tsp. vanilla or almond extract
½ (or more) cup hazelnuts, ground

Cream the butter and sugar until smooth; blend in the other ingredients in order given.

Walnut Filling

½ cup white corn syrup
¾ cup walnuts, ground

Grated rind ½ lemon
¼ cup light brown sugar

Boil the syrup and pour it over the ground walnuts; stir in the juice and sugar.

Almond Filling

½ cup almonds, browned and
   ground
Grated rind of 1 lemon
3 egg yolks

3 egg whites, beaten
⅓ cup light brown sugar

Mix the ground almonds with the rind and egg yolks. Beat the egg whites until stiff, then add the brown sugar and beat until thick. Combine with the almonds.

Streussel For Coffeecake Tops

Two differing ones appear in coffeecake recipes. See pages 46 and 50.

Crème Fraîche

The French have a thick natural cream they serve over fruit and pastries. It is wonderful with raspberries or strawberries when served with pancakes or crêpes. It is matured and has a slight tang. This is a good imitation:

3 ounces cream cheese
⅓ to ½ cup sour cream

1 cup heavy cream

Soften the cheese at room temperature; whisk in the sour cream until it is very smooth, then slowly whisk in the heavy cream. Serve it the traditional French way out of a 6-inch-tall earthen jar with a wooden paddle.

A MISCELLANY OF
GOOD THINGS

Pain Perdu

This "lost bread" makes a fine dish for a festive breakfast or when you are caught without a dessert.

3 eggs, beaten
⅓ cup milk
⅓ cup sour cream
1 tsp. cinnamon, cardamom or anise
2 or 3 Tbsps. honey

¼ cup brandy, Madeira, or rum
8 ½-inch-thick slices of fine white bread
Sweet butter for frying
Powdered sugar, honey or syrup

Beat the eggs until light then add the milk, sour cream, spice, honey, and liquor. Dip the bread on both sides just so it is saturated, but not long enough to break the bread. Have plenty of good butter heating on a griddle and fry the bread on both sides until golden. A little of the dipping mixture may be spooned over the bread before it is turned. Sprinkle with powdered sugar and serve hot with or without syrup. Orange Syrup (see syrups page 136) would be good. Serves 4 or 8, depending on size of bread and when served.

Milk Toast

When we were young and indisposed, we were given toast with boiling milk and a piece of butter in it. We thought it was pretty good but I think this is an improvement. For each serving:

1 or 2 slices buttered toast
1 tsp. flour
1 cup milk

1 tsp. grated cheese
Salt and freshly ground pepper
Poached egg or more grated cheese (optional)

141

Everything must be ready at once. Put the hot buttered crisp toast in a wide soup plate. Blend the flour in a little of the cold milk, then add the rest of the milk and let it come to a boil. Add the cheese, salt and pepper and let it cook gently a minute. Pour it over the toast and top either with a poached egg or a sprinkle of cheese.

Mozzarella Toast

¾-inch-thick slices French or
    Italian Bread
Crushed garlic

Olive oil
Mozzarella cheese, sliced

Day-old bread is used, or sliced crusty rolls. For 6 or 8 slices, crush 4 cloves of garlic in a skillet and add plenty of olive oil. When the garlic colors a little fry the bread on both sides. Add a slice of cheese to the top of each, put the skillet in a 375° F. oven until the cheese melts. This is good with soup and all Italian dishes. Bel Paese, good melting cheese, may be used instead of Mozzarella.

Toasted Cheese Rolls

Firm white bread
⅔ cup grated sharp cheese

¼ cup soft butter
Sour cream

Remove the crusts from (unsliced) firm bread and wrap the bread in a damp towel for 2 hours. Before slicing, spread bread with a layer of paste made of the cheese, butter and sour cream. Slice bread and roll each slice, laying rolls cut side down on wax paper or a damp cloth, in a shallow pan. Cover with paper or a damp cloth and let them stand an hour. If put close together they will stay intact. When ready to serve them, remove from the pan and toast them in a 425° F. oven, not under the flame.

Cheddar Cheese Wafers

⅓ cup soft sharp cheese   ½ cup sifted flour
¼ cup sweet butter   ¼ tsp. mustard

Cream the cheese and butter together and cut in the flour sifted with the mustard as you would for piecrust. Form into a long roll 1½ to 2 inches thick and wrap in wax paper and chill. Just before serving, cut in thin slices and bake about 15 minutes at 375° F. to a golden brown. Serve with salad or cocktails.

Cheese Nut Wafers

3½ ounces cream cheese   1 cup sifted flour
½ cup sweet butter   ¼ cup finely chopped nuts,
½ tsp. salt   almonds, black walnuts or
                                pecans

Cream the cheese and butter until fluffy and smooth. Sift the salt and flour together and cut in the cheese-butter mixture with a wire pastry cutter and blend in the nuts. Chill. Roll into very small balls and put them on an ungreased cookie sheet. Flatten a little and bake 15 minutes at 375° F.

Ingrid's Swedish Flat Bread for Smörgåstårta

Recipe for Baking Powder Biscuits
Make a rich biscuit dough using 2 tsps. of baking powder instead of 3. Divide the dough in 2 parts, rolling each very thin into a 9-inch circle. Put them on a greased, floured cookie sheet for 10 minutes. Punch 12 times over each surface with a sharp-pointed knife. Put them into a preheated 400° F. oven and bake them 10 or 12 minutes until they are ivory colored—they must not brown. If baking too fast, turn the heat to 300° F. Garnish when they are perfectly cool with this filling:

2 pounds tiny shrimp or
   medium shrimp, finely sliced
2 cups homemade oil
   mayonnaise
½ cup or more sour cream
3 Tbsps. fresh chopped dill

GARNISH
Small rolls of smoked salmon
Red or black caviar
Capers
Fluted edge of mayonnaise

This also may be made with fresh cooked flaked crab or lobster meat. Mix 1½ cups of mayonnaise with the sour cream and dill. Mix it with the seafood and spread half of it over one of the flat breads. Put the other on top and cover it with the rest of the seafood mixture. If this is to serve 8 or 9, make 8 or 9 little salmon rolls and place them around the pie an inch from the edge, so that each serving will have a roll. Put a spoon of the caviar in front of each salmon roll and sprinkle 1 or 2 Tbsps. capers over the surface. Make a fluted edge by squirting the rest of the mayonnaise from a pastry tube. This is an elegant first course or a cocktail party dish. Increase the mayonnaise for the edge with additional sour cream if needed.

Pissaladière Provençal

PIZZA DOUGH
1 envelope yeast
½ cup lukewarm water
1 Tbsp. light brown sugar
¾ tsp. salt
2 cups sifted flour
1 egg, beaten
2 Tbsps. olive oil

FILLING
3 cups sliced onions
4 Tbsps. olive oil
1 clove garlic, crushed
1 tsp. thyme
Salt and pepper
8 anchovy fillets
8 strips red pimento
16 black Italian olives
8 cherry tomatoes, halved
3 tablespoons olive oil

For the dough, dissolve the yeast in the lukewarm water and sugar until frothy. Sift the salt and flour together and combine it with the yeast, beaten egg and olive oil. Beat 3 or 4 minutes until the dough is elastic. Set in a warm place covered with a towel to rise double. Beat it down and roll it out ⅛ inch thick and fit it onto an oiled 12-inch pie plate or pizza pan. For the filling, slice the onions very thin and sauté in the olive oil until golden but not burned. Mix them with the seasonings and let cool. Spread the onions over the dough. Arrange the fillets on the onions like the spokes of a wheel. In between decorate with the pimento strips, pitted, halved olives, and halved tomatoes. Sprinkle with the olive oil. Bake about 30 minutes at 375° F. Serves 8 or 4, as the case may be. A good red wine and a green salad goes well with this.

Pizza Napoli

PIZZA DOUGH
Pissaladière Provençal, or
Any unsweetened roll or bread
  dough
2 or 3 Tbsps. olive oil

FILLING
2 Mozzarella cheeses
2 skinned ripe tomatoes, *or*
  8 cherry tomatoes
2 Tbsps. olive oil
1 can anchovy fillets
8 Italian olives, pitted
2 tsps. powdered fennel or ore-
  gano

Prepare the dough and roll it ⅛ inch thick; spread over a 12-inch pizza pan. Brush with olive oil. Slice the cheese very thin and arrange it over the dough. Bel Paese is also a good melting cheese for this. Slice the tomatoes over the cheese or arrange the halved cherry tomatoes over the dough. Sprinkle with an herb and olive oil. Lay the anchovies fan-shape over the top and the pitted olives, halved, between them. Pimento strips may be added if you like. Bake at 375° F. about 30 minutes. Serve hot with red wine and a salad. Serves 4 to 8.

Onion Tart

BISCUIT DOUGH
1¼ cups sifted flour
2 tsps. baking powder
½ tsp. salt
6 Tbsps. vegetable shortening
Milk

FILLING
2½ to 3 cups sliced onions
3 Tbsps. butter
Salt and pepper
¼ tsp. nutmeg
2 eggs, beaten
⅞ cup sour cream
⅓ cup shredded Swiss or Gruyère cheese

Sift the flour with the dry ingredients and cut in the shortening with a wire pastry cutter. Add just enough milk so the dough may be lightly handled and rolled out ½ inch thick. Line a 9-inch pie plate, Pyrex or one that can be brought to the table; bake it 8 minutes at 375° F. Have the hot filling ready. Sauté the thinly sliced onions in the butter until yellow and tender, but not the least burned. Sprinkle with salt and pepper. Add the nutmeg to the well-beaten eggs and mix in the sour cream. Spread the onions over the partially baked crust, cover with the cream mixture and sprinkle the cheese over the top. Bake at 350° F. or 325° F. for about 20 minutes until the filling is set and lightly browned. Serves 6 or 8. Fine with almost any meat course, instead of potatoes.

Bread Cheese Pudding

8 slices homemade bread
  (white)
⅞ cup melted butter
½ pound sharp Cheddar cheese,
  shredded

4 extra large eggs
2 cups milk
Dash of salt
Freshly ground pepper
¼ tsp. nutmeg

This is too good to leave out of a bread book. Any bread except homemade or bread just as good will *not* do for this. If the crusts are hard, remove them. Dice the bread very fine. Grease a good-size baking dish and after each two slices of crumbled bread are put in, sprinkle with ¼ of the butter and ¼ of the cheese to distribute them evenly. Beat the eggs until very light, add the milk, salt, pepper and nutmeg. Pour this over the bread. Add a little more milk if necessary, to make the liquid just visible. Let this stand at least 6 hours or all day. Cover and bake 30 minutes at 350° F. and 30 minutes more at 325° F., removing the cover the last 15 minutes to brown. The bread texture disappears. It is a fine luncheon dish with a mushroom sauce; or an accompaniment to chicken, pork or fish. Serves 8 or 10.

Bread Pudding

8 slices homemade-type bread or
  soft egg rolls
1 cup milk
1 cup light cream
4 large eggs, beaten
⅓ cup light brown sugar
3 Tbsps. sherry or dark rum

CARAMEL
1 cup white sugar
⅓ cup boiling water
CHOICE OF FRUIT
1¼ cups pitted fresh cherries *or*
¾ cup mixed glacé fruits *or*
1 cup sliced stewed dried apricots
3 tablespoons whiskey

This pudding is a real party dessert for which you may experiment with your own favorite fruit. The bread mixture must stand in the caramelized pan 3 hours before baking. Caramelize an 8-inch by 3-inch-deep aluminum baking pan. Cook a cup of sugar in an iron skillet until it is dark brown. Turn off the heat and add the boiling water. Cook it until it is a very heavy syrup then put it in the pan and tip it around until it thickens and stays on the sides, putting it over the flame again if necessary. When the caramel is cold and hard, fill it with the bread mixture. Only the best firm bread is suitable for this. Remove the crusts from 8 or 9 slices and cut them in the tiniest cubes, almost crumbs. Put one-fourth of it in the pan and dot with one-third of the fruit and continue until all is used. End with a layer of bread. Beat the milk, cream, beaten eggs, sugar and sherry or rum together and pour it over the bread. (Other flavorings may be used if you wish, i.e. 2 teaspoons each of rose, almond and vanilla extract.) The liquid should come almost to the top of the bread and if necessary, add 2 or 3 spoons of milk. An hour before serving time set the pudding dish in a pan with a little hot water and bake it an hour at 325°. When it is done loosen the sides with a knife and put a serving plate over it and turn it upside down. Put the whiskey in the pudding dish over a flame to melt it then scrape it over the top of the pudding. Serves 8 or 10.

Puff Pastry

Feuilletage

The chef-owner of one of the oldest and finest restaurants in Paris uses light cream instead of water in his puff pastry. Every amateur interested in fine cooking wishes to experiment. I have purposely cut the recipe in half because this quantity is much easier to manipulate, especially in the beginning. This quantity is enough for a vol-au-vent or 8 or 10 patty shells. One can easily increase the proportions to 3 cups of flour, 1½ cups of butter, and so on.

2 cups sifted bread flour	1 cup sweet butter
½ tsp. salt	GLAZE
½ cup ice water	1 egg yolk
1½ Tbsps. brandy	2 Tbsps. cream

Two sticks of sweet butter are about the right shape to use. Sift the flour with the salt and put it in a mixing bowl. Make a well in the center and pour in ⅓ cup of the water and the brandy, the latter acting as a kind of leavening agent. Mix the dough and knead it on a lightly floured board until it is smooth and elastic, adding a little more water if necessary. Knead it at least 6 or 8 minutes, then refrigerate it. Remove the butter from the refrigerator 10 or

15 minutes before using as it must not be too hard for the initial rolling. Roll the dough ¼ inch thick, into an oblong over twice as long as the butter and over twice as wide. Put the butter on one half of the dough and fold the other half of the dough over the butter. Tuck one side of the dough over the butter and the other side under the butter so that it is completely and evenly enclosed. Now roll it out in a square being careful not to let the butter break through. Fold twice like a handkerchief, roll again, fold, roll again, fold and chill for 15 minutes. This is repeated 6 or 7 times. The greater number of turns, the greater number of layers there will be, hence the higher and lighter the pastry. Now the chilled dough is ready to be prepared for the oven.

FOR TURNOVERS The dough is rolled in a ¼-inch-thick strip 4 or 5 inches wide and cut in squares. They are filled with cherry or apple filling or jam, etc. They are folded so two opposite points meet. Press them together and brush the top with glaze. Chill before baking.

FOR SMALL PATTY SHELLS Roll the dough ¼ inch thick and cut ½ with a cookie cutter and ½ with a doughnut cutter. Remove the tiny centers and lay the solid rounds on an ungreased cookie sheet and top each with a doughnut-cutter round. When baked and puffed they form the shells to hold the prepared food to be served in them. Top with the baked tiny round. Before baking, chill them and brush the top only with the glaze. The little rounds are baked less time on a separate sheet. They are prettier cut with a notched fancy cutter.

FOR VOL-AU-VENT The chilled dough is rolled ¼ inch thick and two rounds are cut the size of a tea plate. Put one on an ungreased baking sheet. The other round has a smaller plate put on it and cut around, leaving a 1½-inch margin or border to lay on top of the round on the cookie sheet. This when baked, forms the sides of the vol-au-vent to receive the food served in it. The smaller round that is left is trimmed with little cutouts from the trimmings of pastry. Little hearts, diamonds, and fluted rounds are arranged over the top. After it and the vol-au-vent are baked, it serves as a lid. Brush the top and the rim of the vol-au-vent with the glaze, being careful not to let any drip on the sides, lest it prevent its rising. Puff pastry is put in a preheated 400° F. oven and the heat immediately turned down to 350° F. This slower baking prevents the inside pastry from being soggy. The pastry bakes in about 38 to 42 minutes. The shells must be watched to see that they do not brown too quickly. They should be golden. They are usually filled with creamed seafood, chicken, turkey, sweetbreads, mushrooms or chicken livers. You will find puff pastry has many other uses too. FOR A PÂTÉ FORM Line the inside of the form with strips to fit, folding ½ inch over the top of the filling. An oblong strip of pastry is cut to fit with notched sides and laid over the top. this is decorated with little diamonds and hearts cut from pastry trimmings. With practice your puff paste productions will gain a professional look.

Flaky Pastry

2¼ cups sifted flour
1 tsp. salt
¼ cup butter

½ cup vegetable shortening
6 or 7 Tbsps. ice water

This quantity is for a 2-crust 9-inch pie. For an 8-inch pie use 2 cups of flour and ⅔ cup of shortening; the ratio is ⅓ cup shortening to 1 cup flour. It is helpful to have all the ingredients chilled before mixing, including the flour.

Sift the sifted flour with the salt and sift into a mixing bowl. Cut the butter and shortening into the flour with a wire pastry cutter until the mixture is like coarse meal. Add just enough ice water and mix into a ball, handling as little as possible. Wrap the ball in wax paper and chill a half hour. Divide the pastry in 2 parts, one part a little larger than the other. Roll out the smaller part very thin, a little larger than a 9-inch pie pan and line it, folding over the edges. Make a few dents with a knife around the surface, and fill it. Roll out the other half of the pastry somewhat larger than the plate, fold in half and lift it over half of the pie plate; then unfold it. Fold over the edge and flute it. Make two sprays of stems and slits for leaves, over the surface. Bake in a 400° F. preheated oven for 15 or 20 minutes, then reduce to 325° F. for the rest of the baking, depending on the directions and filling.

For a single prebaked crust, use 1 cup of flour and ⅓ cup of shortening. When the plate is prepared, make a dozen slits in the bottom surface to prevent blistering.

VARIATIONS

For extra flaky crust, roll the dough half the size it should be, spread with 2 Tbsps. of soft butter, fold twice like a handkerchief then roll out to the required size. This can be done to the top crust only, or to a 1-crust pie.

For another flaky crust, sour cream can be mixed with the dough (the flour and shortening) instead of ice water. About ⅓ cup of sour cream for every cup of flour.

Croutons and Croustades

CROUTONS are made of 2- or 3-day-old bread, cubes of any size you like. Very small ones are used for soup. They are fried in butter and sprinkled with powdered fennel, if you like, and are a fine addition to tomato soup. Inch-cube croutons, or *chapons,* are fried in olive oil and garlic and tossed in salad.

CROUSTADES are made of loaves or buns. They hold creamed fish or chicken. Brioches are also used for *croûtes* or *croustades.* For large ones, a long sandwich loaf is very convenient. The top crust is removed and the inside crumb is cut out, leaving sides and bottom intact to hold the food to be served in it. It is spread completely with very soft butter and dried out to a crisp light gold color in a 250° F. oven. The buns are hollowed out for individual servings the same way. Brioches make fine ones. These are used in the same way *vol-au-vent* shells of puff pastry are used.

II

Whole Grain Recipes

Yeast Breads

WHOLE GRAINS

Whole grain bread and a balanced diet of fresh foods are vastly important for growing children, and the surest preparation for health and well-being for the adult of any age. Pearl S. Buck wrote in her preface to my first whole grain book, "The fact is that natural grain foods, with all the flavors of the good earth in them, are the only proper nourishment for the gourmet—he who demands pleasure above all else in his meals. Rain and sun, the strong sweet properties of minerals and the hidden magic of growth are contained only within the whole grains. They flavor the dishes which they make with that divine touch which man can only weakly imitate. There is a natural affinity between natural foods and the human body. They share the earth as source, and the body so fed holds energies to be found in no other way. We call it health. I commend this book, therefore, first for the pleasure it will give you in its fine food, and second, for the health it will provide for bone and flesh, sinew and muscle. When the body is content and sound, the mind is clear and the soul serene."

Whole Wheat Bread

1 envelope yeast
¼ cup lukewarm water
2 or 3 Tbsps. brown sugar or honey
1 cup boiling water

3 Tbsps. sweet butter
1 Tbsp. salt
3½ cups unsifted whole wheat flour
½ tsp. mace (optional)

Put the yeast, lukewarm water and sweetening in a small bowl until it becomes frothy. Add the hot water to the butter and salt, and when it becomes lukewarm combine it with the yeast mixture. If the flour has been refrigerated, put it in a large mixing bowl, with the spice if used, and set in a dishpan of hot water to bring it to room temperature. Pour the water-yeast mixture into the flour and beat it very hard. As flours differ, a little more lukewarm water can be added to make a not-too-soft, resilient dough. Only experience gives one the "feel" of the way it should be—so the bread won't dip in the center when baked (too much liquid) or won't be too dense (too much flour). Beat the dough 2 or 3 minutes. A hard rubber spatula is very good for this. Set the bowl in a dishpan of quite hot water, cover with a tea towel, and in an hour the dough will rise almost double and be light. Even after this rising if the dough seems very hard to beat, 2 tablespoons of warm water may bring it to a light and spongy consistency. Beat it 3 minutes and put it in an oiled regulation 3 x 5¼ x 9¼-inch bread pan. Set it in a pan of warm water, cover with a towel and let the dough rise for 45 minutes. The second rising takes less time. The dough should be rounding over the pan. Put it in a cold oven. Set oven at 400° F. to complete the rising. Bake 15 minutes then turn the heat to 325° F. and bake 35 minutes more. Turn the bread out onto a breadboard and cover loosely to cool. The mace gives a nice fragrance, as does anise. Raisins may be added to the flour before it is mixed, if desired. Milk gives a blander flavor; water does not take anything away from the flavor of whole grain wheat.

Thanksgiving Cranberry Bread

Recipe for Whole Wheat Bread   ½ cup light brown sugar
1 cup cranberries   ⅓ cup molasses

Wash, dry and cut each cranberry in half. Mix them with the sugar and molasses and let them stand 30 or 40 minutes. Toss the cranberries and syrup into the flour. Cranberries prepared this way resemble sour cherries in color and tartness and make a very good addition to bread for the holidays.

Whole Wheat and Brown Rice Flour Bread

1 envelope yeast   1 Tbsp. salt
¼ cup lukewarm water   2½ cups whole wheat flour
¼ cup honey or brown sugar   1 cup brown rice flour
1½ cups boiling water   ⅓ cup raisins
3 Tbsps. butter   ¾ tsp. mace

This is a fine-grain bread and is better cut after 6 or 8 hours. Proceed as in the recipe for Whole Wheat Bread. It is baked about 50 minutes.

Whole Wheat, Rye, and Oat Flour Bread

1 envelope yeast   3 Tbsps. butter
¼ cup lukewarm water   1½ cups whole wheat flour
⅓ cup honey, molasses or   1 cup rye flour
   brown sugar   1 cup oat flour
1¼ cups boiling water
1 Tbsp. salt

Proceed as in the Whole Wheat Bread recipe. After the dough has risen the second time, put it in a cold oven. Set oven at 400° F. and bake for 20 minutes; turn heat to 325° F. and bake 35 to 40 minutes more.

Whole Wheat and Oat Flour Bread

1 envelope yeast
¼ cup lukewarm water
¼ cup honey or light brown sugar
1⅓ cups boiling water
1 Tbsp. salt

3 Tbsps. sweet butter
2 cups whole wheat flour
1½ cups oat flour
½ cup raisins (optional)

Proceed as in the Whole Wheat Bread recipe. Put in a cold oven. Set oven at 400° F. and bake for 20 minutes; turn heat to 325° F. and bake 35 minutes longer.

Corn and Rye Bread

1 envelope yeast
¼ cup lukewarm water
3 Tbsps. honey or brown sugar
1¼ cups boiling water
1 Tbsp. salt

3 Tbsps. butter
1½ cups rye flour
1½ cups whole wheat flour
½ cup corn meal

Proceed as in the recipe for Whole Wheat Bread. Bake 1 hour.

Buckwheat and Whole Wheat Bread

1 envelope yeast
1 Tbsp. light brown sugar
¼ cup lukewarm water
1 cup evaporated milk
¼ cup water

1 Tbsp. salt
3 Tbsps. brown sugar or molasses
3 Tbsps. butter
2 cups whole wheat flour
1½ cups buckwheat flour

Dissolve the yeast with 1 Tbsp. of sugar in lukewarm water until frothy. Scald the milk and water and add the salt, sweetening and butter. Mix the flours in a large mixing bowl. When the milk mixture is lukewarm mix it with the yeast and add to the flour. Beat very hard for 3 minutes with a rubber spatula. A little more warm water or flour may be needed to make a spongy, not-too-soft dough. Put the bowl in a dishpan of hot water, cover with a tea towel, and let the dough rise an hour or more until it is light. Beat again 2 or 3 minutes; put the dough in an oiled bread pan. Set it in warm water again to rise an hour. Put the pan in a cold oven. Set at 400° F. and bake 15 minutes; turn the heat to 350° F. and continue baking for about 35 minutes more. These breads when at all moist make excellent toast.

Kasha Bread

1 cup kasha (buckwheat groats)
2 cups water
½ tsp. salt
¼ cup butter
⅓ cup or more molasses
1 Tbsp. salt
½ tsp. clove

½ tsp. cinnamon
2 envelopes yeast
3 Tbsps. warm water
1 Tbsp. light brown sugar
1 cup buckwheat flour
2 cups whole wheat flour
⅔ to ¾ cup warm water

If you soak the kasha in 2 cups of water overnight they will take 10 minutes less time to cook. Put them in the top of the double boiler and add ½ tsp. salt, cover and cook over simmering water 20 minutes if soaked; 30 minutes if unsoaked. Take 1¼ cups of it for the bread and put it in a large mixing bowl. (The rest of the porridge makes a wonderful cereal for breakfast with cream and honey.) Add the butter, molasses, salt and spices to the hot kasha. Dissolve the yeast in the warm water and sugar until frothy, then add it to the mixing bowl. Add the flours and ⅔ cup of warm water and no more than is necessary to make a stiff dough. (The water in the cereal counts, so too much water will cause the bread to sink in the middle when baked.) Beat for 3 minutes. Put the bowl in a pan of quite warm water, cover with a towel and let the dough rise a full hour or until light. Beat it down well and put it in an oiled loaf pan and let it rise 50 minutes to an hour. Put it in a cold oven set at 400° F. and bake it 15 minutes. Turn the heat to 350° F. and bake 55 minutes more. Turn the heat off and if the bread is not too brown let it stand in the oven another 10 minutes. Cereal breads take longer to bake. This is a wonderful, nutty bread.

Sunflower and Whole Wheat Bread

A half cup or more of sunflower meal may be added to many breads, replacing the same quantity of other flours. It gives a nutty flavor and texture to the bread.

1 envelope yeast	1¼ cups boiling water
⅓ cup lukewarm water	1¾ cups whole wheat flour
3 Tbsps. honey or brown sugar	1¾ cups sunflower meal
2 tsps. salt	⅓ cup raisins
2 Tbsps. butter	

Dissolve the yeast in the lukewarm water with honey or sugar until frothy. Add the salt and butter to the boiling water and cool to lukewarm; combine with the yeast and the mixed flour, meal and raisins. Follow directions for making any of the breads. After it has risen twice bake it about 45 to 50 minutes, half the time at 375° F. and half the time at 350° F. or 325° F.

Sesame Meal Bread

1 envelope yeast	1 Tbsp. salt
¼ cup lukewarm water	2 cups whole wheat flour
¼ cup honey	1 cup oat flour
¼ cup butter	1 cup sesame meal
1 cup hot water	

Melt the yeast with the lukewarm water and honey until it is foamy. Put the butter in the hot water and when it is melted and lukewarm, mix it with the yeast mixture. Mix the salt and flours in a large mixing bowl with the sesame meal. Instead of oat flour you may use 3 cups of whole wheat flour. Stir in the liquid and mix for 3 minutes adding 1 or 2 spoons of warm water if necessary. The dough should be rather heavy as the meal lends some moisture when baked. Set the bowl in a pan of quite warm water and cover with a tea towel. When it is risen, about an hour, beat it down well and put it in an oiled loaf pan and let it rise until it is over the pan. Bake it at 375° about 50 minutes. This is a very fine, sesame-flavored loaf.

Whole Wheat, Bran and Oat Flour Bread

1 envelope yeast	3 Tbsps. butter
¼ cup lukewarm water	½ cup raisins (optional)
⅓ cup brown sugar or molasses	1½ cups whole wheat flour
1½ cups boiling water	1½ cups oat flour
1 Tbsp. salt	1 cup bran flour

Bran flour is flaky and not like the crumbled cereal. Dissolve the yeast in the water with sugar or molasses until frothy. Boil the water; add the salt and butter and when it is lukewarm mix it with the yeast. Toss the raisins, if used, with the flours in a large mixing bowl and stir in the water-yeast mixture. Beat very hard for 3 minutes, adding a little more warm water if necessary to make a spongy dough. Set the bowl in a dishpan of hot water, cover with a tea towel, and let the dough rise an hour or more until light. Beat it down for 3 minutes, then put it in an oiled bread pan to rise again in warm water. When risen over the top of the pan put it in a cold oven. Set oven at 400° F. and bake 20 minutes; turn the heat to 325° F. and bake 35 minutes more. If when removed from the pan the bread doesn't sound hollow when thumped on the bottom, it can stand 5 or 10 more minutes baking.

Soya and Whole Wheat Bread

1 envelope yeast
¼ cup lukewarm water
1 Tbsp. brown sugar
⅓ cup molasses
1½ cups boiling water
3 Tbsps. butter

1 Tbsp. salt
⅓ cup raisins
1 tsp. cinnamon
2¾ cups whole wheat flour
¾ cup soya flour

What soya lacks in flavor it makes up in food value; so we add plenty of seasonings. Other flours can be used with soya. Use ¼ to ⅓ soya to the amount of other flours used in a recipe. Dissolve the yeast with the brown sugar in lukewarm water. Mix the molasses, boiling water, butter and salt and, when it is lukewarm, combine with the yeast. Mix the raisins and cinnamon with the 2 flours and add the liquid. Stir very hard and if necessary add a little more water to make an elastic dough. Proceed as in the recipe for Whole Wheat Bread. This bread bakes for about 50 minutes. This bread is a little more moist than some breads. It makes excellent toast.

Raisin Whole Wheat Bread with Milk

1 envelope yeast
¼ cup lukewarm water
⅓ cup molasses or honey
2 Tbsps. butter
1 Tbsp. salt

1½ cups scalded milk
3½ cups unsifted whole wheat flour
½ cup seedless raisins
⅛ tsp. powdered clove or cinnamon

Dissolve the yeast with the lukewarm water and sweetening. Put the butter and salt in the hot milk. When it is lukewarm mix it with the yeast. Put the flour in a large mixing bowl and mix the raisins and spice in it. Milk makes a blander bread than water so perhaps you will like the addition of spice. Add more if you like. Mix the yeast-milk mixture with the flour and beat very hard for 2 or 3 minutes. If necessary add a spoon or more of warm milk. Set the bowl in a dishpan of hot water, cover it and let the dough rise an hour or more. When it is double in bulk, beat it down again 2 or 3 minutes, then put the dough in an oiled bread pan and set again in warm water to rise. Put the bread in a cold oven. Set the temperature at 400° F. for 15 minutes; turn the heat to 325° F. and bake 35 minutes more. Turn the bread out onto a board to cool, loosely covered with a tea towel.

Whole Wheat Buttermilk Raisin Bread

1 envelope yeast
¼ cup lukewarm water
¼ cup honey, brown sugar or molasses
1½ cups buttermilk
3 Tbsps. butter

2 tsps. salt
3½ cups unsifted whole wheat flour
½ tsp. soda
½ cup raisins

Dissolve the yeast in the water and sweetening in a small bowl, until it is frothy. Heat the buttermilk just enough to melt the butter in it. When it is lukewarm add it to the yeast mixture. Mix the dry ingredients together and toss the raisins through them. Combine the two mixtures and beat very hard with a hard rubber spatula. If necessary add a little more buttermilk. When the dough is spongy, set the bowl in a dishpan of quite warm water, cover with a tea towel and let the dough rise to double in bulk. This takes an hour, perhaps a little more. Beat it down for 3 minutes and then put it in a greased bread pan. Set the pan in warm water, cover and let the dough rise until it is rounding over the pan. Put the pan in a cold oven. Set at 400° F. and bake 15 minutes; turn the heat to 325° F. and bake 30 or 35 minutes more. Turn out onto a board to cool, loosely covered with a towel.

Whole Wheat Cinnamon Bread

1 envelope yeast
¼ cup lukewarm water
1 Tbsp. light brown sugar
⅓ cup sweet butter
½ cup light brown sugar
3 eggs, beaten

1 cup milk, scalded
2 tsps. salt
3½ to 4 cups whole wheat flour
FILLING
4 or 5 Tbsps. soft butter
½ cup light brown sugar
2 Tbsps. cinnamon
⅓ cup currants
2 Tbsps. rum or Madeira

Dissolve the yeast in the lukewarm water with 1 Tbsp. sugar in a small bowl. Cream the butter and sugar until fluffy and smooth; add the beaten eggs which have been brought to room temperature. Scald the milk and let it become lukewarm. Add the salt. Combine the yeast with the butter-egg mixture and the milk. Put 3½ cups of flour in a large mixing bowl and stir in the liquid. If necessary add more flour to make a soft but firm dough. This can be a little softer than that for other bread. Beat it very hard and set the bowl in a dishpan of hot water, cover with a towel and let the dough rise an hour or more until light. Meanwhile prepare the filling. Soften the butter. Combine the sugar and cinnamon, and add the currants after they have soaked in the liquor an hour. When the dough has risen, beat it 3 minutes with a hard rubber spatula and then roll it out to a scant ½ inch thick on a floured board. Spread with soft butter and sprinkle with the sugar mixture. Roll up the long way and put it in an oiled bread pan. If it is too large cut off 3 or 4 slices for rolls. Put them on an oiled pan, cut side down. Put the pan of bread and rolls in a pan of warm water to rise double. Put them in a cold oven. Set oven at 400° F. and bake for 20 minutes (until the rolls are almost done); reduce the heat to 325° F. and bake the bread 30 minutes more. The rolls may take 5 or 10 minutes more after the heat is turned down.

Whole Wheat Potato Bread

1 envelope yeast	⅓ cup butter
¼ cup lukewarm water	⅓ cup light brown sugar
1 Tbsp. light brown sugar	⅓ cup skim milk powder
1 large potato (11 oz.)	1 egg, beaten
1 cup water	3½ to 4 cups whole wheat flour
1 Tbsp. salt	1½ teaspoon cardamom

Dissolve the yeast in the lukewarm water with sugar. Shred the peeled potato into a saucepan with the water and salt, cover and cook until it is tender, about 8 or 10 minutes. Put it all through a sieve and add the butter, sugar and milk powder. Stir until mixture is smooth. Add the beaten egg. Combine the potato mixture when it is lukewarm with the yeast. Mix the cardamom with 3½ cups of the flour and add the yeast mixture. Beat very hard and if necessary add more flour to make a light, soft dough that is not too dense. Beat 2 or 3 minutes, then set the bowl in a dishpan of hot water, cover with a towel and let the dough rise an hour or until it is double in bulk. Beat down for 4 minutes then put it in an oiled bread pan. If the dough expands a great deal put some of the dough in a small pan. The potato makes the yeast very active. When it has risen put it in a cold oven. Set the heat at 400° F. and bake bread 20 minutes; turn the heat to 325° F. and bake 30 minutes more. Turn out on a board to cool. The small loaf will take 10 minutes less time to bake.

Whole Wheat, Rye and Fig, Raisin or Date Bread

2 cups whole wheat flour
1 cup rye flour
½ cup oat flour
1½ Tbsps. anise seeds
1 tsp. anise powder
¾ cup sliced fruit (figs, raisins, or dates)

1 envelope yeast
⅓ cup lukewarm water
3 Tbsps. brown sugar or honey
1 cup hot water
4 Tbsps. butter
1 Tbsp. salt

This is a wonderful mixture of grains. If the flours are refrigerated, warm them in a mixing bowl set in hot water. Mix all the flours and dry ingredients and toss the fruit through them. If figs are used, use soft ones. Dissolve the yeast in the lukewarm water with sugar or honey. Combine the hot water with the butter and salt. When it is lukewarm and the butter is melted, add the yeast and stir the mixture into the flours. Add enough warm water to make the dough spongy and beat it 3 or 4 minutes. Set the bowl in a pan of hot water, cover with a towel and in an hour or more the dough will be light. Punch it down well and if too stiff, add a spoon or two of warm water. Beat it 2 or 3 minutes, then put it in an oiled bread pan, set in warm water to rise until light and rounding over the pan. Place in a cold oven. Set oven at 400° F. and bake for 15 minutes, then turn the heat to 325° F. and bake 35 minutes more.

Whole Wheat Rolls

1 envelope yeast
¼ cup lukewarm water
1 Tbsp. light brown sugar
1 cup milk, scalded
2 tsps. salt
⅓ cup sweet butter

⅓ cup light brown sugar
Grated rind 1 California orange
3¼ cups whole wheat flour, about
⅓ cup raisins
2 eggs, beaten
Melted butter

Dissolve the yeast with the lukewarm water and 1 Tbsp. of sugar. Scald the milk; add the salt and cool to lukewarm. Cream the butter and sugar until smooth and stir in the orange rind. Toss the raisins with the flour in a large mixing bowl. Combine the yeast, lukewarm milk and creamed butter and sugar. Empty it into the flour and mix well; add the well-beaten eggs. Beat 3 or 4 minutes; set the bowl in a dishpan of quite warm water and cover with a tea towel. When dough has risen double its bulk, beat it down for 2 minutes. Rolls can be dropped from a spoon into oiled muffin tins, half filling them. Or ½ the dough at a time can be rolled ¼ inch thick on a floured board and cut in ovals, brushed with melted butter, folded like a pocketbook and put in an oiled shallow pan; or small rounds can be cut, brushed with butter and another round placed on top. In any case they are set in a warm place to rise double, then baked. Put the pans in a cold oven. Set heat at 400° F. and bake about 25 minutes. If they bake too fast, turn the heat down to 325° F. after 15 minutes. Makes over 2 dozen rolls. This can also be baked in 1 loaf.

Whole Wheat Sally Lunn

1 envelope yeast	4 egg yolks
1 Tbsp. light brown sugar	½ cup light brown sugar
¼ cup lukewarm water	3 cups whole wheat flour
2 cups milk, scalded	1 tsp. cardamom
½ cup sweet butter	4 egg whites, beaten
1 tsp. salt	¼ tsp. cream of tartar

Dissolve the yeast with the tablespoon of sugar in the lukewarm water until it is frothy. Scald the milk, add the butter and salt and cool to lukewarm. Beat the egg yolks and sugar together until thick and creamy. Mix the flour with the cardamom in a large mixing bowl. Combine the yeast, milk and egg and sugar mixtures and beat it into the flour. Beat hard 3 minutes. Beat the egg whites until stiff with the cream of tartar. Stir ¼ of the whites into the flour batter, then fold in the rest. Put the batter into a well-oiled 9-inch tube pan and set it in a dishpan of warm water to rise. When it comes to the top of the pan, gently lift pan into a cold oven. Set oven at 400° F. and bake 20 minutes; turn the heat to 325° F. and bake 20 to 25 minutes longer. Three or four minutes after bread comes from the oven, carefully loosen the sides and around the tube with a sharp-pointed knife, turn it over and let it fall onto a cake plate. While it is still warm it can be sprinkled with a mixture of powdered sugar and cardamom or anise.

Boule de Poilâne

Paris

There is a *boulangerie* at number 8, rue du Cherche-Midi with windows filled with pastries and breads. The pastry is not an uncommon sight but the bread is. Huge dark round loaves, decorated with grapes made of dough, and long breads shaped like twisted staffs. "Maître Boulanger" has an inner office decorated with forty oil paintings (I counted them), gifts of left-bank artists, grateful for his bread. There are also ceramic casseroles (not for sale), exact replicas of the *boules*. The building is on the site of the Présmontrés, a twelfth century monastery. A very steep stair leads to an ancient cellar where the bread rises and bakes. The temperature of this *cave* where the dough is mixed is uncomfortably high. The dough does its final rising in round baskets, then it is emptied onto a long shovel and slid into a very hot oven and baked an hour. The flour is stone-ground, containing all the nutrients with only the cellulose removed. The bread is made exactly the way it was in the Middle Ages. The bread is called for by wives of cabinet ministers, people of the stage and screen, ladies brought in chauffeured cars, housewives and finally M. Edgar Pisani, former minister of Agriculture—all seeking good bread for its taste and health. Père Pierre Poilâne and *fils*

Lionel and Max run this busy establishment with the aid of several bakers. Head baker, Serge Verrier gave me the simple directions for making this bread:

Boule de Poilâne or Pain de Campagne

STARTER
1½ cups whole wheat flour
1 envelope yeast
1½ cups warm water

3 cups whole wheat flour
1 Tbsp. salt
Warm water

Mix the starter in a large bowl 12 hours (at least 8 hours) before mixing the dough for the bread. This is just enough starter for 1 loaf. Set the starter in a warm place covered with a tea towel. When ready to make the bread, add the flour and salt and just enough warm water to make a very stiff dough. Mix it thoroughly and remove 1 cup of starter for the next loaf. Keep it refrigerated and well covered. Knead the dough until smooth and elastic. Set it in a pan of warm water covered with a tea towel and let the dough rise 2 hours. Punch it down a minute or 2, then put it in a smaller greased bowl to rise. If you think it will flatten too much when baked, work in another ½ cup of flour. When dough is risen, gently empty it into a baking pan. Preheat the oven to 450° and bake the bread 20 minutes, then turn the heat to 300° and bake it 40 minutes more. For crisp crust, sprinkle the dough with water when it goes into the oven or set a pan of hot water on the oven floor. Remove water when the heat is lowered. Danish Sour Bread starter can be used in this bread if desired.

Pumpernickel #1

This is a dark, fine-flavored bread the texture and shape of pumpernickel. If you desire a lighter loaf, use 2 envelopes of yeast and add another ½ cup of whole wheat flour and a little more warm water. It is good with baked beans, pork, duck, etc.

1 envelope yeast	1 Tbsp. salt
¼ cup lukewarm water	1 cup buckwheat flour
¼ cup molasses	1 cup crumbled 100% bran
3 Tbsps. butter	1 cup rye flour
1 cup hot water	1 cup whole wheat flour

Put the yeast, lukewarm water and molasses in a small bowl, and let it become frothy. Melt the butter in the cup of hot water and stir in the salt. Mix the flours and bran in a large mixing bowl. Combine the yeast with the water-butter mixture when it is lukewarm, stir it into the combined flours. Beat very hard and add more warm water to make a resilient dough. Beat for 5 minutes. Put the bowl into a dishpan of hot water, cover with a tea towel to rise. It doesn't rise nearly as high as lighter flours. Beat down again and put the dough in an oiled bread pan to rise again in warm water. When it is light bake it 25 minutes at 375° F. and another 25 minutes at 325° F.

VARIATIONS

The only difference in the following pumpernickel breads is the variation of the mixtures of flours. Buttermilk and ¼ teaspoon of soda may replace the hot water. It is warmed with the butter.

PUMPERNICKEL #2

1 cup rye flour	1¾ cups whole wheat flour
1 cup buckwheat flour	

PUMPERNICKEL #3

½ cup coarse corn meal	1 cup rye flour
½ cup oat flour	1¾ cups whole wheat flour

Mr. Uggi Van Hauen, grandson of Reinhard Van Hauen, founder of the "best bakery in Copenhagen," brought to my hotel a bag of a dozen loaves of different breads—the prettiest and most interesting sight for my purposes, I've ever seen. It is said the Swedes come across the water to Copenhagen to buy their bread. The bakery uses only the best ingredients and no chemical preservatives. Mr. Van Hauen gave me several recipes for bread and the famous Danish pastry. I was very glad to receive the recipe for the pastry from the source. As the bakery uses starter and flour by the hundredweight, I had to resort to higher mathematics to reduce quantities and test until the proportions were correct. However, I can say that the results were as excellent as the bread I sampled. The directions for the starter appear at the end of the recipe for the bread.

Danish Sour Bread

2 cups whole wheat flour
½ cup rye flour
¼ cup brown rice flour
1 Tbsp. salt
1 Tbsp. powdered caraway

1 cup starter
¼ cup softened lard or butter
1 envelope yeast
1⅓ cups warm water
Caraway seeds

Mix the flours and dry ingredients in a large mixing bowl. In the center, make a well and add the starter, the lard (or butter) and yeast. (If the starter has been refrigerated, measure a cup of it and bring it to room temperature.) Stir in the warm water, a little at a time, and mix the dough thoroughly for 6 or 8 minutes. Set the bowl in a pan of warm water, cover with a tea towel and let the dough rise an hour. It will double in bulk. If you wish the usual loaf, punch it down well with a hard rubber spatula and put it in an oiled pan. If you wish to make a big round loaf, work in ½ cup of whole wheat flour, or it will flatten too much when it rises again. Roll the dough in caraway seed or sprinkle seed over the top. Let the dough rise in a warm place half an hour. Preheat the oven to 425° F. and bake the bread 15 minutes, then turn the heat to 300° F. and bake the bread 45 minutes more. For a good crust set a pan of hot water on the oven floor and remove it when the heat is turned down. This is a beautiful big round loaf which can be painted with cornstarch liquid when it comes hot from the oven. If you wish to make two loaves, double all the ingredients except the starter.

Starter

1st day:
½ cup warm water
1 cup cultured buttermilk
2 Tbsps. wine or malt vinegar
2 cups rye or whole wheat flour
1 envelope yeast
2nd day: the above starter
1 cup of rye or whole wheat flour
2 Tbsps. Blue Ribbon Malt Syrup
⅔ cup hot water

3rd day: the starter
1 cup rye or whole wheat flour
2 Tbsps. malt syrup
⅔ cup hot water
4th day: the starter
1 cup rye or whole wheat flour
2 Tbsps. malt syrup

Mix the first day's starter in a large bowl and cover it with cheesecloth so that the air may reach it. Set the bowl in a warm, draftless place. Each successive day stir in the warmed ingredients. I say hot water because the malt syrup and the flour are probably refrigerated. Mix the syrup with the hot water and flour and by then it will be lukewarm, the right temperature to mix with the other starter. The fourth day, it is ready to use but it improves with age. Use 1 cup of it for bread. Keep it in large glass screw-top jars in the refrigerator after the fourth day. Bring it to room temperature by setting a cup of it over warm water before making bread. Starter makes all kinds of delicious and interesting breads. It keeps for weeks and is at its best when it ferments.

South Jutland Rye Bread

Reinhard Van Hauen, Copenhagen

1 cup starter	4 tsps. salt
2 Tbsps. lard *or* bacon fat	2 cups rye flour
1¾ cups warm water	½ cup brown rice flour
1 envelope yeast	¾ cup whole wheat flour

Remove 1 cup of starter from the refrigerator and bring it to room temperature. It may be set in a bowl of quite warm water. Melt the lard or bacon fat in ½ cup of the water and add the yeast. Mix this with the warmed starter. Mix the salt with all the flours in a large mixing bowl; make a well in the middle and add the yeast-starter mixture. Stir in the rest of the warm water to make a stiff dough. Punch it 5 minutes with a hard rubber spatula so it is well mixed. Set the bowl in a pan of warm water, cover with a tea towel and let the dough rise 2 hours. Punch it down with the spatula and put it in an oiled bread pan and let it rise in a warm place 45 minutes. If you wish to bake the bread in a ball shape you will have to knead in ½ cup of flour, either rye or whole wheat, otherwise the dough will flatten too much when it rises the second time. Preheat the oven to 400° F. and bake the bread 15 minutes with a pan of hot water on the oven floor. Turn the heat to 300° F., remove the water, and bake the bread 45 minutes more. This combination of flours results in a fine-flavored bread.

Georg's Oldenburger Sauerbrot

An old friend in Munich sent me this fine bread and he makes it himself.

1 cup starter	2 cups rye flour
1 envelope of yeast	1 cup bran
3 Tbsps. lukewarm water	1 cup white flour
¼ cup molasses	4 tsps. salt
3 Tbsps. good fat	1⅔ cups warm buttermilk

Bring the starter (page 172) to room temperature. Melt the yeast in the lukewarm water with the molasses and add the fat, either softened butter or bacon fat. Mix the flours in a large mixing bowl. Use bran flakes from the mill, not breakfast food. Add the salt. Make a well in the center of the flours and add the buttermilk and yeast mixture. Mix well 2 or 3 minutes. Set the bowl in a pan of hot water covered with a tea towel. Let the dough rise an hour, then punch down well and again let it rise an hour. It will be much lighter the second time it rises. Oil a very little bread pan and a regular size pan and let the dough rise in them 45 minutes. Preheat the oven at 400° F. for ten minutes. Bake the bread at 400° F. for 10 minutes, then turn the heat to 350° F. and bake the larger loaf 50 minutes more and the small loaf 40 minutes more. The bread has a slightly sour flavor due to the buttermilk. It may be made with water, or half water and half buttermilk.

South Jutland Black Rye Bread

Reinhard Van Hauen, Copenhagen

3 cups rye flour	1¼ cups lukewarm water
½ cup brown rice flour	¼ cup lard or butter
1 Tbsp. salt	1 cup starter
¼ cup malt syrup	1 envelope yeast

Mix the flours and salt together in a large mixing bowl. Put the syrup, water and fat in a saucepan and heat it until the syrup and fat are melted. Cool to lukewarm. (If it is impossible to obtain malt syrup, use 3 or 4 Tbsps. of brown sugar instead, in both bread and starter.) The starter, if refrigerated, must be brought to room temperature. Combine the water mixture, yeast and starter. Make a well in the center of the flour and stir in the mixture. Mix thoroughly several minutes. It will be a stiff dough. If you desire to make the usual loaf, add 2 or 3 Tbsps. of warm water. If a large round loaf is desired, leave the dough stiff. Set the dough to rise for 2 hours in a bowl in a pan of hot water, covered with a tea towel. Then punch the dough down 2 or 3 minutes and let it rise again for about 40 minutes. Punch it down and make it into a ball; put it on a lightly oiled pan to rise about 30 minutes. Preheat the oven to 400° F. and bake the bread 30 minutes with a pan of hot water on the oven floor. Turn the oven to 300° F., remove the water and continue baking the bread 30 minutes more. Caraway powder or seeds can be added to the dough if desired. It is well to let the bread cool 6 hours before cutting. It is a fine bread for sandwiches, to eat with cheese, and for everyone who likes a dark, rugged bread.

Whole Wheat Meal Bread

Reinhard Van Hauen, Copenhagen

3 cups whole wheat flour
½ cup brown rice flour
½ cup fine wheatmeal groats
1½ Tbsps. salt

2 Tbsps. malt syrup
1¾ cups hot water
1 cup starter (rye or whole wheat)
1 envelope yeast

Mix the flours and groats with the salt in a large mixing bowl. Melt the syrup in the hot water. Bring the starter to room temperature and mix it with the yeast and then combine with the water-syrup. Make a well in the center of the flour and stir in the starter mixture; beat hard for 3 minutes. This is a stiff dough; if necessary add a spoon or 2 of warm water. Set the bowl in a pan of very warm water, cover with a tea towel and let the dough rise an hour, then punch it down again. Stiff whole grain dough like this should rise 2 hours but it facilitates rising if after the first hour it is punched down and set to rise again. Punch it down after the second hour and empty it in a large ball onto a pan sprinkled with corn meal. Let it rise ½ hour lightly covered with a towel. Preheat the oven to 400° F. and bake the bread 25 minutes, then turn the heat to 300° F. and bake it 30 to 35 minutes more. Let it cool thoroughly 4 or 5 hours before cutting it. This is a fine, rugged bread.

Johanna's Schwäbisches Schrotbrot

Swabian Bran Bread

1 cup starter
1 envelope yeast
¼ cup molasses
¼ cup bacon fat or butter
1¼ cups warm water or buttermilk
2 cups rye flour

1 cup whole wheat flour
1 cup flaky bran
1 Tbsp. salt
Corn meal
Caraway seeds or powder

Bring the starter (see Danish Sour Bread) to room temperature by putting it in a bowl set in warm water. When it is warm, mix in the yeast. Melt the molasses and fat in 1 cup of either warm water or buttermilk, heating it just until the fat is melted. Mix the flours with the salt in a mixing bowl. Combine the liquid mixture with the starter and add it to the flours. Mix very hard with a rubber spatula, adding no more liquid than is necessary to incorporate all the flour. It is too sticky to knead. Set the bowl in a pan of hot water, cover with a towel and, after 45 minutes, punch the dough down. Let it rise another hour then punch it down again and put it in an oiled 7-inch bowl (5-cup volume) to rise ½ hour until it is over the top. Preheat the oven to 425° F. Sprinkle a 12-inch tin pie plate with corn meal and gently turn the dough onto the corn meal so it won't fall; sprinkle the top with caraway seeds or powder and put it in the hot oven immediately. This round loaf won't be much over 2 inches thick and, if you prefer, it can be baked in an 11-inch-long sandwich pan. It is good in either shape. Bake it 15 minutes; turn the heat to 300° F. and continue baking 45 minutes more. This is a great lunch bread with hors d'oeuvres such as sausage, herring, cheese, etc.

Swedish Limpor

This is a wonderful bread with a fascinating flavor. The Swedes make it for Christmas and it is called *Vörtlimpor*.

1 envelope yeast
¼ cup lukewarm water
2 Tbsps. light brown sugar
1½ cups whole wheat flour
1 tsp. salt
1 Tbsp. aniseed

1 tsp. powdered fennel
Grated rind of 1 orange
⅓ cup molasses
1½ cups beer, ale or stout
1 Tbsp. butter
2 cups rye flour

Combine the yeast, lukewarm water and brown sugar and let stand until frothy. Put the whole wheat flour in a large mixing bowl and stir in the salt, aniseed, fennel and grated orange rind. Make a well in the center and add the molasses. Put the beer (or ale or stout) in a saucepan with the butter and heat it just so it melts the butter. Stir this into the molasses and flour and beat very hard. Set the bowl in a dishpan of quite warm water, cover with a tea towel and let the sponge rise until light, 45 minutes to an hour. After it has risen add the rye flour and beat until it is light, spongy and elastic. If necessary add 2 or 3 spoons of lukewarm water. Beat hard with a hard rubber spatula or wooden spoon 4 minutes, set again in hot water, covered, to rise until double in bulk. Beat down again and put the dough in an oiled bread pan, set in warm water to rise again. When it is rounding over the pan set the bread in a cold oven. Set the heat at 400° F. and bake 15 minutes, then turn the heat to 325° F. and bake about 25 minutes more.

Rye Meal Bread

1 cup rye meal
1⅓ cups boiling water
3 Tbsps. butter
⅓ cup molasses
2 envelopes yeast

⅓ cup lukewarm water
2 cups rye flour
1 Tbsp. salt
1½ to 2 Tbsps. caraway powder
¾ cup lukewarm water, more
   or less

Put the meal in a saucepan and pour the boiling water over it, cover and let it cook 10 minutes, over low heat. Add the butter, cover and let it steam until it is lukewarm. This softens it. (Rye meal is not the hard grain sometimes sold in health stores, but is a coarse cereal which needs an hour's cooking if served for that purpose.) Put some of the molasses with the meal and the rest over the yeast with the lukewarm water to dissolve. Put the rye flour in a big mixing bowl; add the salt and caraway powder and mix it through the flour. When the yeast has dissolved, mix it with the meal, then add it to the flour. Stir until you obtain a moist, rather heavy dough adding lukewarm water, a little at a time. Beat the dough hard with a stiff rubber spatula. The dough must not be too heavy, only practice will tell you. The dough hasn't the resilience and sponginess that whole wheat flour has. Set the bowl in quite warm water and let the dough rise an hour. If it is still too heavy to beat, add a spoon or 2 of lukewarm water. Beat well. Oil a bread pan, add the dough and let it rise again in warm water, covered with a towel. Put the dough in a cold oven. Set oven at 375° F. and bake it an hour. If the oven is too hot, turn the heat to 325° F. for the last 20 minutes. You'll have a fine rye loaf.

Rye Meal and Whole Wheat Bread

1 cup rye meal	2 tsps. anise powder
1½ cups water	1 Tbsp. salt
3 Tbsps. butter	2 envelopes yeast
⅓ cup molasses	1 cup whole wheat flour
1 Tbsp. aniseeds	1 cup rye flour

Soak the meal 4 or 5 hours or overnight in 1 cup of water. Add ½ cup of hot water, cover and cook over simmering water 40 minutes in a double boiler. Do not let it cool before making the bread because it thickens and water will have to be added. While it is hot add the butter, molasses, aniseeds, anise powder and the salt. When it is lukewarm add the *rapidmix* yeast. Stir in the flours and beat 2 or 3 minutes. Set the bowl in a pan of hot water, cover with a towel and let the dough rise an hour. When it is light, beat it down, then put the dough in an oiled bread pan to rise again 45 to 55 minutes. Put the bread in a cold oven. Set the heat at

400° F. and bake ½ hour, then turn the heat to 300° F. and bake another ½ hour. This is a rough bread with a fine flavor that men like. This bread is better if cut after 8 or 10 hours.

VARIATIONS

Replace ½ or more cup of rye flour with the same amount of:

Whole wheat flour	100% bran crumbles
Oat flour	Wheat germ
Brown rice flour	Buckwheat flour
Sunflower meal	Corn meal

Rye and Oat Bread

2 envelopes yeast	1 Tbsp. salt
¼ cup lukewarm water	1 egg, beaten
⅓ cup molasses	½ cup oat flour
1 cup boiling water	3 cups rye flour
2 Tbsps. butter	½ tsp. mace *or* 2 tsps. caraway powder

Melt the yeast in the lukewarm water with the molasses until frothy. Mix the boiling water with the butter and salt and when it has cooled to lukewarm, add it to the frothy yeast. Beat the egg until light and add to the yeast. Mix the flours and add the mace. Combine the liquid and flours and beat very hard. Proceed as in the recipe for Whole Wheat Bread (page 156). This bakes 55 minutes.

Rye and Oat-flour Bread and Rolls

2 envelopes yeast
⅓ cup lukewarm water
⅓ cup brown sugar *or* ¼ cup
  honey
1 cup scalded milk
⅓ cup butter
1 Tbsp. salt
3 eggs, beaten

⅓ cup raisins or currants
1 tsp. clove
2 cups rye flour
2 cups oat flour
Cinnamon
Soft butter
Brown sugar

Soak the yeast in the water with sugar or honey until it is frothy. Scald the milk and add the butter and salt. When the butter is melted and the milk is lukewarm, mix it with the frothy yeast. Beat the eggs until light. Toss the raisins or currants through the mixed flours and clove. Combine the eggs with the yeast-milk mixture, stir into the flour and beat very hard. If necessary add a spoon more of liquid or flour. The dough must be light and spongy. Beat 3 or 4 minutes. This dough hasn't the spring of that which contains whole wheat flour. Set the bowl of dough to rise in a dishpan of quite hot water, covered with a towel for about 1 to 1½ hours. When the dough is light, beat it down again about 4 minutes. Take ½ of it to make a small loaf and use the rest for rolls. Flour a board well for this dough is sticky. Roll out the dough for bread a scant ½ inch thick, the length of your bread pan, spread lightly with soft butter and sprinkle with a mixture of cinnamon and light brown sugar, roll up and lay it in the bread pan which has been well oiled. The rest of the dough is rolled out and cut in ovals, spread with a little butter, cinnamon and sugar and folded over in half like pocketbook rolls. Put them close together in an oiled pan. Set bread and rolls to rise in a warm place, loosely covered. When raised and light put them in a cold oven. Set the heat at 400° F. and bake 20 minutes; remove the rolls. Turn the heat to 325° F. and bake the bread 20 to 25 minutes more.

Rye, Oat and Rice-flour Bread

1 envelope yeast
⅓ cup lukewarm water
¼ cup brown sugar or honey
1¼ cups boiling water
1 Tbsp. salt
2 Tbsps. butter

1½ cups rye flour
1 cup oat flour
1 cup brown rice flour
1 tsp. clove, mace or caraway
⅓ cup raisins

Melt the yeast in the lukewarm water or honey. Pour the boiling water over the salt and butter and cool to lukewarm. Mix the flours with the spice and raisins. Mix the yeast and water mixture and combine with the flours. Beat hard for 2 or 3 minutes. Two or 3 spoons of warm water may be needed to make a pliable dough. Set in a pan of warm water, cover with a towel and let the dough rise until light. Beat down again and put the dough in an oiled bread pan to rise again. When it is rounding over the pan, put the bread in a cold oven. Set heat at 400° F. for 10 minutes, then reduce it to 350° F. for 40 or 45 minutes more. This is a fine bread.

Rye and Buckwheat Bread

1 envelope yeast
¼ cup lukewarm water
1 Tbsp. brown sugar
1¼ cups boiling water
2 Tbsps. butter
1 Tbsp. salt

⅓ cup molasses
½ cup buckwheat flour
1 cup whole wheat flour
2 cups rye flour
¼ tsp. clove

You can use 3 cups of rye flour and ½ cup of buckwheat and omit the whole wheat but the bread will not be quite so light. Proceed as for the recipe for Whole Wheat Bread (p. 156). This bakes 50 to 55 minutes.

Rye with Wheat Germ Bread

1 envelope yeast
¼ cup lukewarm water
3 Tbsps. brown sugar or molasses
1½ cups boiling water
3 Tbsps. butter

1 Tbsp. salt
2 cups wheat germ
2 cups rye flour
2 tsps. anise or caraway powder or seeds
½ cup raisins (optional)

Proceed as in the recipe for Whole Wheat Bread (p. 156). Toss the raisins, if used, through the flours and spice. This bread takes longer to rise as it hasn't whole wheat in it, that old stand-by with its leavening qualities. However, it is a good bread, somewhat like pumpernickel, and should be sliced thin but not until it has cooled ½ a day. This bread should bake 1 hour.

Corn, Whole Wheat and Rye Bread

1 envelope yeast
¼ cup lukewarm water
⅓ cup molasses
1½ cups boiling water
3 Tbsps. butter

1 Tbsp. salt
1½ cups corn meal
1 cup whole wheat flour
1 cup rye flour

Proceed as in the recipe for Whole Wheat Bread (p. 156).

A Mixed-Bag Bread

This bread happened in an effort to use up the diminishing contents of 4 or 5 bags of grains. It proved to be of fine flavor—nutty and delicious—and demonstrates how versatile the grains are and how inventive one can be.

1½ cups steel-cut oats
3 cups water
¼ cup butter
¾ tsp. cinnamon
¼ tsp. clove
2 envelopes yeast
¼ cup lukewarm water

⅓ cup brown sugar
1 Tbsp. salt
⅓ cup sunflower meal
1 cup oat flour
½ cup corn meal
2 cups whole wheat flour
¾ cup warm water, more or less

Soak the oats in water overnight. In the morning cook them in the double boiler until they are soft. They cook much faster when they have been soaked. Put 1½ cups of the porridge in a large mixing bowl and add the butter and the spices. When the porridge is lukewarm add the yeast which has been dissolved in the warm water. Mix the sugar and the salt, meals and flours together and work in the porridge mixture. Porridge bread dough must be very thick because the water in the porridge must be counted. Add no more warm water than is necessary to mix all the flour, else the bread will be too moist. Work the dough 2 or 3 minutes then set it to rise. After an hour punch it down and it will be lighter the second rising. This is done in a pan of hot water, pan and bowl covered with a tea towel. After the dough has risen the second time, put it in oiled bread pans, one regular size and one small one, and let it rise again until light. Bake the smaller one 50 minutes in a 375° F. oven and the large one 1 hour and 5 minutes.

Rye, Bran and Buttermilk Bread

1 envelope yeast
¼ cup lukewarm water
¼ cup brown sugar or molasses
1½ cups buttermilk
1 Tbsp. salt

3 Tbsps. butter
1¼ cups flaky bran flour
2 cups rye flour
1 cup whole wheat flour

Melt the yeast in the lukewarm water with sweetening. Warm the buttermilk with the salt and butter hot enough to melt the butter;

when lukewarm, mix with the yeast and combine with the flours. If bran is not available use 100% crumbled bran. Proceed as in the recipe for Whole Wheat Bread (p. 156). Bake a full hour.

Swedish Rye Bread

1 envelope yeast
1 Tbsp. brown sugar
¼ cup lukewarm water
1 cup scalded milk
2 Tbsps. butter
1 Tbsp. salt

¼ cup molasses
2½ cups rye flour
1 cup whole wheat flour
1 tsp. powdered anise
1 tsp. powdered fennel

Melt the yeast with the brown sugar in lukewarm water. Scald the milk and add the butter, salt and molasses. When the mixture is lukewarm add the yeast. Mix the flours with the anise and fennel and combine with the liquids. Proceed as in the recipe for Whole Wheat Bread (p. 156). Bake 55 minutes.

Bohemian Rye Bread

1 10- or 11-ounce potato
1 cup water
1 Tbsp. salt
1 envelope yeast
2 Tbsps. brown sugar
¼ cup lukewarm water

2 Tbsps. butter
2½ cups rye flour
1 Tbsp. caraway seeds *or* 2 tsps.
  caraway powder
1 cup whole wheat flour
Lukewarm water

Peel the potato and cut it in paper-thin slices. Cook it in 1 cup of water with the salt. When it is tender, mash it and the water through a sieve. Dissolve the yeast and sugar in the lukewarm water. Stir the butter into the hot potato and when mixture is lukewarm combine it with the yeast. Mix the flour with the caraway and stir in the yeast-potato mixture. Stir in lukewarm water to make a spongy dough and beat hard for 3 minutes. Set the bowl in a dishpan of hot water, cover with a tea towel and let the dough rise an hour. When light, beat it down again for 3 minutes, then put the dough in an oiled bread pan and set it in warm water again to rise. When the dough is rounding over the pan, put it in a cold oven. Set the heat at 400° F. and bake for 20 minutes, then turn the heat to 300° F. and bake 50 minutes or an hour.

Onion Rye Bread

Recipe for Bohemian Rye Bread   ¾ cup sour cream
2½ cups thinly sliced onions   2 eggs, beaten
2 Tbsps. butter   ¾ tsp. salt

Make the recipe for Bohemian Rye Bread (p. 184). Sauté the onions in the butter until yellow but not burned. Mix with the sour cream, beaten egg and salt. Take the dough after it has risen and roll ⅔ of it ½ inch thick. Put it in an oiled shallow pan and spread with the onion mixture. Let it rise 30 minutes in a warm place then bake about 30 minutes in a 375° F. oven. The rest of the dough may be made into rolls. Put it in oiled muffin tins, let it rise and bake about 20 to 25 minutes at 375° F. Serve onion bread hot.

Soya, Rye and Oat-flour Bread

1 envelope yeast   ¾ cup soya flour
⅓ cup lukewarm water   1¼ cups rye flour
4 Tbsps. light brown sugar *or*   1½ cups oat flour
   3 Tbsps. honey   1 tsp. cardamom powder
1½ cups boiling water   1 tsp. caraway powder
1 Tbsp. salt   ⅓ cup raisins
2 Tbsps. butter

Oat flour makes fine light bread when combined with the sticky flours such as soya, rye and buckwheat. Follow the directions for

Whole Wheat Bread (p. 156) or most of the other yeast breads. The seasonings may be changed to suit one's taste in this or in other breads. Bake about 55 minutes to an hour at 375° F.

Corn Bread and Rolls

1 envelope yeast	3 Tbsps. butter
1 Tbsp. light brown sugar	4 tsps. salt
¼ cup lukewarm water	⅓ cup light brown sugar
2 cups water	3 cups corn meal
½ cup milk	2 cups whole wheat flour

Dissolve the yeast and the brown sugar in lukewarm water until frothy. Scald the water and milk and pour it over the butter, salt, sugar and corn meal and mix until smooth. Combine yeast with corn meal mixture. Add the whole wheat flour. Beat hard for 3 or 4 minutes and if necessary add a spoon or 2 of lukewarm water. Set the bowl in hot water, cover with a towel and let the dough rise until light. Beat down and put dough in 6 oiled muffin tins and the rest in an oiled loaf pan. Let rise again. Bake at 375° F., the rolls about 20 minutes and the bread about 50 minutes.

Orange, Oat and Soya Bread and Rolls

1 envelope yeast	¾ cup orange juice
⅓ cup lukewarm water	Grated rind 2 oranges
¼ cup honey	¾ cup soya flour
½ cup boiling water	3¾ cups oat flour *or* 1¾ cups
2 Tbsps. butter	oat flour and 2 cups whole
2 tsps. salt	wheat flour

Dissolve the yeast in the lukewarm water and honey. Pour the boiling water over the butter and salt to melt the butter, then add the orange juice. Mix the rind through the flours. The all-oat flour called for makes a fine bread but part whole wheat makes a somewhat lighter bread. Mix the yeast with the liquid and combine with the flours. A spoon or 2 of lukewarm water may be necessary to make a light, spongy dough. Set the bowl of dough in a pan of hot water to rise. Cover with a tea towel. When light beat down again for 2 or 3 minutes. Put the dough in 6 oiled muffin tins, ⅔ full. The rest of the dough is put in an oiled bread pan. Let the dough rise in a warm place and when light bake at 375° F.; the rolls 18 to 20 minutes, the bread 50 minutes.

Cracked Oats and Oatmeal Bread

1 envelope yeast	2 Tbsps. butter
¼ cup lukewarm water	¾ tsp. mace
3 Tbsps. honey or brown sugar	⅓ cup raisins
1 cup cracked oats porridge*	1¼ cups whole wheat flour
1 cup boiling water	1½ cups oat flour
2 tsps. salt	

Dissolve the yeast in the lukewarm water with honey or sugar until frothy. See below for the porridge. Mix the boiling water, salt and butter and let it stand until it is lukewarm. Combine with the yeast, porridge and the mace and raisins mixed with the two flours. Beat 2 or 3 minutes, adding a spoon or 2 of water if necessary. Let dough rise in a pan of warm water, beat it down again and put in an oiled bread pan and let it rise again in a pan of water, covered with a towel. Put the pan in a cold oven. Set the heat at 375° F. and bake the bread for 20 minutes. Turn the heat down to 325° F. and bake 40 minutes more. This is a fine, slightly moist bread. These moist breads make wonderful toast.

* *Cracked or steel-cut oats porridge:* 1 cup oats, 2 cups boiling water and 1 tsp. salt. Put the ingredients in the top of the double boiler and let it come to the boil over the flame for 2 or 3 minutes, then cook over simmering water for 30 minutes, covered. Stir occasionally. There is nothing better for children or adults on a cold morning than this porridge with butter, cream and honey. Sometimes there is some leftover, which makes a fine bread.

Oatmeal Bread

2 cups rolled oats
½ cup molasses
1 Tbsp. salt
1 Tbsp. butter
2 cups boiling water

1 envelope yeast
¼ cup lukewarm water
1 cup oat flour
2⅓ cups whole wheat flour

Mix the first 5 ingredients and stir until well mixed. Dissolve the yeast in the lukewarm water until frothy. Stir the oat flour into the rolled oats mixture and when it is lukewarm add the yeast. Beat well and add the whole wheat flour. Beat 2 or 3 minutes, then set it to rise in a pan of warm water, covered with a towel. When the dough is light and double in bulk, beat it down and put it in two small greased bread pans; set in a warm place to rise again. When risen put the pans in a cold oven. Set the heat at 375° F. and bake 25 minutes, then turn the heat to 350° F. and bake 20 minutes more. This is a fine bread.

Italian Fruit Bread

½ cup sweet butter
¾ cup light brown sugar
2 envelopes yeast
⅓ cup lukewarm water
2 Tbsps. brown sugar or honey
1 cup milk
3 egg yolks
3½ cups graham or whole
wheat flour
1 tsp. salt

2 tsps. anise powder
¼ cup currants marinated in
3 Tbsps. rum or Marsala
1 cup sliced glacé fruits: cherries, angelica, pineapple, citron
3 egg whites, beaten
Honey
Anise or cinnamon
Powdered sugar

Cream the butter and sugar until smooth. Melt the yeast in the lukewarm water with sugar or honey. Scald the milk and let it cool to lukewarm, then combine with the yeast, creamed butter and sugar and egg yolks. Mix the liquid with 2 cups of the flour sifted with the salt and anise. Beat for 5 minutes. Mix the rest of the flour with the marinated currants and fruits and beat it into the sponge. Beat for 2 minutes, then fold in the stiffly beaten egg whites. Mix well and set the bowl in a dishpan of hot water, cover with a towel and let the dough rise until light, about 1½ hours. Beat the dough down a little and put it in a well-oiled 9-inch tube pan; let it rise again in warm water until it rises to the top of the pan. Bake at 375° F. for 30 minutes, then at 325° F. for 20 to 25 minutes. After it comes from the oven, let it stand for 3 minutes, then loosen the sides with a sharp-pointed knife, turn it upside down onto a cake plate. Dribble the top with honey and dredge with powdered sugar mixed with a little anise or cinnamon. These fruit breads are fine with sweet butter.

Russian Fruit Bread

1 tsp. saffron
3 Tbsps. dark rum
¼ cup currants
¼ cup white wine
2 envelopes yeast
¼ cup lukewarm water
4 Tbsps. honey
¾ cup milk, scalded
¾ cup sweet butter
½ cup light brown sugar
1½ tsps. salt
4 egg yolks

1 cup sliced candied fruit (cherries, citron, pineapple)
4 cups whole wheat flour
¼ cup browned sliced almonds
8 bitter almonds, ground
Grated rind of 1 lemon
2 egg whites, beaten
1 tsp. anise extract or powder
2 tsps. almond extract
Honey
Powdered sugar

Soak the saffron in the rum and the currants in the wine several hours. Dissolve the yeast in the lukewarm water and honey until frothy. Scald the milk and add the butter, sugar and salt. When lukewarm, add the yeast and whisk in the egg yolks. Toss the fruits through the flour. Some of the coarse husks may be sieved out of the flour if you like but it isn't really necessary. Add the nuts and grated rind. Combine with the yeast mixture and beat very hard for 5 minutes; then fold in the stiffly beaten egg whites mixed with the seasonings. Add the currants and saffron, un-drained. Set the bowl in a pan of hot water, cover with a tea towel and let the dough rise until light, about 1½ hours. Beat it down a little. Now oil a 9-inch tube pan and put the dough in it; let it rise until it comes to the top of the pan. Bake the cake at 375° F. for 20 minutes, then turn the heat to 350° F. and bake for about 30 minutes more. After the bread comes from the oven let it stand 3 or 4 minutes, then loosen the sides with a sharp-pointed knife, turn the loaf upside down over a cake plate and it will drop to the plate. Dribble the top with honey and dredge with powdered sugar, or cover with a simple sugar and water icing when it has cooled.

Sunflower Potato Bread

1½ cups finely diced potato
¾ cup water
3 Tbsps. butter
1 Tbsp. salt
1 envelope yeast

¼ cup lukewarm water
3 Tbsps. brown sugar
1 cup sunflower meal
2½ cups whole wheat flour

Put the potato and water in a heavy pot, cover and cook until the potato is tender, about 10 minutes. Put a sieve over a large mixing bowl and mash the potato and water through. Melt the butter in it with the salt. Dissolve the yeast and sugar in the lukewarm water until frothy. Add the sunflower meal and whole wheat flour to the potato and the yeast. Beat very hard for 4 minutes. Try not to add any more water or the bread will be very moist. The dough is quite thick. Put it to rise in a pan of warm water, covered with a towel, for 1 hour. Beat the dough down and put it in an oiled bread pan; set in a pan of warm water again, covered, and let it rise 1 hour. Put the pan in a cold oven. Set heat at 400° F. and bake the bread 15 minutes. Then turn the heat to 325° F. and bake 25 to 30 minutes more. As I have remarked before, there is something about sunflower that bakes fast. This is a very fine bread.

Quick Breads

Bran Bread

This is one of the finest and most delicious quick breads imaginable. If you can't get flaky bran flour in a health store or mill, use wheat germ. When I was young we used to go to the local flour mill and get it. They fed it to horses in those days. It was what was left when they refined the flour to make it white.

1½ cups bran flour *or* wheat germ
2½ cups whole wheat flour
1 tsp. salt
¼ cup brown sugar

½ cup raisins
1½ tsps. soda
1¾ cups buttermilk
½ cup molasses

Mix the dry ingredients together and toss the raisins through them. Mix the soda with a little of the buttermilk, then add the rest of the buttermilk and the molasses. Stir the liquids into the flours. Bake at 350° F. 1 hour in an oiled bread pan.

Apricot Bread

1 cup dried apricots
Grated rind of 1 orange
⅓ cup orange juice
½ cup light brown sugar
3 cups whole wheat flour
1½ tsps. salt

½ tsp. soda
3 tsps. baking powder
1½ cups buttermilk
1 egg, beaten
3 Tbsps. melted butter

Cut the apricots in small pieces and put them in a saucepan with the orange rind, juice and sugar. Cover and simmer gently 5 minutes, more steaming than cooking them. Mix the dry ingredients together. Mix the buttermilk, beaten egg and butter. Beat in the apricot mixture. Combine with the flour and bake in an oiled bread pan 50 to 55 minutes at 350° F.

Buckwheat Bread

2⅓ cups buckwheat flour
½ tsp. baking powder
1 tsp. salt
1½ tsps. soda

½ cup brown sugar
½ cup raisins or soaked,
chopped prunes
1¾ cups buttermilk

Mix the dry ingredients and toss the fruit through them. Stir in the buttermilk. Bake at 350° F. about 50 minutes. This is a fine-grained bread. Half whole wheat and half buckwheat flour could be used if desired.

Caraway Rye Bread

1 Tbsp. caraway seeds
2½ cups rye flour
½ cup corn meal
2 tsps. salt

2½ tsps. baking powder
¼ cup honey or ⅓ cup molasses
1⅔ cups buttermilk

Mix the seeds with the dry ingredients. Mix the honey or molasses with the buttermilk and add to the dry ingredients. Bake in an oiled bread pan about 55 minutes at 350° F.

Fruit Rye Bread

2½ cups rye flour
½ cup whole wheat flour
1 tsp. salt
4 tsps. baking powder
1 egg, beaten

⅓ cup brown sugar or molasses
1½ cups milk or buttermilk
¾ cup soaked, chopped prunes,
 sliced dates, sliced soft figs, or
 raisins

All rye flour may be used but it won't be quite so light a bread. Mix the dry ingredients together. Beat the egg until light, then add the sugar or molasses and beat until thick. Add the milk or buttermilk. More or less liquid depends on the flour used so add 1 cup of liquid to the egg mixture first and add what is needed at the end. Toss the fruit through the dry ingredients, then combine with the liquids. Bake in an oiled. bread pan 50 to 60 minutes at 350° F.

Prune, Date, or Raisin and Nut
Whole Wheat Bread

2 eggs, beaten
1 cup brown sugar
2 cups milk or buttermilk
½ tsp. salt
3¼ cups whole wheat flour

4 tsps. baking powder
½ cup coarsely chopped nuts
1 cup sliced dates, raisins, or
 soaked, chopped prunes

Beat the eggs until light, then add the sugar and beat until thick. Add the milk. Mix the dry ingredients and toss the nuts and fruit through them, then combine with the liquids. If necessary add a spoon or 2 of buttermilk (if used) to make a soft dough. Milk is more a thinning agent than buttermilk. Oil a large bread pan or two small ones and bake 50 minutes to an hour at 350° F. The small loaves may take 10 minutes less time to bake.

VARIATIONS One may change the flours; for instance, 1 cup of oat, rye, or corn can replace 1 cup of whole wheat flour. There are infinite variations. Honey and molasses can replace the brown sugar. If honey is used, cut the quantity in half. Some cinnamon, mace, allspice, nutmeg, anise, or clove can be added. Dried, soaked, sliced apricots or sliced soft figs can also be used for the fruit.

Banana Bread

1 cup light brown sugar
½ cup butter
2 egg yolks, beaten
2 Tbsps. buttermilk
1 tsp. soda
¼ tsp. salt

1½ cups mashed bananas
½ cup coarsely chopped almonds or pecans
½ tsp. cinnamon
1¾ cups whole wheat flour
2 egg whites, beaten

Cream the sugar and butter until smooth, then mix in the rest of the ingredients in order given. Dissolve the soda in the buttermilk. Fold in the stiffly beaten egg whites last. Bake at 350° F. one hour.

Whole Wheat Buttermilk Bread

2½ cups whole wheat flour
½ cup corn meal
½ cup raisins (optional)
1 tsp. salt

1½ tsps. soda
½ cup molasses
½ cup sour cream
1⅓ cups buttermilk

Mix the dry ingredients with the raisins, if used. Mix the molasses with the sour cream and buttermilk. Combine the 2 mixtures. Bake in an oiled bread pan 1 hour at 350° F.

Christmas Mincemeat Bread

1 cup mincemeat
2 or 3 Tbsps. dark rum
½ cup 100% bran crumbles
2 cups whole wheat flour
½ cup wheat germ

1 egg, beaten
¾ to 1 cup buttermilk
¼ cup light brown sugar
3 tsps. baking powder

If you are using homemade mincemeat, then just add the rum. If it is commercial, use a scant cup of it and add 5 or 6 sliced dates and 2 spoons of apricot jam or orange marmalade, and the rum. Mix with the dry ingredients and the beaten egg. Mix the buttermilk, sugar and baking powder and add to the flour mixture. The batter should be soft and moist but not thin. Bake bread in a greased bread pan 1 hour at 350° F. Slice after it has cooled. This is nice to have during the holidays for tea.

Steamed Corn Bread

2 cups stone- or water-ground
corn meal
½ cup wheat germ
½ cup 100% bran crumbles
1 cup whole wheat flour
1 Tbsp. salt

2 tsps. baking powder
⅔ cup raisins or sliced dates
¾ cup molasses
2¼ cups buttermilk
1 tsp. anise, mace, cinnamon, or
allspice

Mix all the dry ingredients together and toss the fruit through them. Mix the molasses with the buttermilk and a spice and stir it into the flours. Light molasses is best for baking, not the very dark bitter kind. Oil the molds. This recipe will fill two 1-pound cylinder coffee cans ⅔ full. Use those that come with plastic lids. Put the batter in the cans, cover with the lids and put them in a large kettle. Add boiling water ⅔ of the way up the cans. Cover the kettle and simmer gently for 3 hours, keeping the water replenished when necessary. Time the bread so it will be hot for dinner. Serve it whole, with butter, cutting it at the table. It has been a tradition to serve it with baked beans but it goes with other dishes too: pork, duck or goose. It is a grand bread which has gone rather out of fashion and should be restored to our repertoire. When it has thoroughly cooled, wrap it well in wax paper and refrigerate it. It can be reheated or served cold.

Steamed Carrot and Potato Bread

1 cup whole wheat flour	1 cup shredded raw potato
1 tsp. cinnamon	1 tsp. soda
1 tsp. mace	2 Tbsps. hot water
1 cup sliced dates	½ cup brown sugar
¼ tsp. salt	1 egg, plus 2 whites, beaten
1 cup shredded raw carrots	3 Tbsps. melted butter

Mix the flour and spices and toss the dates through. Shred the vegetables on a disk shredder so they look like coconut—not grated. It makes a lighter bread. Add the salt to the carrots and potatoes and add them to the flour. Mix the soda and hot water and stir it into the mixture. Add the sugar to the beaten egg and beat until thick and creamy. Add it to the rest of the mixture and put it in a greased container ⅔ full to allow for expansion. Pour the melted butter over the top. Cover with a lid. This is too much for a 1-pound coffee can so use an 8-inch melon mold. Put it in a large kettle with boiling water halfway up the mold, cover the kettle and boil gently for 3 hours. This is a fine bread to serve with chicken, baked beans, pork, etc.

Steamed Rye, Corn and Whole Wheat Bread

2 cups corn meal	1 tsp. soda
1 cup whole wheat flour	1½ tsps. salt
1 cup rye flour	1 cup molasses
1 tsp. cinnamon	3 cups sweet milk or buttermilk
1 tsp. clove	½ cup raisins

Mix all the ingredients together. Steam 3 hours in greased coffee cans set in a large kettle of simmering water, kept halfway up the sides of the cans. The big kettle is closed tight. The cans with lids, are filled ⅔ full. One-pound coffee cans with their plastic lids are good for this.

Carrot Tea Bread

This is a delicious, fine-textured bread and just the thing to serve with tea or coffee.

1⅓ cups whole wheat flour
1 cup wheat germ
2 tsps. salt
1 tsp. cinnamon
½ cup nuts, chopped
Grated rind of 1 large California
   orange

1 cup light brown sugar
2 large eggs, beaten
3 tsps. baking powder
½ cup buttery vegetable oil
½ cup orange juice
2 cups shredded raw carrot
Nuts (optional)

Mix all the dry ingredients in a large bowl. Beat the eggs very light and add the baking powder. Stir into the dry ingredients with the oil, juice and carrots. Walnuts, pecans or hazelnuts can be used. If hazelnuts are used, blanch and skin them, then brown them in the oven a little. They are very good in this bread. Put the batter into an oiled bread pan and bake it 10 minutes at 400° F., then turn the heat to 325° F. and bake it 1 hour and 5 minutes more—an hour and 15 minutes altogether.
VARIATION Use 1 cup of shredded potatoes and 1 cup of shredded carrots and the bread will not be quite so sweet. You can cut the amount of sugar in half, also. This bread, sliced and heated in the oven is very good, as it is moist.

Prune Bread

¼ cup butter	1 tsp. baking powder
1 cup light brown sugar	1 tsp. cinnamon
1 cup cooked, mashed prunes	½ tsp. nutmeg
½ cup sour cream	½ tsp. clove
3 egg yolks	½ tsp. allspice
1 cup sifted whole wheat flour	3 egg whites, beaten

Cream the butter with the sugar until very smooth. Add the mashed prunes, sour cream and egg yolks. Beat until smooth. Sift the coarse husks from the flour and measure it. Mix all the dry ingredients and combine with the liquid mixture; fold in the stiffly beaten egg whites last. This may be baked in 1 long pan about 35 minutes at 350° F. or it can be baked in 2 8-inch layer pans 28 to 30 minutes and filled with:

1 egg, beaten	½ cup finely chopped nuts
½ cup sour cream	½ cup raisins
½ cup light brown sugar	

Put all the ingredients in the top of the double boiler and cook over simmering water, stirring until mixture thickens. Let it cool then fill a cooled cake.

Hot Breads

Gingerbread

½ cup butter
1 cup brown sugar
⅔ cup molasses
2 egg yolks
½ cup sour cream
1⅛ cups whole wheat flour
¼ cup brown rice flour

1 tsp. cinnamon
1 tsp. ginger
½ tsp. nutmeg
½ tsp. clove
1 tsp. soda
3 Tbsps. hot water
2 egg whites, beaten

Cream the butter and sugar until smooth. Add the molasses. If the molasses is strong, use half molasses and half honey or corn syrup. Beat in the egg yolks and sour cream. Mix the flours with all the spices. Combine with the liquids. Dissolve the soda in the hot water and add it. Fold in the stiffly beaten egg whites. Bake in a greased, floured 8 x 11-inch pan at 350° F. about 28 or 30 minutes. Serve hot with sweet butter.

Orange Gingerbread

½ cup light brown sugar
½ cup butter
½ cup molasses (light)
1 egg, beaten
Juice of 1 orange
Rind of 1 California orange,

grated
½ cup cold tea
1⅓ cups whole wheat flour
¼ cup brown rice flour
¾ tsp. soda
1 tsp. ginger

Cream the sugar and butter until fluffy and smooth and add the molasses, beaten egg, juice and rind and the tea. If you wish the cake as delicate as any white flour gingerbread, sift the whole wheat to remove the coarsest husks. I like it the way it is. Mix all the dry ingredients and combine with the liquids. Bake at 350° F. about 25 to 30 minutes. Serve hot with butter.

Hot Cinnamon Bread

⅓ cup butter
¾ cup light brown sugar
3 egg yolks
1 cup sifted whole wheat flour
Few grains salt
2 tsps. baking powder

½ cup milk
3 egg whites, beaten
TOP
3 Tbsps. light brown sugar
1 Tbsp. cinnamon
2 Tbsps. butter

Cream the butter and sugar until smooth and add the egg yolks. Sift some of the coarse husks out of the flour, if you wish. Mix the flour with the dry ingredients and add the butter-egg mixture and the milk alternately. Fold in the stiffly beaten egg whites. Put the batter in a greased, floured 8 x 11-inch pan and sprinkle with the mixed ingredients for the top. Bake 20 minutes at 350° F.

VARIATION

APPLE CINNAMON BREAD
Recipe of Hot Cinnamon Bread
2 peeled tart apples, thinly sliced
SAUCE
1½ cups brown sugar
1 cup boiling water

1 Tbsp. butter
1 Tbsp. cornstarch
2 Tbsps. cold water
2 tsps. vanilla *or* 2 Tbsps. brandy or rum

Put the batter for cinnamon bread in the pan with the cinnamon top and insert rows of apple ½ inch into the dough. If the apples are small you may need three. Bake at 350° F. 20 minutes and another 5 minutes at 300° F. Serve hot with the sauce: Boil the sugar and water 2 minutes; add the butter and the cornstarch dissolved in the cold water. Cook until it thickens, then add the flavoring. Serve in a sauceboat.

Soya and Corn Meal Bread

1 cup corn meal	3 egg yolks
1 cup soya flour	1½ cups buttermilk
2 tsps. baking powder	3 Tbsps. melted butter
2 Tbsps. brown sugar	3 egg whites, beaten
1 tsp. salt	

Mix the dry ingredients together. Beat the yolks and add the buttermilk and melted butter; add them to the dry ingredients. Fold in the stiffly beaten egg whites. Bake in a greased, floured 8 x 11-inch pan in a 375° F. oven for 15 to 18 minutes. This excellent and nourishing bread will serve 6 to 8 persons. Serve hot with butter and jam. When cold it is better reheated before serving.

Whole Wheat Corn Meal Bread

¾ cup whole wheat flour	1 egg, beaten
¾ cup corn meal	1 cup sour cream
1½ tsps. baking powder	2 Tbsps. melted butter
1 tsp. salt	½ cup milk
3 Tbsps. brown sugar	

Mix the dry ingredients, then combine with the mixed liquid ingredients. Bake in a greased, floured 8 x 11-inch pan at 375° F. for about 15 or 20 minutes. Serve hot with butter.

Skillet Batter Bread

1¼ cups mixed flours: whole
  wheat, oat, rye, buckwheat
  flour, semolina, corn meal
1 tsp. salt
3 tsps. baking powder
2 large eggs, beaten

½ cup sour cream
2¼ cups milk
1 Tbsp. brown sugar
½ tsp. cinnamon
1 tsp. aniseeds
3 Tbsps. oil and butter

You may use any mixture of flours you like, the more variety the better. One half cup of buckwheat with a mixture of the others is very good and unusual. Put the unsifted flours in a mixing bowl and stir in the dry ingredients. In another bowl beat the eggs until very light, then beat in the rest of the ingredients. Combine with the flour mixture. Melt 3 Tbsps. of oil and butter in a 10-inch iron skillet, turning it so the sides are oiled. Empty the batter into it and bake in a 375° F. oven for 15 minutes, turn the heat to 325° F. and bake 15 minutes more. Serve hot with butter, cut in wedges. This always excites great enthusiasm. Serves 6. This bread should be a little soft and custardy in the center.

Ethel's Batter Bread

6 Tbsps. whole wheat flour
6 Tbsps. rye or buckwheat flour
6 Tbsps. corn meal
1 tsp. salt

4 tsps. baking powder
1 Tbsp. brown sugar
2 eggs, beaten
3 cups milk

The flours may be changed; oat flour is very good in this, just so 1 cup plus 2 or 3 tablespoons of mixed flours are used. Put them all in a mixing bowl and stir in the dry ingredients so they are well mixed. Beat the eggs until very light and add the milk, then combine the liquids and dry ingredients. Melt 2 or 3 Tbsps. of good fat in a 10-inch iron skillet, turning it so the sides and bottom are well greased. Pour in the batter and bake 30 to 35 minutes, ½ the time at 375° F. and the other ½ at 325° F. It is custardy in the center. Serve hot with plenty of butter.

French Toast

5 or 6 slices whole grain bread	2 or 3 eggs, beaten
1 cup milk	Butter
Vanilla, almond extract or rum	Powdered sugar
	Honey or brown sugar

Season the milk with flavor and sweetening to taste. Beat the eggs until light. Dip the bread in the milk, then in the egg and fry to a golden brown in plenty of butter. Sprinkle with powdered sugar and serve as is or with brown sugar, syrup or honey.

Creole Toast

Slices of whole grain bread	Clotted cream, sour cream,
Sweet butter	*crème fraîche* or yoghurt
Molasses	

Spread ¾-inch-thick slices of bread with butter on both sides. Put light molasses in a frying pan and fry the bread in it on both sides. Serve the toast with the cream you choose. Children like this for dessert and so do adults.

Muffins, Biscuits, Popovers

MUFFINS

Whole Wheat Muffins

1¼ cups whole wheat flour
3 tsps. baking powder
1 tsp. salt
2 Tbsps. brown sugar
⅓ cup raisins

2 Tbsps. melted butter
1 cup buttermilk
2 egg yolks
2 egg whites, beaten

Mix the dry ingredients. Toss the raisins through them. Mix the melted butter with the buttermilk and the egg yolks. Mix the liquids with the dry ingredients, stirring as little as possible, and fold in the stiffly beaten egg whites. Bake in greased muffin tins 20 minutes at 375° F.

Blueberry Whole Wheat Muffins

1 cup cleaned, dry blueberries
2 cups whole wheat flour
3 tsps. baking powder
1 tsp. salt
Grated rind of 1 orange

(optional)
2 Tbsps. honey
2 egg yolks
1 cup sour cream (or more)
2 egg whites, beaten

There are two ways of mixing the blueberries with muffin batter. One is to toss them through the mixed dry ingredients or put ½ the batter in greased muffin tins, add 1 Tbsp. of blueberries, then add the rest of the batter. Mix the dry ingredients together and mix the grated rind through them. Rind is optional but it gives a bland berry a good flavor. Mix the honey, yolks and sour cream together and add them to the flour. A little more sour cream may be necessary to make a soft batter, not as thick as quick bread dough. Mix as little as possible, then fold in the stiffly beaten egg whites. Bake 20 to 25 minutes at 375° F. If your oven bakes fast, reduce the heat after 15 minutes. Serve all muffins hot with butter. Other fruits can be used in these muffins, such as 1 cup of sour, pitted cherries, blackberries, or raspberries. If fruit is sour add more honey to the batter, and mix the fruit through the dry ingredients.

Wheat Grits Muffins or Hot Bread

1 cup wheat grits porridge*	⅔ cup whole wheat flour
¼ cup buttermilk	2 tsps. baking powder
2 egg yolks	1 tsp. salt
2 Tbsps. honey	½ tsp. allspice
2 Tbsps. melted butter	2 egg whites, beaten

Mix the porridge with the liquids until smooth. Combine with the mixed dry ingredients. Fold in the stiffly beaten egg whites last. Bake in 9 greased muffin tins or in an 8 x 11-inch pan 20 to 25 minutes at 375° F. Turn down the heat to 325° F. after 15 minutes if baking too fast.

* Put 1 cup of wheat grits in the top of the double boiler with 2 tsps. of salt and 3 cups of boiling water. Cook over the flame for 10 minutes, stirring frequently; cover and cook over simmering water 20 minutes more. All the whole grain porridges are excellent for children, served with syrup or cream and honey.

Buckwheat Muffins

1 cup buckwheat
½ cup corn meal
2½ tsps. baking powder
¾ tsp. salt
2 Tbsps. brown sugar or molasses

2 egg yolks
1¼ cups milk *or* 1½ cups
  buttermilk
4 Tbsps. melted butter
2 egg whites, beaten

Mix the dry ingredients. Mix the egg yolks, milk or buttermilk and butter. Add them to the flours, stirring as little as possible. Fold in the stiffly beaten egg whites and bake in greased muffin tins 20 minutes at 375° F.

Rye Grits Muffins

1 cup rye grits porridge*
¼ cup buttermilk
2 egg yolks
2 Tbsps. honey
2 Tbsps. melted butter

⅔ cup rye or whole wheat flour
2 tsps. baking powder
1 tsp. salt
½ tsp. clove
2 egg whites, beaten

Mix the porridge with the buttermilk, egg yolks, honey and butter until smooth. Mix the dry ingredients and combine with the porridge mixture. Stir very little and fold in the stiffly beaten egg whites. Bake in greased muffin tins 25 minutes, ½ the time at 375° F. and ½ at 325° F.

---

* Like Rice Grits Porridge, rye grits porridge is fine for breakfast with syrup or cream and honey. Put 1 cup of rye grits in the top of a double boiler with 2 tsps. salt and 3 cups of boiling water. Cook over the flame for 10 minutes, stirring frequently, then cover and cook over simmering water for 35 minutes more. Makes over 3 cups of porridge.

Rice Grits Muffins

1 cup rice grits porridge*	⅓ cup brown rice flour
¼ cup buttermilk	⅓ cup whole wheat flour
2 egg yolks	2 tsps. baking powder
2 Tbsps. melted butter	1 tsp. salt
2 Tbsps. honey or brown sugar	2 egg whites, beaten

Mash the porridge into the buttermilk until smooth, then add the egg yolks, butter and honey or sugar. Mix the dry ingredients and add them to the grits mixture, stirring very little. Fold in the stiffly beaten egg whites. One third cup of raisins can be added if desired. Bake in 9 greased, floured muffin tins at 375 ° F. for 20 minutes.

Rye and Rice Flour Muffins

½ cup brown rice flour	¼ cup currants
1½ tsps. baking powder	½ cup sour cream
1 tsp. salt	1 egg, beaten
2 Tbsps. brown sugar	¾ cup buttermilk
1 cup rye flour	

Mix all the dry ingredients together and toss the currants through them. Mix the cream with the beaten egg and ½ cup of buttermilk. Combine with the dry ingredients. Add the rest of the buttermilk if needed to make a fluffy dough. Stir as little as possible. Bake in 9 greased, floured muffin tins 15 minutes at 375° F. and 5 minutes at 325° F. These are filling and delicious muffins. Serve hot with butter.

* Brown rice grits makes a fine porridge for children or adults, served with cream and honey. Put 1 cup of brown rice grits in the top of the double boiler with 2 tsps. salt and 3 cups of boiling water, and let the mixture come to a boil over the flame. Cover and cook over simmering water for 20 minutes. Makes 3 cups of porridge.

BISCUITS

Whole Wheat Biscuits

2 cups sifted whole wheat flour   6 Tbsps. shortening
4 tsps. baking powder   ⅔ cup milk (about)
1½ tsp. salt

Sift the flour. Return the coarse husks to the flour bag for bread. Mix the dry ingredients; cut in the lard or vegetable shortening with a wire pastry blender. Stir in the milk adding just enough to make a soft, light dough, stirring as little as possible. Drop from the spoon onto a greased, floured baking sheet, let stand 3 minutes then bake at 375° F. about 10 minutes. Makes about 12 to 16 biscuits.

Barley Flour Drop Biscuits

1 cup barley flour.   2 Tbsps. butter
¾ teaspoon salt   1 egg, beaten
2 tsps. baking powder   ½ cup buttermilk
2 tsps. brown sugar

Mix the dry ingredients and cut in the butter with a wire pastry cutter. Add the egg with ½ the buttermilk. Add enough buttermilk to make a soft dough but one that is thick enough to drop from a spoon onto a greased pan. Bake 12 to 15 minutes at 400° F. ½ the time, and 375° F. ½ the time. Barley does not have the rising characteristics of wheat but barley recipes are given for those on restricted diets.

Böhmische Dalken

Bohemian Whole Wheat Puffs

1 envelope yeast	3 Tbsps. butter
3 Tbsps. lukewarm water	½ tsp. salt
2 Tbsps. light brown sugar	2 cups sifted whole wheat flour
3 egg yolks, beaten	3 egg whites, beaten
1½ cups lukewarm milk	Jam and powdered sugar

Melt the yeast and sugar in the lukewarm water until foamy. Beat the egg yolks and add them to the milk which has been warmed enough to melt the butter. Sift the salt with the flour. Some of the husks can be sifted out. Combine the yeast, milk, flour and stir until well blended. Fold in the stiffly beaten egg whites. Let the batter stand a few minutes to become a little light. Butter and oil munk forms and heat them a little. Put 2 Tbsps. batter in each and fry until the tops are a little dry. Brush lightly with a little melted butter. With 2 sharp-pointed knives, turn the puffs over and cook 1 minute on the other side. Split them and fill with a little jam. Roll the puffs in powdered sugar. They are very light and nice for tea.

Fruit Shortcake

1 cup sifted whole wheat flour	About ⅓ cup milk
2 tsps. baking powder	4 cups strawberries, raspberries,
¾ tsp. salt	sliced peaches, cherries, etc.
4 Tbsps. butter and vegetable shortening, mixed	¼ cup honey
	Heavy cream or *Crème Fraîche*

Sift the flour and measure. Some may prefer to discard the husks. They may be put back in the container for use in bread. Mix the dry ingredients together and cut in the butter and shortening with a wire pastry cutter. Add just enough milk to make a soft dough, stirring as little as possible. The dough can be dropped in 4 cakes onto a greased, floured pan or patted into an 8-inch cake pan. Let it stand 2 minutes then bake it at 375° F. about 20 minutes. Split the cakes through, insert a little soft butter between the halves and put back the tops. Cover with crushed honey-sweetened berries or other fruit and serve hot with heavy cream or *crème fraîche*.

POPOVERS

Whole Wheat Popovers

1 cup whole wheat flour	1¼ cups milk
¾ tsp. salt	1 tsp. vegetable oil
1 tsp. brown sugar or honey	3 large eggs, beaten

The flour, salt, sugar or honey, milk and oil are beaten together until smooth, or they can be mixed in an electric blender. The eggs are beaten by hand with a rotary beater until very light. The blender is not suitable for beating eggs as it liquefies them, removing the air that should be beaten into them. Beat the eggs into the liquid mixture. This can stand or it can be baked immediately in 11 well-greased iron popover forms at 375° F. for 40 minutes. Or they can be put in a cold oven, then baked at 425° F. for 50 minutes. See that your oven doesn't burn them. If it bakes very fast turn the oven down to 325° F. for the last 15 minutes. Do not open the oven door while they are baking. Serve immediately with plenty of sweet butter. Remember these are made with whole wheat instead of white flour so they are somewhat different.

Doughnuts, Fritters, Dumplings

DOUGHNUTS

Whole Wheat Doughnuts

2 eggs, beaten
1 cup light brown sugar
½ tsp. salt
⅔ cup sour cream
2 tsps. baking powder

¾ cup buttermilk
3 cups (about) whole wheat
    flour
Deep fat for frying
Powdered sugar

Beat the eggs until light; add the sugar and beat until thick and creamy. Add the salt, sour cream, baking powder and buttermilk. Add flour to make a dough that can be rolled out ½ inch thick and cut with a doughnut cutter. Add no more flour than necessary to make a light doughnut. Fry at 375° F. until brown on both sides. Drain on brown paper and sprinkle thickly with powdered sugar. These should be stored in a covered earthenware jar. They keep amazingly well.

Rye and Whole Wheat Fritters

1 cup rye flour
½ cup whole wheat flour
1½ tsps. baking powder
½ tsp. salt
1 egg, beaten

¼ cup molasses
Buttermilk
Oil for deep frying
Powdered sugar

Mix the dry ingredients. Beat the egg and add the molasses and ⅔ cup of buttermilk. Combine the two mixtures and add more buttermilk if necessary to make a stiff dough that can be dropped in teaspoonfuls into deep fat. Fry at 370° F. until brown. Drain on paper, roll in powdered sugar. Serve hot with jam or syrup.

FRITTERS

Corn Fritters

1 cup corn
4 or 5 Tbsps. corn meal
1 tsp. light brown sugar
¼ tsp. pepper

1 tsp. salt
1½ tsps. baking powder
1 large egg, beaten
Oil for deep frying

Mix all the ingredients together. Drop from a spoon into 370° F. oil and fry until a golden brown. Sprinkle with powdered sugar or serve with syrup. Excellent with fried chicken.

Fruit Fritters

⅓ cup whole wheat flour
½ cup brown rice flour
1 tsp. light brown sugar
½ tsp. salt
¾ tsp. baking powder
2 egg yolks

¼ cup sour cream
2 egg whites, beaten
Sliced bananas, strawberries, peaches
Deep oil for frying
Powdered sugar

Sift the flour if you like and discard the husks, then measure it. Sift all the dry ingredients together. Mix the yolks with the cream and combine the 2 mixtures. A spoon or 2 of milk can be added if the batter is too thick. Fold in the stiffly beaten egg whites. Drop 2 or 3 pieces of fruit or whole berries at a time into the batter and, when well covered, spoon out and fry in deep oil at 365° F. to 370° F. until golden brown. Drain on brown paper, sprinkle with powdered sugar and serve immediately with sour cream.

VARIATION

CORN FRITTERS A half cup of sweet corn kernels may be added to the batter and fried to serve with chicken. It may be necessary to thin a little with milk or buttermilk but not much as the batter must hold its shape.

DUMPLINGS
Corn Meal Dumplings

¾ cup corn meal	¼ tsp. soda
¼ cup whole wheat flour	1 egg, beaten
3 tsps. baking powder	3 Tbsps. sour cream
1 tsp. salt	Milk

Mix the dry ingredients together very well. Beat the egg, add the cream and 2 Tbsps. milk. Combine with the dry ingredients and add more milk if necessary to make a soft dough but one that is stiff enough to hold its shape. Chopped chives or fresh dill can be added if desired. Drop from a spoon on simmering stew with plenty of liquid. Cover and cook 12 to 15 minutes without lifting the lid. Makes 6 large dumplings.

Whole Wheat Dumplings

¾ cup whole wheat flour	1 egg, beaten
2 tsps. baking powder	2 tsps. melted butter or lard
1 tsp. salt	Milk

Mix the dry ingredients. Beat the egg until light, add the butter or lard and ¼ cup of milk. Stir lightly into the flour and add more milk to make a thick but soft dough, one that can be dropped with a kitchen spoon over simmering stew. Cover tight and cook gently for 12 minutes without lifting the lid. Serves 4.

Pancakes, Waffles

PANCAKES

All these pancakes are filling and delicious, and you feel as though you had really eaten. Served with a good syrup or honey for breakfast they start off both children and adults for a good day. For lunch or supper, try them with ham or sausage. This amount will serve two or three but the recipe can easily be doubled or trebled. If you prefer a thinner pancake, add a little buttermilk to the batter.

Whole Wheat Pancakes

1½ cups whole wheat flour
2 or 3 Tbsps. brown sugar
1 tsp. salt
3 tsps. baking powder

2 egg yolks
3 Tbsps. melted butter
1¼ cups milk
2 egg whites, beaten

Mix the dry ingredients together and combine with the mixed liquids. Fold in the stiffly beaten egg whites last. Fry on a well-greased griddle set over a moderate heat until the cakes bubble over the top. Turn once.

Whole Wheat Buttermilk Pancakes

⅞ cup whole wheat flour	2 egg yolks
1½ tsps. baking powder	2 Tbsps. melted butter
½ tsp. salt	1 cup buttermilk
1 Tbsp. light brown sugar	2 egg whites, beaten

Mix the dry ingredients. Beat the egg yolks, add the melted butter and buttermilk and stir into the flour. Fold in the stiffly beaten egg whites last. Fry on a well-greased, medium-hot griddle. When they bubble across the top, turn them once. Serves 2 to 3.

VARIATION

BLUEBERRY WHOLE WHEAT PANCAKES   Add ½ cup of cleaned, dry blueberries to the dry ingredients and mix. Add the beaten yolks mixed with the butter and buttermilk and fold in the stiffly beaten egg whites last. Fry on a well-greased, medium-hot griddle, cooking a little more slowly than fruitless pancakes. These can be served with honey-sweetened sour cream with 1 cup of blueberries added. The plain pancakes (above) can be served with sweetened berries and a big bowl of sour cream. Raspberries, strawberries, sliced apricots or peaches can replace blueberries.

Whole Wheat Cottage Cheese Pancakes

½ cup whole wheat flour	½ tsp. salt
½ tsp. baking powder	2 eggs, beaten
2 tsps. light brown sugar	1 cup creamed cottage cheese

Mix the dry ingredients and add the beaten eggs. Sieve the cottage cheese and add it to the mixed flour and eggs. Fry on a well-greased, medium-hot griddle. These cakes do not spread but are fluffy and moist. Serve with sweet butter, sour cream and honey or syrup.

VARIATION

RYE COTTAGE CHEESE PANCAKES Use rye flour instead of whole wheat in the foregoing recipe.

Grits Porridge Pancakes

1⅓ cups grits porridge and
milk (rice, whole wheat, rye,
or oatmeal)
1 tsp. baking powder
1 Tbsp. brown sugar or honey

1 tsp. salt
1 Tbsp. melted butter
3 egg yolks
3 egg whites, beaten

These can be made of leftover porridge or the porridge can be made of ½ cup of grits cooked in 2 cups milk. Boil it up, then cook over simmering water 20 minutes. Add the other ingredients to 1⅓ cups of porridge, folding in the stiffly beaten egg whites last. This makes a very light pancake. If one with more body is desired, add 2 or 3 Tbsps. of the same kind of flour as grits used. A little grated lemon rind can be added to the batter. Fry on a buttered griddle. When they brown, turn them once.

Paul's Rye Pancakes

1 cup rye flour
1 cup water
1 envelope yeast
2 egg yolks
¾ tsp. salt

2 Tbsps. honey or brown sugar
½ cup sour cream
2 egg whites, beaten
Oil and butter for frying

Soak the flour and water several hours. Sprinkle the yeast into the flour-water mixture 15 minutes before you fry the pancakes. The ingredients should be at room temperature. Mix in the rest of the ingredients, folding in the stiffly beaten egg whites last. These incredibly light pancakes are delicious with honey or maple syrup.

Fry them on a rather hot griddle in plenty of oil and butter until they are quite brown on one side, then turn them and cook until they are light brown on the other side. They don't need butter and are too delicate to spread anyway. Makes 18 or 20 cakes.

Rye Pancakes

1 cup rye flour	1 egg, beaten
1 tsp. baking powder	2 Tbsps. melted butter
1 tsp. salt	1¼ cups (or more) buttermilk
3 Tbsps. brown sugar	

Mix the dry ingredients. Beat the egg until light and add the butter and buttermilk. Combine the mixtures and add more buttermilk to thin the batter if necessary. Fry on a well-greased, medium-hot griddle.

Buckwheat Pancakes

1 envelope yeast	1 tsp. salt
½ cup lukewarm water	1 Tbsp. molasses
¾ cup boiling water	4 Tbsps. butter, melted
2 cups buckwheat flour	¼ tsp. soda
2 eggs, beaten	¼ cup boiling water
1 cup milk, warmed	1 Tbsp. molasses

Dissolve the yeast in the lukewarm water. Add the boiling water to the buckwheat flour and when lukewarm add the rest of the ingredients except the last three. Stir in the yeast and when well mixed, wrap bowl well in 2 tea towels and set in a warm place to rise overnight. In the morning when ready to fry the cakes, dissolve the soda in the boiling water and add it and the molasses to the batter. The batter is rather thin. Fry on a hot well-greased griddle and serve with maple syrup.

Quick Buckwheat Pancakes

1 cup buckwheat flour
¾ cup whole wheat flour
2½ tsps. baking powder
1 tsp. salt
1 Tbsp. molasses

2 egg yolks
⅓ cup melted butter
1⅔ cups sweet milk *or* 1¾ cups buttermilk
2 egg whites, beaten

Mix the dry ingredients and combine with the mixed liquids. Fold in the stiffly beaten whites last. Fry on a well-greased hot griddle.

Buckwheat Crèpes

Galetous

2 cups buckwheat flour
1 Tbsp. olive oil
¼ cup fruit brandy

1 tsp. salt
1⅛ cups buttermilk
4 large eggs

Put the flour in a mixing bowl and make a well in the center and add the oil, brandy, salt and buttermilk. When it is mixed, whisk in the four eggs, 1 at a time. Fry small cakes on a well-greased griddle. This is a Breton dish.

Barley Flour Pancakes

1 egg, beaten
⅓ cup sour cream
⅓ cup buttermilk
1 cup barley flour

1½ tsps. baking powder
¾ tsp. salt
1 Tbsp. brown sugar or honey

Beat the egg and add the cream and buttermilk. Mix the dry ingredients and combine with the liquids. Let stand 2 minutes, then fry on a buttered, fairly hot griddle until light brown and puffy. Turn once and finish frying. Serve with butter and one of the syrups listed. Makes 8 pancakes.

Swedish Blinis with Caviar

Blinis Med Löjrom
Den Gyldene Freden, Stockholm

Den Gyldene Freden (The Golden Peace) was so christened to express the longing of the Swedish people at the close of the great war of 1700–1721. This inn is in Stockholm's old town and was founded in 1725. Its rooms and cellar are filled with medieval furniture and relics of the past. Carl Michael Bellman (1740–1795) the "poet of peace" composed his songs and ballads here, singing to the motley company. Every year on his birthday a festival is celebrated in the Bellman Room. The inn is a sort of unofficial headquarters for the Pen Club and for the traditional Thursday dinner parties of the Swedish Academy. Today the inn has an international clientele. People come to eat fine food and drink wines from its famous cellars. Mr. S. Moquist, Maître d'Hotel, gave me this delicious blini recipe for this book.

BLINIS	GARNISH
2 cups buckwheat flour	Melted butter
2 cups warm milk	Sour cream
2 Tbsps. light brown sugar	Caviar
1 envelope yeast	
3 large eggs	
1 Tbsp. salt	
Oil and butter for frying	

Begin the batter 4 hours before you are ready to fry the blinis. Put the flour in a large mixing bowl and stir in the lukewarm milk, sugar and yeast. Set the bowl in a pan of warm water, cover with a tea towel and let batter rise 2 hours. Have the eggs at room temperature, separate them and stir in the yolks and set the pan again in warm water to rise another 2 hours. Stir in the salt and the stiffly beaten whites of the eggs. Melt the oil and butter on a pancake griddle and fry the cakes over a medium-hot flame. When the top of the cakes dries, they are done as they are not to be turned. If the griddle is too hot, the bottom of the cakes will brown before the top is done, in which case you can turn them for only a second to prevent the top from being too moist. The melted butter is added to the top, then a dollop of sour cream and a spoon of caviar. Makes 16 to 20 pancakes depending on their size. For a dinner party, one pancake is a sufficient serving. Any leftover batter can be refrigerated, well covered, and used later. Let it stand at room temperature so it can rise again, before frying.

WAFFLES

Whole Wheat Waffles

2 cups whole wheat flour
4 tsps. baking powder
½ tsp. salt
2 egg yolks
½ cup melted butter

1¾ cups sweet milk or butter-milk
2 egg whites, beaten
Big bowls of berries or sliced fresh fruit and sour cream

Mix the dry ingredients and combine with the beaten egg yolks, butter and milk. A little more buttermilk may be needed. Fold in the stiffly beaten egg whites. Waffles make a fine lunch or supper dish accompanied by bowls of fresh sweetened berries or other fruit and sour cream.

VARIATION

BUCKWHEAT WAFFLES For the waffles follow the recipe for Quick Buckwheat Pancakes increasing the melted butter to ½ cup.

Wheat Grits and Rye Grits Porridge

If 1 cup of grits are soaked in 1 cup of water several hours or overnight, they will cook in half the time when the porridge is made. The following directions are for unsoaked grits.

1 cup grits   1½ tsps. salt
3 cups boiling water

Put the grits and water in the top of the double boiler. Stir it over the direct flame until mixed and smooth. Cover and cook over simmering water for 10 minutes before adding the salt. Then continue cooking the wheat grits for 30 to 35 minutes or until tender; the rye grits are cooked 45 minutes. They are served with brown sugar or honey and hot milk or cream. A pinch of powdered clove makes rye grits fragrant.

Corn Bread,
Spoon Bread

CORN

Wheat has long been the synonym for bread, a natural treasure closely related to human life. Corn is much younger, for America had yet to be discovered before the New World could add a new folklore to the Biblical story of Joseph and the wheat of Egypt. The saga now of American corn, or maize, has reached every civilized land taking a place with rice, wheat and rye in the eating habits of many peoples. It began with the Indian tribes of the Americas which had been growing *mahis* or *maize* long before the Spanish or British voyages of discovery were even thought of. Coronado, Columbus, Captain John Smith and Governor Bradford—all of them owe their fates to the humble Indian maize. The first two, under the pressure to discover gold, neglected a treasure far greater in corn; the last two, learning the value of maize just in the nick of time, brought their Virginia and Massachusetts colonists through a decimating winter by using corn bought from the Indians or raised by themselves. Indeed, it was the cultivation of corn that turned our Indians from nomadic to agrarian habits. Our forefathers in Jamestown and in Plymouth relied on corn, first for physical survival, and increasingly since for the sheer pleasure of its eating—in forms of such variety and enjoyment as to assure corn forever a place both fundamental and economical in the world's dietary.

As corn lovers know, it has a taste of its own, but it is willing to combine with a variety of other foods. It is never submerged, but lends new virtue to other ingredients. It is gladly acceptable from the humble porridge to epicurean dishes.

Cream Corn Bread

This may be made with light cream or half light and half heavy. It is a very good corn bread with either.

1 cup cream	1 Tbsp. light brown sugar
1 cup corn meal	2 egg yolks
¾ tsp. salt	2 egg whites, beaten
1 tsp. baking powder	

Mix the cream with the dry ingredients which have been well mixed together. Stir in the yolks and then fold in the whites, beaten stiff. Bake in a small greased pan about 15 minutes at 375° F.

Carrot Corn Bread

2½ cups stone-ground corn meal	2 eggs, beaten
2½ tsps. salt	1 cup sour cream
2 tsps. baking powder	2 Tbsps. honey or brown sugar
1 cup carrot juice	½ cup buttermilk

Mix all the dry ingredients in a mixing bowl. Stir in the juice. Beat the eggs until light then add the cream, sweetening and buttermilk. Stir the mixture into the meal. Liberally grease a pan or 10-inch iron skillet, empty the batter into it and bake in a 400° F.

223

oven for 10 minutes and another 15 or 18 minutes at 325° F. This is a delicious, nourishing bread to be served with plenty of sweet butter and jam.

Nebraska Corn Bread

1 tsp. soda
2 cups buttermilk
1 tsp. salt
2 cups yellow stone-ground
   corn meal

¼ cup lard or butter, melted
1 Tbsp. light brown sugar
2 eggs, beaten

Mix the soda until frothy with a little of the buttermilk. Mix all the ingredients together and bake in a greased 11 x 8-inch pan about 25 minutes at 350° F. Serve hot with butter.

Southern Corn Bread

2 cups white corn meal
1 cup boiling water
2 egg yolks, beaten
1 Tbsp. melted butter or lard

½ tsp. baking soda
¾ cup buttermilk
1 tsp. baking powder
2 egg whites, beaten

Scald the corn meal with the boiling water and add the yolks, melted fat and soda dissolved in the buttermilk, and the baking powder. Fold in the stiffly beaten egg whites last. Southern corn bread is not supposed to be sweet but 1 tsp. of brown sugar makes it brown better and taste better to some of us. Bake in a greased pan 25 or 30 minutes at 350° F.

Apricot Corn Bread

¾ cup dried apricots
2 cups corn meal
1½ tsps. salt
¼ cup light brown sugar
2 Tbsps. melted butter
1 cup buttermilk

1 cup sour cream
1 tsp. soda
2 Tbsps. hot water
2 egg yolks
2 egg whites, beaten

Soak, drain and slice the apricots. Mix the corn meal, salt, and sugar, and toss the apricots through them. Combine the melted butter, buttermilk and sour cream. Dissolve the soda in the hot water and add it to the liquids; add the egg yolks. Combine the liquids with the corn meal and fold in the stiffly beaten egg whites last. Bake in a greased, floured pan about 25 minutes at 350° F. Serve hot with butter.

Sour Cream Corn Bread

1½ cups corn meal *or* ¾ cup corn meal and ¾ cup whole wheat flour
1 tsp. soda
1 tsp. salt

3 Tbsps. light brown sugar
1 cup sour cream
1 egg, beaten
½ cup milk
2 Tbsps. melted butter

Mix the dry ingredients and combine with the mixed liquids. Bake in a greased pan 15 or 20 minutes at 375° F. Brown rice flour can replace half of the whole wheat. This can be experimented with, using various flour combinations. Sour milk, cream and buttermilk are fine for baking because they make breads of light and rich texture.

Plantation Corn Meal and Hominy Bread

1 cup corn meal	1 tsp. salt
½ cup cooked hominy	2 Tbsps. honey
1½ cups boiling milk	1 tsp. baking powder
1 egg, beaten	2 Tbsps. butter or lard

Put the corn meal and hominy in a bowl, mix them then stir in the boiling milk. Mix the egg with the salt, honey and baking powder and mix it into the hot mixture. Melt the butter or lard in a skillet, tip it so bottom and sides are covered with fat and pour in the batter. Bake about 25 minutes, or until done, at 350° F. Serve hot with plenty of sweet butter.

Georgia Egg Bread

2 cups corn meal	1 tsp. salt
1 cup boiling water	¼ tsp. baking soda
2 Tbsps. soft butter	2 egg yolks
1 cup buttermilk	2 egg whites, beaten

Pour the boiling water over the corn meal and add the butter, then the buttermilk, salt, soda and egg yolks. Beat so the ingredients are well mixed, then fold in the stiffly beaten egg whites. Bake 25 or 30 minutes at 350° F. in a greased pan.

Corn Meal and Rice Bread

1 cup boiling milk	½ cup corn meal
1 tsp. salt	1 tsp. baking powder
⅓ cup butter	1 cup cooked rice
1 Tbsp. light brown sugar	2 eggs, separated

Pour the boiling milk over the salt, butter and sugar. When the butter is melted, pour mixture over the corn meal which is mixed with the baking powder. Add the rice and egg yolks and mix well.

Fold in the stiffly beaten whites last. Bake in a greased pan or shallow baking dish 20 minutes at 375° F. If the eggs are small use 3. Serve hot with butter. This is a very good bread.

Nebraska Spider* Corn Bread

1¼ cups corn meal
1 Tbsp. light brown sugar
1 tsp. soda
1 tsp. salt

3 Tbsps. melted butter
2 eggs, beaten
2 cups buttermilk
3 Tbsps. fat for spider

Mix the dry ingredients and add the liquids which have been mixed together. Melt the fat in a 10-inch spider, tip pan so sides are greased and add the batter. Bake 20 minutes at 375° F. Serve hot with butter.

White Corn Bread

2 cups white corn meal
1 cup boiling water
1½ tsps. salt
1 Tbsp. light brown sugar or
   honey

1 cup heavy cream
4 egg yolks
¼ cup melted bacon fat or
   butter
4 egg whites, beaten

Put the corn meal in a mixing bowl and pour the boiling water over it and mix until smooth. Stir in the salt, brown sugar or honey and cream which has been beaten with the egg yolks. Add the bacon fat or butter, then fold in the stiffly beaten egg whites last. Bake at 350° F. about 25 minutes. Serve hot with butter.

* In the Middle West an iron skillet is sometimes called a spider.

Pimento Corn Bread

2 cups corn meal
2 tsps. baking powder
1 tsp. salt
1 tsp. brown sugar
2 eggs, beaten
1 cup heavy sour cream

½ cup milk or buttermilk
½ cup diced red canned pimentos
½ cup sweet corn (fresh or canned)

Mix the dry ingredients together. Beat the eggs until light and mix them with the liquids. Combine the two mixtures. Drain both the pimentos and corn, if canned is used. Lightly stir them into the batter. Bake in a greased 11 x 9-inch pan 10 minutes at 375° F. and 15 minutes more at 325° F. Serve hot with butter. You can serve this with fish or chicken instead of potatoes. You also can use 1½ cups of corn meal and ½ cup brown rice flour instead of all corn meal.

SPOON BREADS

Connecticut Spoon Bread

2 cups milk
1 cup corn meal
¼ cup heavy cream
¼ cup sweet butter

1½ to 2 tsps. salt
4 egg yolks, beaten
4 egg whites, beaten stiff

Moisten the corn meal with ½ cup of the cold milk to prevent it from lumping. Scald the rest of the milk and add it to the meal with the cream, butter, salt and egg yolks. Beat vigorously. Fold in the beaten whites. Bake in a greased baking dish 30 minutes at 375° F. ½ the time and 350° F. ½ the time. Serve hot with butter.

Cream Spoon Bread

1 cup corn meal   2 tsps. salt
1 cup heavy cream   4 eggs, beaten
3 cups boiling milk   3 Tbsps. melted butter
1 Tbsp. light brown sugar

Mix the corn meal with the cold cream in the top of the double boiler. Boil the milk and add it to the corn meal with the sugar and salt. Cook over simmering water to a porridge. Remove and beat in the very well-beaten eggs. Beat for 2 minutes. Bake in a greased baking dish 45 minutes at 350° F. When it is done pour the melted butter over the top. This spoon bread is rich enough without serving with butter.

Kentucky Spoon Bread

2 cups scalded milk   1 tsp. salt
1 cup corn meal   3 eggs, beaten
3 Tbsps. butter

Pour the boiling milk over the corn meal and add the butter and salt. Beat the eggs until light and add them to the mixture. Bake at 375° F. 20 to 25 minutes in a greased baking dish.

VARIATION

CHEESE SPOON BREAD   1 cup shredded cheddar, Gruyère, *or* Emmenthaler cheese
Recipe for Kentucky Spoon Bread   (added before the eggs)
1 additional cup of boiling milk
¼ tsp. nutmeg

This gives the right zip to spoon bread and is a delicious addition to a meal of chicken or pork. It is also good with ham.

Nebraska Spoon Bread

¾ cup corn meal
4 cups milk
2 tsps. salt

⅓ cup butter
1 tsp. baking powder
3 eggs, beaten separately

Moisten the corn meal with 1 cup of cold milk in the top of the double boiler and stir until smooth. Add 3 cups of scalded milk and the salt and cook until it thickens. Add the butter, baking powder and egg yolks. Beat well then fold in the stiffly beaten whites. Bake in a buttered casserole at 350° F. until set, about 30 minutes. It should be moist inside. Serve with butter.

Rhode Island Spoon Bread

4 cups milk
2 cups corn meal
¼ cup butter

2 tsps. salt
2 egg yolks
2 egg whites, beaten

Moisten the meal with 1 cup cold milk, then add the rest of the milk, scalded, the butter, salt and egg yolks. Beat very hard. More salt may be added to taste. Fold in the whites and bake in a greased baking dish at 400° F. for 30 minutes. Serve with plenty of butter.

Polenta

Taverna la Fenice, Venice

My favorite restaurant in Venice serves warm polenta with *Fegato Veneziana* (liver and onions Venetian style). As they make the polenta in the morning for lunch, it is served while still a little soft and warm; at night after it has become stiff and cold, it is toasted and served hot with the *Fegato*. Everything Signore Alfredo Zoppi serves in this lovely outdoor restaurant reflects his own imagination and style.

2 cups fine water-ground yellow
  corn meal
1 Tbsp. salt

1 cup cold water
4 to 6 cups boiling water

Mix the corn meal with the salt and cold water so that it does not become lumpy. This is done in the top of the double boiler. Put it over simmering water and stir in the boiling water, 4 cups at first. Cover and cook 30 minutes, stirring occasionally. When necessary, if it becomes too thick, add more boiling water. Polenta thickens as it cools. When it is done, spread it ¾ inch thick on a slab to cool and thicken. When ready to serve, cut in oblong slices, 2 x 5 inches.

VARIATION

POLENTA WITH SAUSAGES
Recipe for Polenta
4 Italian sausages, 2 sweet, 2 hot
  or 6 or 8 pork sausages

1 cup tomato sauce
1 tsp. powdered fennel
Butter
Parmesan cheese

Make the polenta as directed. Prick the sausages with a needle 3 times. Bake them in the oven at 350° F. for 18 minutes. Skin them if necessary, and cut them in inch lengths. Mix them with the sauce and fennel. Butter a baking dish and spread half the hot mush over it, then spread all the sauce over it and spread the rest of the mush over the top. The mush must not be too thick. Dot the top with butter and liberally sprinkle with cheese. Brown in a hot oven. A grand supper main dish or an accompaniment to chicken or pork.

Corn Meal Cheese Soufflé

1 cup milk, scalded　　　　½ tsp. salt
3 Tbsps. corn meal　　　　¼ tsp. nutmeg
1 cup shredded sharp cheese　4 or 5 eggs, separated

Scald the milk and pour it over the corn meal, cheese and seasonings. Let it cook until it thickens and the cheese melts. Add the beaten yolks and stir a moment longer. Let it cool a little. Beat the egg whites until stiff and fold them into the cheese mixture. Empty into a greased 7½-inch soufflé dish. Set it in a pan with a little boiling water and bake 30 minutes at 375° F. If it is baking too fast, turn the heat to 325° F. Serves 4 to 6 depending on whether it is the main lunch or supper dish or an accompaniment to the meat. It should be a little moist inside.

Corn Meal "Yorkshire" Pudding

¼ cup corn meal　　　2 egg yolks
1 cup milk　　　　　2 egg whites, beaten
½ tsp. salt　　　　　Beef drippings

Cook the corn meal, milk and salt until mixture thickens. Let it cool a little and stir in the yolks. Fold in the stiffly beaten whites. Grease muffin tins with 1 Tbsp. of beef drippings. Bake the muffins about 15 minutes at 350° F. After 10 minutes put 1 tsp. of drippings on each muffin and continue baking until done. They are good with beef or pork.

Corn Pancakes, Waffles, Porridge

CORN PANCAKES

Corn Cakes

1 cup ground fresh corn
⅓ cup corn meal
1½ tsps. baking powder
Pinch light brown sugar

¾ tsp. salt
⅓ to ½ cup sour cream
3 egg yolks
3 egg whites, beaten

Cut the corn from the ears and grind it. Mix the dry ingredients together and stir in the corn. Add ⅓ cup of sour cream, the egg yolks and, if the batter is too thick, add a little more sour cream. Fold in the stiffly beaten whites last. Fry in plenty of butter on a moderately hot griddle. These are delicious for a supper dish or with poultry or pork.

Corn Pancakes

1 cup corn meal
½ tsp. baking soda
¾ tsp. salt
½ cup sour cream

1 egg, beaten
1 Tbsp. butter, melted
Buttermilk

Mix the dry ingredients. Mix the sour cream, egg and butter and mix with the corn meal. Add enough buttermilk, ⅔ cup or more, to make a light pancake batter. Fry on a hot greased griddle. Serves 4. If the recipe is doubled, separate the eggs and add the stiffly beaten whites last.

Corn Meal Rice Pancakes

1 cup corn meal	2 Tbsps. melted butter
¾ tsp. baking soda	½ cup cooked rice
1 tsp. salt	1 cup buttermilk
1 Tbsp. light brown sugar	2 egg whites, beaten
2 egg yolks, beaten	

Mix the dry ingredients. Beat together egg yolks, butter, rice and ½ the buttermilk. Combine the 2 mixtures and add enough buttermilk to make a light pancake batter. Fold in the whites stiffly beaten. Fry on a hot greased griddle. When the pancakes have bubbles on the top turn once. Serve with honey or one of the syrups listed.

Corn Batter Cakes

2 cups corn meal mush	2 egg yolks, beaten
1 tsp. salt	Milk or buttermilk
1 Tbsp. light brown sugar	2 egg whites, beaten

This may be made from scratch or from left over corn meal mush. Mix the mush with salt, sugar and egg yolks. Add enough milk or buttermilk to make a light pancake batter. If buttermilk is used add 3 Tbsps. melted butter. Fold in the stiffly beaten egg whites last. Fry on a liberally greased hot griddle. When the tops bubble turn once.

CORN WAFFLES
AND PORRIDGE

Corn Meal Waffles

2 cups yellow or white corn
   meal
1 tsp. salt
1 Tbsp. light brown sugar
1 tsp. baking soda
1 tsp. baking powder

⅓ cup melted butter
3 egg yolks, beaten
½ cup sour cream
1½ or more cups buttermilk
3 egg whites, beaten

Mix the dry ingredients. Combine with the melted butter, egg yolks, sour cream and 1 cup of buttermilk. Beat together and, if necessary, add more buttermilk to make a batter like heavy cream. Fold in the stiffly beaten egg whites. More melted butter and sour cream can be added for a crisp waffle that doesn't stick to the irons.

VARIATION

CORN MEAL AND RICE WAFFLES Make Corn Meal Waffles and replace ½ cup corn meal with ½ cup cooked rice.

Corn Meal Mush or Porridge

1 cup corn meal
2 tsps. salt
1 cup cold milk or water

2½ to 3 cups boiling milk or
   water

Milk or water can be used or a mixture of both. Put the corn meal in the top of the double boiler and add the salt; mix with 1 cup of cold liquid. This prevents it from being lumpy. Stir in the boiling liquid, cover and cook over simmering water for 30 minutes. Stir occasionally. If porridge is desired, a little more liquid may be necessary. If polenta is to be made, use water instead of milk. Serve porridge with brown sugar and butter or brown sugar or honey and cream. Various things to do with mush follow.

VARIATIONS

FRIED MUSH Make a recipe of Corn Meal Mush. Pour it 1 inch thick onto a greased platter and let it cool and harden. Cut in strips, roll in corn meal and fry in plenty of bacon fat and butter. Serve with honey or syrup.

CORN MEAL MUSH WITH CHEESE is excellent to serve with meats instead of potatoes. Before removing from the fire add ½ cup shredded or grated Cheddar or Parmesan cheese. Spread on a greased platter. When it is cool and hard, spread with soft butter and sprinkle with more cheese. Cut in 2-inch squares, put them in a baking dish and reheat 10 minutes in a hot oven.

POLENTA is another variation. Cook the mush with cheese. Serve the dish with Italian or pork sausages and tomato sauce. Or ½ the cheese mush can be put in a greased shallow baking dish, covered with sliced cooked sausages, a cup of tomato sauce and covered with the rest of the mush. If this is not served immediately it will thicken too much, so the original mush must have plenty of liquid in it to be rather soft when put together with the sausage and tomato sauce. Reheat 10 minutes in a hot oven. The polenta can be covered with sour cream if you like.

PULISKA is another variation, a delicious Hungarian dish using *Lekvar,* a jam of puréed prunes or apricots. Put ½ the plain mush in a baking dish, cover with a thick layer of jam, the rest of the mush and cover the top with sour cream. This makes a fine supper dish or it may be served with chicken or pork. Heat for 10 minutes in a hot oven so the cream is ivory colored.

CORN MEAL MUSH WITH CHEESE AND SOUR CREAM is a fine dish to serve instead of potatoes. Put ½ the mush in a baking dish and sprinkle over it 1½ cups shredded sharp cheese. Cover with the rest of the mush and top with a thick layer of sour cream. Reheat 10 minutes in a hot oven.

Miscellaneous Corn Breads

CORNPONE, HOECAKE, JOHNNYCAKE, MUFFINS

Corn Meal Pone

1 cup stone-ground corn meal
¾ tsp. salt
½ tsp. baking soda
½ tsp. baking powder

3 Tbsps. sour cream
Buttermilk to make a batter
3 Tbsps. butter and oil

Mix the dry ingredients and add the sour cream and buttermilk to make a soft batter, one that won't spread when dropped from a spoon into an iron skillet on the melted butter and oil. Oil is necessary to prevent burning. Cover tightly with a lid and cook on top of the stove over the lowest flame 25 to 30 minutes. This makes 5 or 6 simple but delicious pones, and their goodness depends on the quality of the stone-ground meal used. Variations can be made by using ⅓ of the quantity of meal with rye, oat or whole wheat flour.

Hoecake

2 cups corn meal   Boiling water
2 or 3 tsps. salt

This old plantation dish was originally baked on a hoe over the fire. Up at the big house they added 1 cup of milk, 2 Tbsps. butter and 1 tsp. of baking powder. In either case add enough scalding water to make a batter to form into cakes on a greased griddle, or bake in the oven on a greased sheet 30 minutes very slowly, at about 325° F.

Corn Meal Munks

1 cup corn meal   1 tsp. brown sugar or honey
½ cup boiling water   2 eggs, beaten
¾ tsp. salt   ⅓ cup sour cream, about
1 tsp. baking powder   Butter or oil for frying

Mix the corn meal and water. Combine the salt, baking powder and sugar or honey with the lightly beaten eggs and mix with the corn meal. Mix enough sour cream into the mixture to make a light but thick batter. Put 2 tsps. of butter or oil in each munk mold and fill with batter to the top. Fry over a medium flame, turn once, using two pointed knives, and cook until the underside is brown. They are very good served hot with butter. Makes 10 or 11 munks.

Corn Oysters

2 cups fresh corn   ¼ tsp. freshly ground pepper
⅓ cup corn meal   ½ cup melted butter
⅓ cup whole wheat flour   3 egg yolks, beaten
2 tsps. salt   3 egg whites, beaten

Three 8-inch (closely packed kernels) ears of corn yield 2 cups of corn cut from the ears. Put the corn on the cob in warm water, bring to the boil and, after 45 seconds, remove it and cut it from the ears. Instead of fresh corn a small white kernel corn in cans may be used. Le Sueur shoe peg is very good. It must be drained. Add the corn to the mixed dry ingredients then stir in the butter and egg yolks. Fold in the stiffly beaten whites last. Drop by spoonfuls into hot fat and fry until brown. Delicious with chicken or pork. Serves 6.

Johnnycake

1 cup corn meal
1 tsp. salt
1 Tbsp. light brown sugar

¾ cup milk
1 beaten egg

Mix the dry ingredients. Add the milk to the beaten egg and combine with the corn meal. Bake on a greased griddle in small cakes over a slow flame. Turn when the crust is golden. Serve with butter, and syrup if they are for breakfast.

Buttermilk Johnnycake

1 cup corn meal
½ tsp. soda
1 tsp. salt

½ tsp. baking powder
⅔ cup buttermilk or more
4 Tbsps. butter, melted

Mix the dry ingredients and then add the buttermilk and melted butter. The batter should be stiff enough to hold its shape when dropped onto a greased sheet. Bake 15 minutes at 400° F. Makes 8 cakes.

Maryland Johnnycake

2 cups corn meal
1 tsp. salt
3 Tbsps. butter

½ cup milk
2 or more cups boiling water

Mix the meal, salt, butter and milk. Add enough boiling water to make a soft batter but one that will hold its shape when dropped by spoonfuls onto a hot greased griddle. Flatten to ½ inch thick and when they are brown around the edges, turn them and fry until done. Use ½ butter and ½ lard for frying. These are good served with pork chops or sausage.

Rhode Island Johnnycake

2 cups white corn meal
1 tsp. salt
1 Tbsp. brown sugar

2 cups boiling water
1¼ cups milk, about

Mix the dry ingredients and scald them with the boiling water. Thin with milk so the batter stays in shape when dropped from a spoon onto a hot well-greased griddle. Have the griddle hot at first, then lower the heat and cook the cakes slowly, turning but once when the crust is a golden brown. Serve with butter or syrup. Serves 4 or more.

Cheese Corn Muffins

1 cup corn meal
1 tsp. salt
1 tsp. light brown sugar
½ tsp. baking soda
1 egg, beaten

1 cup buttermilk
3 Tbsps. melted butter
2 tsps. grated sharp cheese for
each muffin

Mix all the dry ingredients and combine them with the mixed liquids. Pour into greased muffin tins and cover each with 2 tsps. of grated cheese. Bake 15 minutes at 375° F. Muffins made of corn bread batters do not take so long to bake.

Corn Meal Potato Muffins

1 cup corn meal
4 tsps. baking powder
1 tsp. salt
1 Tbsp. light brown sugar

1 egg, beaten
1 cup mashed potatoes
2 Tbsps. melted butter or bacon fat
1 cup milk

These may be made of leftover mashed potatoes. The potatoes should be rather soft. Mix the dry ingredients together, then add the rest of the ingredients. Bake in greased muffin tins about 35 minutes at 350° F.

Tartles

1 cup white corn meal
1 tsp. salt

Boiling water
Melted butter or bacon fat

Mix the meal and salt and scald with just enough boiling water so the dough can be handled. Form into fingers an inch thick and roll in melted butter or bacon grease and bake at 350° F. for 30 minutes.

Corn Dodgers #1

1 cup corn meal
1 tsp. salt

2 Tbsps. melted butter
Cold water

Mix the meal with the salt and butter. Add just enough water so you can form into little rolls with your hands. Put them on a greased baking sheet and bake them 30 minutes in a 325° F. oven. If the heat is too high turn it down to 300° F.

Corn Dodgers #2

1 cup corn meal
1 cup boiling water
2 Tbsps. butter, melted

1 tsp. salt
2 egg yolks
2 egg whites, beaten

Scald the meal with the boiling water, then add the butter, salt and egg yolks. Beat until smooth, then fold in the stiffly beaten whites. Drop by spoonfuls onto a greased baking sheet and bake 35 minutes at 325° F.

Hominy

USES OF HOMINY

Hominy has been useful and good for making hot breads and cereal in the Middle West and the South for generations. As many have not used it some rules for its preparation are in order.

Boiled Hominy

1 cup hominy or samp   2 tsps. salt
3 cups boiling water

Soak the hominy in several cups of water overnight. Drain it and add the boiling water and salt. Cook in the top of the double boiler over simmering water for 2 hours. Hominy expands about 3 times its bulk. It is now ready for use as cereal, served with cream and sugar, or it can be served instead of potatoes, with butter added and a sprinkle of cheese if desired, or for the hot breads which follow.

Hominy Grits

1 cup hominy grits   1 tsp. salt
3 cups boiling water

The grits are finer than hominy and are soaked an hour. Drain the grits, add the boiling water and salt, and cook in the double boiler from 1 to 2 hours or until they are tender. Some grits may take less time to cook. They swell about 2½ times their bulk.

Hominy Pancakes

1½ cups cooked hominy   ½ cup corn meal
2 Tbsps. butter, melted   2 egg yolks
1 tsp. salt   Milk or buttermilk
1 tsp. baking powder   2 egg whites, beaten

Mix the hominy with the melted butter and combine with the mixed dry ingredients and the egg yolks. Add enough milk or buttermilk to make a medium pancake batter, then fold in the stiffly beaten egg whites. Fry the pancakes on a well-greased hot griddle. When the tops bubble, turn them once and fry until a golden brown. Serve with honey or maple syrup.

VARIATION

HOMINY WAFFLES
Recipe of Hominy Pancakes   More melted butter

Use 6 Tbsps. of melted butter for waffles instead of the 2 Tbsps. called for in the pancakes. Waffle batter is usually a little thinner.

Hominy Cakes

1½ cups cooked hominy
⅓ cup corn meal or whole
    wheat flour
2 tsps. baking powder
1 tsp. salt

2 egg yolks
Milk
2 egg whites, beaten

Mix the dry ingredients and add the egg yolks and milk to make a stiff dough; fold in the stiffly beaten egg whites. These are dropped by spoonfuls and fried in plenty of hot fat or in deep oil at 370° F. Drain on brown paper and serve with chicken or pork. They may be sprinkled with powdered sugar or Parmesan cheese.

Hominy Soufflé

1½ cups cooked hominy or grits
2 Tbsps. melted butter
½ cup grated sharp cheese
¼ tsp. nutmeg

1 cup milk, scalded
½ tsp. salt
4 or 5 egg yolks
4 or 5 egg whites, beaten

Put the hominy or grits, butter, cheese and nutmeg in a saucepan and pour the scalded milk and salt over it. Stir until well mixed and add the egg yolks. If more than 4 people are to be served, use 5 eggs. Stir until mixture thickens a little over a slow flame, then fold in the stiffly beaten egg whites. Bake 25 or 30 minutes in a greased baking dish set in a pan of water, ½ the time at 375° F., ½ at 325° F. This is good with meats or poultry instead of potatoes.

Hominy Hot Bread

1 cup cooked hominy
¼ cup melted butter
1½ cups buttermilk
1 Tbsp. brown sugar
1 tsp. salt

1 tsp. baking powder
½ tsp. soda
½ cup corn meal, rye or whole wheat flour
2 eggs, beaten separately

Mix the hominy with the butter and buttermilk. Add the mixed dry ingredients and the egg yolks. Fold in the stiffly beaten egg whites last. Bake at 350° F. about 20 minutes. Raisins can be added if desired.

Hominy Batter Bread

This is one of the most delicious lunch or supper hot breads. Serve with plenty of butter. Any mixture of whole flours or meal can be used with the hominy, just so there is a total of 1 cup. The spices give a fascinating flavor to this bread.

1 cup cooked hominy or hominy grits
⅓ cup rye flour
⅓ cup whole wheat flour
⅓ cup corn meal
1 tsp. salt

4 tsps. baking powder
½ tsp. anise (optional)
½ tsp. cinnamon (optional)
2 eggs, beaten
3 cups milk
1 Tbsp. brown sugar

Put the hominy or grits in a big bowl and stir in the mixed dry ingredients. Beat the eggs until light, add the milk and sugar and beat again. Combine the liquids with the dry ingredients and pour into a large well-greased 10-inch iron skillet and bake 30 minutes at 350° F. If it is done sooner remove from the oven, it should be soft in the center.

Hominy Corn Bread

¾ cup cooked hominy   1½ tsps. baking powder
2 Tbsps. butter   1 Tbsp. brown sugar
1 cup warm milk   ¾ cup corn meal
3 egg yolks, beaten   3 egg whites, beaten
1 tsp. salt

Mix the hominy with the butter and warm milk and the egg yolks. Mix the dry ingredients and add them to the hominy. Fold in the stiffly beaten egg whites last. If a richer bread is desired use 1 cup light cream instead of milk. Bake in a greased 8 x 11-inch pan about 25 minutes at 350° F. Serve hot with butter.

Tortillas

There are two ways of making tortillas, with hominy and corn meal or with just corn meal. The East Indians make a bread they call chipati the same way as the Mexicans, using whole wheat flour instead of corn.

3 cups drained hominy   ¼ cup corn meal
1 tsp. salt

Grind the hominy very fine then mix it with the salt and corn meal. Mix into a paste with 2 or 3 Tbsps. of plain water or hominy water. Form into small balls and roll as thin as possible. These are fried without grease on a griddle until golden. For all-corn-meal tortillas, add boiling water to a cup of corn meal and make a paste. More water will be needed. Add salt. Roll and fry the same way. They can be served with butter and syrup. The Mexicans dress them with sausages, frijoles (beans), and tomato sauce.

Oat Breads

OATS

*Oatcakes are a delicate relish
when eaten warm with ale.*—Burns

Midlothian oats are unsurpassed the world over but whether we obtain them imported from Scotland or as steel-cut oats and oat flour, stone-ground, from our own mills, they are the sweetest grain to cook with. They are part and parcel of fascinating Scottish history and from the Shetlands to the Borders and Highlands they are used to make scones, bannocks, baps and buns. The simple rugged fare contributed to the making of the stalwart Scot and prepared him for the battle or the hunt, and the rigorous climate of his country. Besides this little collection of old favorites, there are other breads containing oats throughout the book. Bannocks and scones are the same dough, but bannocks are made plate-size and scones are small cakes.

Scottish Oat Cakes

1¼ cups oat flour
¼ tsp. baking soda
½ tsp. salt

1 egg, beaten
2 Tbsps. melted butter
¼ cup water

Mix the dry ingredients and combine with the mixed liquids. If necessary add a little more water so the dough can be rolled on a floured board to ⅓ inch thickness. Cut in squares or rounds and fry over a medium flame on a well-greased griddle about 10 minutes. Turn once. These are good served with Scotch smoked salmon or herring and a green salad.

Oatmeal Scones

⅞ cup oat flour
½ tsp. baking soda
1 tsp. baking powder
1 tsp. salt

1 Tbsp. honey or syrup
3 Tbsps. sour cream
1 Tbsp. melted butter
1 egg, beaten

Mix the dry ingredients and combine with the mixed liquids. This may be dropped like biscuits on a greased pan or patted onto a hot greased griddle into a round and baked about 12 minutes in a hot oven. Cut in pie-shaped pieces and serve hot with butter.

Oat Shortcakes

1 cup oat flour
¾ tsp. salt
3 Tbsps. light brown sugar
1½ tsps. baking powder

½ tsp. baking soda
3 Tbsps. melted butter
1 egg, beaten
¼ cup buttermilk, more or less

Mix all the dry ingredients together well, then add the melted butter, beaten egg and as much buttermilk as needed to make a batter that won't run. Put a good quantity of melted fat and butter in an iron skillet, make 4 large cakes of the batter, cover and cook slowly for 12 minutes, then turn the cakes and they will be done in less than a minute. These light and tender cakes may be split, spread with soft butter and filled with berries sweetened with honey for shortcake or served with maple syrup or honey. Serves 4.

Oatmeal Wafers

1 cup oat flour
½ cup whole wheat flour
½ tsp. salt
2 Tbsps. light brown sugar

¼ tsp. soda
¼ cup butter and lard, mixed
⅓ cup boiling water

Mix the dry ingredients together very well. Melt the shortening in the boiling water and combine the mixtures. Roll out on a floured board to ⅛-inch thickness. Cut in small rounds or strips and bake in a 375° F. oven about 10 minutes. These have a nutty flavor and are very good served with a spread for canapés.

Oatmeal Pancakes

2 cups boiling milk
1 cup oat flour
Grated lemon peel *or* dash of
    nutmeg

1 tsp. salt
1 Tbsp. light brown sugar
3 eggs, separated

Add the hot milk to the oat flour and cook a moment until it thickens; add the lemon peel or nutmeg, salt, sugar and egg yolks. Fold in the stiffly beaten whites and fry on a hot greased griddle. If you prefer a thinner batter, add a little milk before folding in the egg whites. Orange syrup is excellent with oat flour dishes.

Oatmeal Potato Cakes

½ cup milk, scalded
¼ cup oat flour
Scant tsp. salt
¾ cup mashed potatoes

1 tsp. baking powder
1 egg, beaten
2 Tbsps. chopped parsley or
    fresh dill

Scald the milk, add the oat flour and salt and cook a moment until mixture thickens. Add the rest of the ingredients. Form into patties and fry to a crusty brown on both sides in plenty of fat. The quantities can easily be doubled.

Derbyshire Oatcakes

1 envelope yeast
¾ cup warm water or butter-
    milk
1 cup oat flour

1 Tbsp. honey or brown sugar
½ tsp. salt
1 egg, beaten

Dissolve the yeast in the water or buttermilk until it is frothy; beat in the flour. Cover and let it stand in a warm place for an hour. Beat the sugar, salt and egg together until light and stir it into the batter. Beat well, then let it stand again an hour. Fry on a hot greased griddle and serve with fruit compote or syrup and butter. Makes 6 cakes. Twelves cakes can be made by doubling all the ingredients except the yeast.

Oatmeal Sour Cream (or Buttermilk) Pancakes

2 cups oat flour
2 tsps. baking powder
½ tsp. baking soda
1 tsp. salt
1 Tbsp. light brown sugar

2 egg yolks, beaten
¾ cup sour cream
Milk
2 egg whites, beaten

Mix all the dry ingredients. Beat the yolks into the sour cream and stir this into the flour. Buttermilk can be used instead of sour cream if you wish. In this case add 3 Tbsps. melted butter. A little milk may be necessary to make the batter thin enough to your taste. Fold in the stiffly beaten whites. Fry on a well-greased griddle, turning the cakes once. Serve with maple or orange syrup.

Oatmeal Date Muffins

1½ cups oat flour
2 tsps. baking powder
½ tsp. salt
2 Tbsps. light brown sugar
½ tsp. baking soda

12 sliced dates
3 Tbsps. melted butter
2 egg yolks, beaten
½ cup buttermilk, more or less
2 egg whites, beaten

Mix the dry ingredients together and toss the dates through them. Mix the butter, egg yolks and buttermilk together and add them to the flour. Do not stir any more than is necessary. Fold in the stiffly beaten egg whites. Bake in 9 greased muffin tins at 375° F. about 18 minutes.

Oatmeal Muffins

2 cups oat flour
2 Tbsps. light brown sugar
3 tsps. baking powder
1 tsp. salt

½ tsp. baking soda
4 Tbsps. melted butter
1 or more cups buttermilk
1 egg, beaten

Mix the dry ingredients. Add the butter to ½ cup of the buttermilk and the beaten egg. Add more buttermilk to make a batter like cake, stirring as little as possible. Bake at 375° F. about 15 minutes in greased muffin tins.

Scotsman's Oat Grits Porridge

1 cup steel-cut oats
2 cups boiling water
1 tsp. salt

Cream
Honey

Mix the grits and water in the top of a double boiler. Let it come to the boil for 2 minutes over the flame, then cover and cook for 10 minutes over simmering water before adding the salt. Continue cooking 15 minutes longer. If the grits are soaked in 1 cup of water several hours or overnight, the porridge will take less time to cook. If soaked, add less water for cooking. Serves 4. Serve with cream and honey.

Oats and Consommé

(and other grits)

This is not bread but it may be served instead of bread. While the subject is oats I feel this is too good not to mention.

1 cup cracked or steel-cut oats
½ cup finely diced onions

3 cups boiling consommé
2 Tbsps. butter

The oats are coarsely ground. Put them in a heavy pot over a medium to low flame and stir them until they brown lightly and become fragrant. Add the onions. Slowly pour the boiling consommé over them, cover very tight and cook slowly about 40 minutes. They will absorb the liquid and be fluffy. If the consommé is well seasoned salt will not be required. Stir in the butter and serve instead of potatoes. This is marvelous with chicken or pork. Browned pieces of chicken can be laid on top of the oats when you pour in the consommé and cooked with it. This will serve 4 and can easily be increased. If 2 cups of oats are used with chicken, use 4 cups of consommé. After 20 minutes see if more consommé should be added. Other grits may be cooked this way, such as rice, rye, wheat, buckwheat (kasha), corn, hominy, millet, soy and barley. The top of the steamed dish may be decorated with chopped green onions and crisp crumbled bacon.

Rice Breads

RICE AND ITS USES

There are other recipes using rice in the book but a few added words here on this world-wide grain may be useful. Most people use polished rice because they are told by purveyors of food that it tastes better and cooks faster. That it tastes better is entirely untrue; that it cooks faster may be true. If you know ahead of time when you are going to have rice, you can soak whole-grain rice all day in the liquid it is to be cooked in, and it will cook in no time. White rice is lacking in flavor; brown, patna and various types of India rice are full of flavor and nourishment. I wouldn't dream of cooking any rice dish, including the elegant Rice Imperatrice, with any rice except patna or Indian rice, as well as brown rice. Indian Basmatti rice, for instance, is as fine and delicate as any white rice ever dreamed of being. As rice is the principal food of half the human race, it is important to use it in its whole and nourishing state. The Orient is fully aware of this, and it is high time for the West to get this message.

To Cook Rice

1 cup brown, patna or Indian rice	*or*
	1 cup patna rice or Indian rice
with	with
2 cups consommé or water	2 cups consommé or milk
or	*or*
1 cup brown rice	1 cup wild rice
with	with
4 cups skim milk	2½ cups consommé or water

Brown rice is fat resistant, because it is unhusked, so that skim milk is used for cooking it for puddings and porridge. It is excellent cooked in a quart of skim milk in a double boiler an hour for porridge. Serve it with cream and honey or brown sugar. Raisins, egg yolks and cream can be added to make a pudding. It is excellent for children. Brown rice cooked in 2 cups of chicken consommé is excellent to serve instead of potatoes; or it can be made into risotto with the called-for additions. Patna rice cooks perfectly in milk, as does Indian rice. They are wonderful for porridge and puddings too.

Unless brown rice is soaked several hours before cooking, it takes 15 minutes longer to cook than patna or Indian rice. Patna and Indian rice take about 25 minutes to cook unless previously soaked. Rice is cooked in twice its bulk in liquid in a heavy pot with a tight lid over a flame of pilot-light strength. When it is done, the heat is turned off and it remains covered for 10 minutes. It fluffs up and no rice sticks to the bottom of the pot. Of course, whole rice is *never* drained. The water is absorbed into the grain.

Wild rice is another genus entirely, the latin name is *zizania aquatica*. It grows wild on single stems 5 to 10 feet tall in 2 to 8 feet of water and seeds itself. It must be washed thoroughly in several waters. The rice is cooked until it is tender. More boiling liquid can be added if it needs it. Let it steam a little also, covered with the heat turned off, when it is done.

Philpy

⅓ cup patna or Indian rice
1 cup milk
½ cup brown rice flour
2 egg yolks
1 tsp. salt

1 or 2 Tbsps. honey
⅓ cup milk
⅓ cup sour cream
2 egg whites, beaten

I have changed this old Carolina recipe a bit; this is a lovely hot bread. Put the washed rice in a heavy pot, add the milk, cover tight; inspect in about 20 minutes. Cook until the milk is absorbed and the rice is soft. This is done over very low heat. Stir in the rice flour, the yolks, salt, honey and milk. It should be fluffy and smooth. Add the sour cream and fold in the stiffly beaten egg whites. Put the batter in a very well-greased (butter and oil are the best) 9-inch Pyrex pie plate and bake at 375° F. for 20 to 25 minutes. Serve immediately with sweet butter. Syrup or honey is very good on it too. It makes a grand supper or luncheon dish; or serve it with chicken or pork.

Patna or Brown Rice and Whole Wheat Muffins

1 cup cooked rice
1¼ cups whole wheat flour
2 tsps. baking powder
1 tsp. salt

2 Tbsps. brown sugar or
   molasses
¼ cup butter, melted
2 eggs, beaten
¾ cup buttermilk or more

Add the rice to the mixed dry ingredients; add the sugar or molasses mixed with the melted butter and beaten eggs. Add enough buttermilk to make a soft but firm muffin batter. Bake at 375° F. in 9 or 10 greased and floured muffin tins about 20 minutes. These whole grain hot breads are so nourishing that one muffin is usually enough for each serving, especially with a complete meal.

Brown Rice Flour and Whole Wheat Biscuits

⅓ cup brown rice flour
1 tsp. baking powder
¼ tsp. baking soda
¾ tsp. salt
½ cup whole wheat flour

1 Tbsp. light brown sugar
1 Tbsp. butter
1 Tbsp. lard
¼ cup sour cream
¼ cup milk, about

Mix all the dry ingredients together well and cut in the shortening with a wire pastry cutter. Mix in the cream and milk to make a very soft light biscuit dough, handling as little as possible. Form 11 or 12 biscuits with your hands and put them on a greased, floured baking pan and bake them at 400° F. about 18 minutes.

Rice Dumplings for Stews

1¼ cups cooked brown rice
⅔ cup brown rice flour
2 tsps. baking powder
1 Tbsp. light brown sugar
¾ tsp. salt

1 egg, beaten
¼ cup milk
1 Tbsp. melted butter or oil
Chopped dill or mint

Mix all the ingredients together to make a stiff but light dough, one that can be handled. For lamb stew, 1 or 2 Tbsps. of chopped fresh mint can be added to the dough. Fresh dill is delicious with chicken stew. Form into balls and roll in rice flour, then drop on top of gently simmering stew. Cover tight and cook 12 minutes without lifting the lid. Lift the dumplings into the center of a large platter and surround with the stew. Serves 4 to 6.

Brown Rice Pancakes

1 cup cooked brown or patna
rice
2 cups milk
1 cup whole wheat flour
1½ tsps. baking powder
1 tsp. salt

3 Tbsps. light brown sugar
2 egg yolks, beaten
¼ cup sour cream *or*
2 Tbsps. melted butter
2 egg whites, beaten
Butter and oil for frying

This makes 18 or 20 marvelous pancakes. The recipe can be cut in half to serve 3. Soak the cooked rice in the milk for 2 hours. Mix the dry ingredients together and stir into the rice. Mix the egg yolks and sour cream or butter and add them. Beat the egg whites until they are stiff and fold them into the batter. Fry in mixed butter and oil on a hot griddle. Serve with syrup, honey or thinned apricot or damson jam.

Rice Batter Cakes

1 cup cooked brown or patna
rice
Milk
⅓ cup whole wheat flour
2 tsps. light brown sugar
1 tsp. salt

1½ tsps. baking powder
2 egg yolks, beaten
3 Tbsps. melted butter
2 egg whites, beaten

Mix the rice with ¼ cup of milk. Mix all the dry ingredients together and mix them with the rice; add the egg yolks and melted butter. Add sufficient milk to make the batter thin enough to suit your taste. Fold in the stiffly beaten egg whites. Fry on a well-greased griddle. Serve with honey or maple syrup.

Patna Rice Croquettes

1 cup patna rice
1 quart milk
1½ tsps. salt
2 egg yolks, beaten
1 Tbsp. chopped parsley

Beaten egg
Crumbs
Parmesan cheese
Hot fat for frying

Wash the rice, put it in the top of the double boiler with the milk, let it boil up then put it over simmering water. Cover and cook it 1 hour, stirring occasionally. Add the salt, beaten yolks and parsley. Cook a minute longer. Spread it an inch thick on a greased platter to cool and stiffen. Before serving, cut it in small squares, dip in beaten egg and mixed crumbs and cheese and brown in hot fat. Serves 6.

VARIATION ⅓ cup of grated cheese, Cheddar, Gruyère, Swiss, or Parmesan, can be stirred into the rice after it has cooked. The cheese should then be omitted from the crumbs. Leftover risotto is excellent for these croquettes. Brown rice can be used, in which case use skim milk for the cooking. Brown rice's outer husk resists fat sometimes but it cooks beautifully in skim milk.

Cottage Cheese Rice Cakes

1½ cups cooked brown rice
1 cup sieved cottage cheese
Salt and pepper
½ tsp. nutmeg
1 tsp. light brown sugar

1 Tbsp. whole wheat flour
1 or 2 eggs, beaten
½ cup corn meal
⅓ cup Parmesan cheese
Fat for frying

Mix together first six ingredients. Form into 12 or 14 cakes. Dip them in beaten egg then in a mixture of corn meal and cheese. Chill the cakes and, when almost ready to serve, fry them brown in plenty of good fat and serve hot. These are fine with poultry or pork.

Brown Rice Fritters

1 cup cooked brown rice
½ tsp. salt
Pinch light brown sugar
⅓ cup whole wheat flour

2 eggs, beaten
Crumbs
Parmesan cheese
Oil for deep frying

Mix the rice, salt, sugar, flour and eggs together. The mixture must be stiff enough to roll into little balls. Roll the balls in a mixture of crumbs and cheese and fry at 370° F. until a golden color. Drain and serve instead of potatoes.

Sunflower Breads

SUNFLOWER SEEDS

Because sunflower seeds and meal are not in very common use, a few words about them will show their importance in cookery and in nutrition. They make the most delicious hot breads and loaf breads, and their richness in food value is an extra bonus.

A few years ago three researchers in the laboratory of chemistry and bacteriology at Indiana University in Bloomington sent me this analysis: ". . . sunflower meal contains approximately 150% more preformed nicotinic acid than does the best grade of wheat germ analyzed, and it is approximately 500% richer in this vitamin than is corn germ or solvent-extracted soybean meal . . . sunflower meal produced at low temperatures is in the same class as oats, wheat and barley in regard to the dietary quality of protein."

Sunflower is an important crop in Russia and Argentina. When sunflower in this country becomes a comparable crop to other grains, its price too may win it a place among the favorite meals used in our cookery. Its rich food value makes it an important addition to the normal diet. It mixes well with other grains and it appears in other recipes in this book. It cooks quickly; perhaps the sun itself has something to do with this.

Sunflower Drop Biscuits #1

½ cup whole wheat flour
½ cup sunflower seed meal
2 tsps. baking powder

¾ tsp. salt
⅓ cup sour cream
Milk

Mix the dry ingredients together and cut in the cream as you would fat, with a fork. Moisten with just enough milk, 2 or 3 Tbsps., to mix the dough so it can be dropped from a spoon. Bake 8 or 10 minutes on a greased, floured pan at 375° F. Makes 12 small biscuits.

Sunflower Baking Powder Biscuits #2

½ cup sunflower meal
½ cup whole wheat flour
¾ tsp. salt
1¾ tsps. baking powder

2 or 3 Tbsps. shortening
⅓ cup (about) milk or butter-
milk

Mix the dry ingredients and cut in the shortening with a wire pastry cutter. Two Tbsps. fat make a little lighter biscuit. Mix just enough liquid with the flour to make a light dough that doesn't spread. Drop from a spoon onto a greased pan and bake 10 or 12 minutes at 375° F.

Sunflower Sour Cream Muffins

¾ cup sunflower seed meal
1 cup rye, whole wheat or oat
   flour
2½ tsps. baking powder
1 tsp. salt
½ tsp. soda

¼ cup currants
1 egg, beaten
¾ cup sour cream
2 Tbsps. honey
⅓ cup buttermilk (about)

Mix all the dry ingredients and toss the currants through them. Mix the egg, cream and honey together and combine the 2 mixtures. Mix as little as possible. Flours differ so add enough buttermilk to make a soft dough. Bake in greased, floured muffin tins about 15 minutes, ½ the time at 375° F. and ½ at 325° F. Makes 9 large muffins.

Sunflower Whole Wheat Muffins

1 large egg, beaten
3 Tbsps. butter, melted
¾ cup milk
1¼ cups whole wheat flour

3 Tbsps. brown sugar
½ cup sunflower seed meal
¾ tsp. salt
3 tsps. baking powder

Mix the liquids and add the mixed dry ingredients, stirring as little as possible. Bake in greased, floured muffin tins 12 to 15 minutes at 375° F. Serve hot with butter. Makes 9 muffins.

Sunflower Meal and Rye Muffins

These muffins have an unusual flavor and are wonderful for supper or lunch for growing children.

3 Tbsps. butter, melted
1 large egg, beaten
¾ scant cup milk
3 Tbsps. brown sugar
1 cup unsifted rye flour

¾ cup sunflower meal
¾ tsp. salt
2½ tsps. baking powder
½ tsp. cinnamon
½ tsp. anise (optional)

Mix the liquids and add the mixed dry ingredients. Stir as little as possible. The spices give a fragrance to the muffins. Bake in greased, floured muffin tins 14 or 15 minutes at 375° F. Makes 9 muffins.

Sunflower Seed Meal and Oat Flour Muffins

3 Tbsps. brown sugar or honey
3 Tbsps. butter, melted
1 large egg, beaten
⅔ cup milk

1 cup oat flour
¾ cup sunflower meal
¾ tsp. salt
3 tsps. baking powder

Mix the sugar with the liquids, then combine with the mixed dry ingredients, stirring as little as possible. Bake in greased, floured muffin tins for 15 minutes at 375° F. Makes 9 marvelous muffins. These, as do other sunflower seed meal hot breads, have a nutty rich flavor.

Sunflower Pancakes

¾ cup sunflower meal
¾ cup whole wheat flour
1¾ tsps. baking powder
¾ tsp. salt

2 eggs, beaten
1 Tbsp. honey or brown sugar
2 Tbsps. butter, melted
1½ cups buttermilk

Mix the dry ingredients together and combine with the mixed liquids. Fry to a delicate brown on both sides on a well-buttered griddle. This amount makes about 22 pancakes. They are very tender and are good with just butter. They would be fine filled with creamed chicken or seafood. They could be either rolled or spread with the creamed mixture and topped with a small pancake, and kept warm in the oven.

Sunflower Corn Bread

1 cup sunflower meal
1 cup corn meal
2 tsps. baking powder
1 tsp. salt
½ tsp. soda

2 egg yolks, beaten
⅓ cup sour cream
2 Tbsps. honey
⅓ cup buttermilk
2 egg whites, beaten

Mix all the dry ingredients together and combine with the mixed liquids, folding in the stiffly beaten egg whites last. Bake in a greased, floured pan about 15 minutes at 375° F. It will be seen how fast sunflower meal bakes. Serve hot with butter. Any left over is good cold.

Sources of Supply

Your nearest health food store carries stone-ground cereals and flours beside many health food items. There are too many health food stores to list so only a few specialty shops have been chosen and some mills scattered over the country. Their catalogues are sent on request.

H. Roth & Son
1577 First Avenue
New York, N.Y. 10028
Complete line of foreign and domestic cooking equipment. Spices, nuts, herbs, dried and candied fruits, lekvar, and flours.

Bazar Francais
666 Sixth Avenue
New York, N.Y. 10011
Complete kitchen equipment especially from France.

L. E. Robert Co.
792 Union Street
Brooklyn, N.Y. 11215
Sunflower and sesame seeds and meals, nut butters and candies.

MILLS

Mill O'Milford
Milford, Conn.

The Great Valley Mills
Quakertown
Bucks County, Penna. 18951

Collegedale Distributors
Collegedale, Tennessee

Elam Mills
Broadview, Ill.

Old Fashioned Millers
Enright's
540 East 7th Street
St. Paul 1, Minnesota

Brownville Mills
Brownville, Nebraska

The Bridge Company
498 Third Avenue
New York, N.Y. 10016
Kitchen equipment.

Brownies
21 East 18th Street
New York, N.Y. 10003
Restaurant and bakery
Natural food specialties from
mills from all parts of the
country.

The Grist Mill
524 West 8th Street
Los Angeles, California 90014
Complete line of baked products
and health foods.

El Molino Mills
P.O. Box 2025
Alhambra, California 91803

Comparison of nutrients in wheat flour and wheat bread

Minimum and maximum enrichment levels for the three B vitamins—thiamine, niacin and riboflavin—and iron are given in the table below

One Pound	Protein (grams)	Fat (milligrams)	Calcium (milligrams)	Iron (milligrams)	Thiamine (milligrams)	Riboflavin (milligrams)	Niacin (milligrams)
FLOUR							
Unenriched (all purpose)	47.6	4.5	73	3.6	.28	.21	4.1
Enriched (all purpose)	47.6	4.5	73	13-16.5	2-2.5	1.2-1.5	16-20.
Whole Wheat	60.3	9.1	186	15.0	2.49	.54	19.7
BREAD							
Unenriched (white) (3 to 4% nonfat dry milk)	39.5	14.5	381	3.2	.31	.39	5.0
Enriched (white) (3 to 4% nonfat dry milk)	39.5	14.5	381	8-12.5	1.1-1.8	.7-1.6	10.0-15.0
Whole Wheat (2% nonfat dry milk)	47.6	13.6	449	10.4	1.17	.56	12.9

Sources: Composition of Foods, U. S. Department of Agriculture, Handbook No. 8, Washington, D. C., Revised, December, 1963. Definitions and Standards, Part 15, Cereal Flours and Related Products; Part 17, Bakery Products, Food and Drug Administration, U. S. Department of Health, Education and Welfare.

HOW FLOUR IS MILLED

IT STARTS HERE...

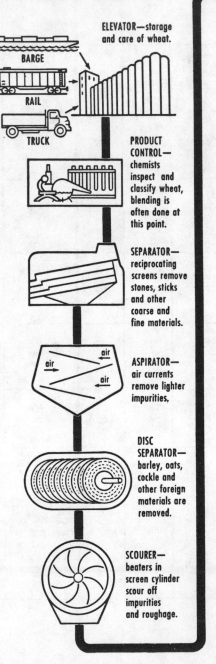
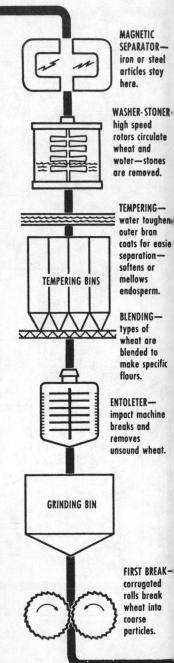

BARGE

RAIL

TRUCK

ELEVATOR—storage and care of wheat.

PRODUCT CONTROL—chemists inspect and classify wheat, blending is often done at this point.

SEPARATOR—reciprocating screens remove stones, sticks and other coarse and fine materials.

ASPIRATOR—air currents remove lighter impurities,

air   air

air

DISC SEPARATOR—barley, oats, cockle and other foreign materials are removed.

SCOURER—beaters in screen cylinder scour off impurities and roughage.

NOTE:
This chart is greatly simplified.
The sequence, number and complexity of different operations vary in different mills.

MAGNETIC SEPARATOR—iron or steel articles stay here.

WASHER-STONER—high speed rotors circulate wheat and water—stones are removed.

TEMPERING—water toughen outer bran coats for easie separation—softens or mellows endosperm.

TEMPERING BINS

BLENDING—types of wheat are blended to make specific flours.

ENTOLETER—impact machine breaks and removes unsound wheat.

GRINDING BIN

FIRST BREAK—corrugated rolls break wheat into coarse particles.

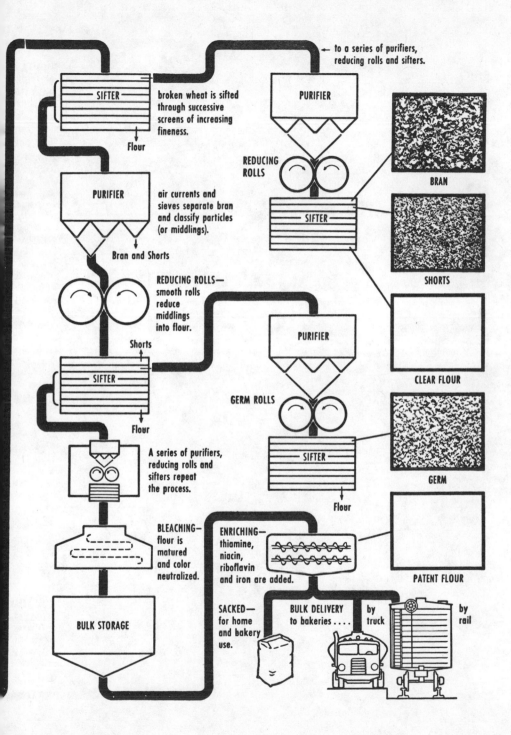

to a series of purifiers, reducing rolls and sifters.

SIFTER — broken wheat is sifted through successive screens of increasing fineness.

Flour

PURIFIER

BRAN

PURIFIER — air currents and sieves separate bran and classify particles (or middlings).

Bran and Shorts

REDUCING ROLLS

SIFTER

SHORTS

REDUCING ROLLS— smooth rolls reduce middlings into flour.

Shorts

SIFTER

Flour

PURIFIER

CLEAR FLOUR

GERM ROLLS

A series of purifiers, reducing rolls and sifters repeat the process.

SIFTER

GERM

BLEACHING— flour is matured and color neutralized.

ENRICHING— thiamine, niacin, riboflavin and iron are added.

Flour

PATENT FLOUR

BULK STORAGE

SACKED— for home and bakery use.

BULK DELIVERY to bakeries . . . .

by truck

by rail

Index